Trade Unions

private sector unions survive in Great Britain?
can unions respond to the challenges posed by performance related
, public–private partnerships and the Internet?
at lessons can be learned from trade unions' experience in Germany
d the USA?

Unions: resurgence or demise? is the third book in the important Future
de Unions in Britain series. Featuring original research underpinned
heory drawn from economics, organizations theory, history and social
ology, the authors offer readers a comprehensive analysis of trade unions'
p ects in the new millennium. Case studies deal with such topical issues
as: ions and the gender pay gap, the private finance initiative, performance
related pay and unions' use of the Internet. Topics covered include:

- the reasons for the loss of 5 million members in the 1980s and 1990s
- the way in which unions' own structures inhibit their revitalization
- the apparent failure of the unions to thrive in the benign times since
  1997
- the extent to which use of the Internet will permit unions to break with
  their tradition of organizing by occupation or industry
- the prospects for real social partnership at national level
- the way in which high-performance workplaces in the US give voice to
  workers without unions

Written by some of the leading scholars in the area, *Trade Unions: resurgence
or demise?* provides readers with an insight into union prospects for the
future and has important policy implications for all parties to industrial
relations: unions, employers and government.

Sue Fernie is Lecturer in Industrial Relations at the London School of
Economics. **David Metcalf** is Professor of Industrial Relations at the London
School of Economics.

The Future of Trade Unions in Britain
The Centre for Economic Performance

This groundbreaking new series on trade unions and employment relations is the result of the largest research grant ever awarded by the Leverhulme Trust, and the three series titles both analyse and evaluate the nature of unionization in Britain. With a multidisciplinary approach, the series brings together experts in the field of employment relations to offer three of the most informed, broad ranging and up-to-date studies available. Essential reading for anyone studying or working professionally with employment relations in Britain.

Representing Workers
Trade union recognition and membership in Britain
Edited by Stephen Wood and Howard Gospel

Union Organization and Activity
Edited by John Kelly and Paul Willman

Trade Unions
Resurgence or demise?
Edited by Sue Fernie and David Metcalf

Trade Unions

Resurgence or demise?

Edited by
Sue Fernie and David Metcalf

Routledge
Taylor & Francis Group

LONDON AND NEW YORK

First published 2005
by Routledge
2 Park Square, Milton Park, Abingdon, Oxon OX14 4RN

Simultaneously published in the USA and Canada
by Routledge
270 Madison Ave, New York, NY 10016

Routledge is an imprint of the Taylor & Francis Group

© 2005 Sue Fernie and David Metcalf, selection and editorial matter;
individual chapters, the contributors

Typeset in Sabon by
HWA Text and Data Management, Tunbridge Wells
Printed and bound in Great Britain by
TJ International Ltd, Padstow, Cornwall

British Library Cataloguing in Publication Data
A catalogue record for this book is available from the British Library

Library of Congress Cataloging in Publication Data
Trade unions : resurgence or demise? / [edited by] Sue Fernie and
  David Metcalf.— 1st ed.
    p. cm.
    Includes bibliographical references and index.
  1. Labor unions—Great Britain.   I. Fernie, Sue. II. Metcalf, David.
  III. Title.

  HD6664.T72335 2005
  331.88´0941—dc22   2004029209

ISBN 0–415–28411–2 (hbk)
ISBN 0–415–28412–0 (pbk)

In memory of

Helen and Nigel

who both contributed immensely to the wider labour movement, fought for social justice and, sadly, died much too young.

Contents

Figures

Tables

Contributors

Stephen Bach is Reader in Employment Relations and Management at the Management Centre, King's College, London.

Richard Belfield is a doctoral candidate in Industrial Relations at LSE and research assistant at the Centre for Economic Performance, LSE.

Andy Charlwood is Lecturer in Industrial Relations and Human Resource Management at Leeds University Business School; Research Associate, Centre for Economic Performance, London School of Economics.

Sue Fernie is Lecturer in Industrial Relations; Research Associate, Centre for Economic Performance, London School of Economics.

Richard Freeman is the Ascherman Professor of Economics at Harvard University; Program Director, Labor Studies at National Bureau of Economic Research; Visiting Professor at London School of Economics.

Rebecca Kolins Givan is a Research Officer in the Centre for Economic Performance, London School of Economics.

Howard Gospel is Professor of Management, King's College, London; Research Associate, Centre for Economic Performance, London School of Economics; Fellow, Said Business School, University of Oxford.

John Kelly is Professor of Industrial Relations in the School of Management, Birkbeck College, University of London.

Morris M. Kleiner is Professor at the Humphrey Institute of Public Affairs and the Industrial Relations Center at the University of Minnesota; Research Associate, National Bureau of Economic Research.

David Marsden is Professor of Industrial Relations, London School of Economics; Associate of the Centre for Economic Performance.

David Metcalf is Professor of Industrial Relations, London School of Economics; Director of the Future of Trade Unions in Modern Britain research programme.

Claus Schnabel is Professor of Economics, Friedrich-Alexander University, Erlangen-Nürnberg, Germany.

Robert Taylor is an adviser to the European Trade Union Confederation in Brussels; Associate of the Centre for Economic Performance; former Labour Editor of the *Financial Times*.

Paul Willman is the Ernest Button Professor of Management Studies at Oxford University; Research Associate in the Centre for Economic Performance, London School of Economics.

Foreword

Profound changes have taken place during the last quarter of a century in both employee representation and voice. Union membership has declined by over five million, the closed shop is almost extinct, half the present workforce has never belonged to a union and now, in the private sector, under one worker in five is a member. Simultaneously there has been a big move away from representative voice to direct voice. Representative voice occurs via a recognized trade union or works council. Direct voice bypasses these intermediate institutions. Instead, management and employees communicate directly with one another through, for example, team briefings, regular meetings between senior management and the workforce, and problem solving groups such as quality circles.

The Leverhulme Trust realized that these alterations in employment relations required more attention and initiated a research programme on the Future of Trade Unions in Modern Britain. This research is being carried out in the Centre for Economic Performance and the Industrial Relations Department at the London School of Economics, and includes colleagues from other institutions like King's College London, Oxford and Sheffield Universities and the Policy Studies Institute. The team is very grateful to the Leverhulme Trust for this financial support. In particular the successive Directors, Barry Supple and Sir Richard Brook, have greatly helped us with their wisdom and flexibility.

Programme research is organized around a number of themes: membership, interaction with employers and the state, adapting to change, performance outcomes, and public sector and public policy (see http://cep.lse.ac.uk/future_of_unions). The various outputs have been distilled into a trilogy published by Routledge. The first volume, edited by Stephen Wood and Howard Gospel was published in 2003 and focused on trade union recognition and membership. It analysed the reasons for the decline in membership, what unions do for younger workers and women, the willingness to unionize among non-union workers and the impact of new laws governing trade union recognition and information and consultation. The second volume, edited by John Kelly and Paul Willman, dealt with union organization and activity. It covered organizing campaigns, union structures, representing workers in the new economy and interactions with employers including social partnership.

This third volume, edited by Sue Fernie and myself, presents different approaches to the future of unions and examines challenges unions face and their response. The approaches include organization theory, social movements and standard economic analysis. The challenges include the public finance initiative and greater use of performance related pay. In addition the future of British unions is analysed by comparing unions' experience in the European Union and the USA.

David Metcalf
Director
Leverhulme Trust Programme on
Future of Trade Unions in Modern Britain

Acknowledgements

This book is based on research conducted as part of the Leverhulme funded research programme on the Future of Trade Unions in Modern Britain based at the Centre for Economic Performance, London School of Economics. We would like to thank the Leverhulme Foundation for their financial support for the programme and the Centre for Economic Performance for administrative support.

The team much appreciates the cooperation and input from Francesca Heslop and Emma Joyes of Routledge in bringing this volume to fruition. Finally, Linda Cleavely has been the programme administrator for its five-year term; her calm efficiency has contributed importantly to its success.

Chapter 1

The future of British unions
Introduction and conclusions

Sue Fernie

In the heyday of trade unions in the late 1970s before Mrs Thatcher was elected, over half of all employees were union members and more than 70 per cent of workers had their pay and conditions set by collective bargaining. Those figures have been whittled away to present day equivalents of 29 per cent and 35 per cent respectively. In the first part of this chapter, we analyse the various factors associated with the decline of trade unions in Britain in the last two decades of the twentieth century. The second part then goes on to describe what the likely fortunes of the unions are in the new millennium.

The past: membership and its decline in the 1980s and 1990s

Membership

Union membership rose by 4 million between 1950 and 1979. At its peak in 1979 it stood at 13.2 million but haemorrhaged 5.5 million in the subsequent two decades. Presently union membership is 7.4 million, consisting of 7.1 million employees and 0.3 million self-employed people. Since the Blair government came to power in 1997 the number of employees who are members has been roughly constant at around the 7 million mark. This is equivalent to a density figure (i.e. per cent unionized) of 29 per cent.

Density alters by demographic, job and workplace characteristics. It varies little by gender or ethnic origin but rises with age. Those with higher education have density levels substantially above those with fewer qualifications. Teachers, nurses and other professional workers have the highest density of any occupation (48 per cent) and sales occupations the lowest (11 per cent). Density rises sharply by tenure, a mirror image of the well known finding that labour turnover is lower in workplaces which recognize a union.

Public sector aggregate membership is larger than that in the private sector and in the public sector 3-employees-in-5 are members but the corresponding figure for the private sector is fewer than 1-in-5. But for the relatively high membership in the privatized transport, communications and utilities, private sector density would now be just 16 per cent. Even manufacturing now has a union density (27 per cent) below that for the whole economy (29 per cent). Small workplaces (under 25 employees) have density levels less than half those of larger establishments. And an individual is more likely to belong to a union if she or he lives in the northern part of the UK than in southern regions.

The number and structure of unions has altered dramatically too. A century ago there were 1,300 unions and at the end of World War II there were still nearly 800. Mergers, takeovers and the decline of unions for specific craft groups, like the Jewish Bakers and Sheffield Wool Shearers Workers Union, have reduced this figure to 226. Indeed, the 11 unions each with over 250,000 members now account for almost three-quarters of total membership. But some small unions do survive – including the Association of Somerset Inseminators and the Church and Oswaldtwistle Power Loom Overlookers Society.

Going hand in hand with the decline in union penetration has been a profound change in the type of mechanisms that provide employees with a voice – a big switch away from representative voice to direct voice. Representative voice occurs via a recognized trade union or works council. Direct voice bypasses these intermediate institutions. Instead, management and employees communicate directly with one another through, for example, team briefings, regular meetings between senior management and the workforce and problem solving groups, such as quality circles. Between 1984 and 1998, the proportion of workplaces with only representative voice arrangements halved, while those relying just on a direct voice nearly trebled. What happened was that unionized workplaces added complementary direct communication systems hedging their voice mechanisms rather than switching away from recognition, while nearly all new workplaces opted for direct communication methods without recognizing unions.

Whichever way one looks at it the last two decades of the twentieth century were a period of relentless, sustained corrosion of British unionization. Membership fell by 5.5 million and density from over half to under one-third of employees. The fraction of workers whose pay was set by collective bargaining halved from around 70 per cent to 35 per cent. The traditional explanations of growth and decay in membership involve: alterations to the composition of workforce and jobs; business cycle; and the roles of the state, employers, individual employees and of unions themselves. These six factors will be studied separately but we recognize that there is considerable interaction among them, particularly the last three. Union structures and policies – espousing single workplace unions and partnerships, for example – affect employers' attitudes towards treating with unions, and vice versa, and will also influence individual workers' membership decisions. It is also likely that the stance of the state – which affects the tone of labour relations – will help determine the degree of affection or hostility towards unions shown by employers and workers.

Changes in composition of workers and jobs, and the business cycle

Shifts in the composition of the workforce and jobs are normally put forward as a key ingredient of any explanation for declining membership or density. The argument is straightforward: more highly unionized sectors like manufacturing or the public sector and individuals with a greater likelihood of being a member – males or full-time workers for example – now account for a smaller proportion of total employment. So, as a matter of arithmetic, union membership also falls. This 'explanation' begs the question why unions cannot get recognition and membership in their non-traditional areas of employment.

Although the composition argument is simple and seductive it is less important than is commonly realized: alterations to the composition of the workforce and employment played a fairly modest role in accounting for the fall off in density and membership in the 1980s and 1990s. This is not surprising: manufacturing now has a lower unionization rate than the rest of the economy; similarly density is identical for men and women. Therefore the two most commonly cited composition factors – loss of manufacturing jobs and the rise of the female workforce – are in fact irrelevant to the composition argument. Union membership fell by over 5 million in the 1980s and 1990s. Evidence from the British Social Attitudes Survey and the Labour Force Survey suggests that only between 1 million and 1.7 million of this loss is attributable to the changed structure of the workforce and employment. The remainder simply reflects lower membership rates for given characteristics.

Carruth and Disney (1988) analysed the role of cyclical factors by constructing a model of union density for the period 1890–1984 and using it to predict density over the period 1971–84. They found strong links between the fall in density during 1979–84 and cyclical factors: notably steady real wage growth, low inflation and persistent unemployment. But now such explanations based on the trade cycle no longer stand up to scrutiny. Since 1993 unemployment has fallen continuously and so has union density – the reverse of the key prediction from models based on the economic cycle.

Role of the state

Activities and policies of the state affect union membership both directly, for example by legislation promoting or undermining union security, and indirectly, via its influence on the environment in which employers and unions operate.

In the 1980s and 1990s the environment in which the social partners conducted their activities was profoundly affected by the onslaught on public sector activities, the undermining of collectivism, and a greater emphasis than previously on product market competition. Public sector unions faced, for example, privatization, compulsory competitive tendering, contracting-out and derecognition at GCHQ. Collectivism was damaged by, for example, taking a million nurses and teachers out of collective bargaining and simultaneously breaking up the central control of education and health by introducing local management of schools and health service trusts. The state also promoted company-based payment systems like profit sharing and employee share ownership schemes through tax breaks (although there was surely no market failure to justify this) while disabling public protection for the lower paid by abandoning both Fair Wage Resolutions and wages councils. Product markets were altered forever by abandoning state subsidies to sectors like coal, steel and shipbuilding, axing exchange controls and, less obviously, by policies such as selling rather than allocating commercial TV franchises and building the channel tunnel. Each of these policies had the side effect of rupturing the previous sometimes cosy relationships between capital and labour.

Industrial relations legislation plays a more direct role in the ebb and flow of membership. In the 1980s legislation impaired union security by weakening and then outlawing the closed shop and interfering in check-off arrangements. The strike threat, a fundamental source of union power, was weakened by a succession of laws which permitted a union to be sued, introduced ballots prior to a strike, and outlawed both secondary and unofficial action. This legislation both raises the cost of organizing and reduces the costs employers face in opposing unions. Freeman and Pelletier (1990) calculated a 'legislation index' according to how favourable or unfavourable various strands of labour law were to unions in each year. These changes in the law were shown to be central to the decline in density in the 1980s. Further, the post-entry closed shop was outlawed in 1988 and the pre-entry shop in 1990. This axing of the closed shop then fed through directly into declining density in the 1990s.

Employers and employees

Did employers become more hostile to unions in the 1980s and 1990s? There is no evidence that union activity – the wage premium causing higher labour costs for example – resulted in a higher rate of closures among union plants compared with their non-union counterparts. Nor did management embark on wholesale derecognition of trade unions. Although derecognition in some national newspapers, TV and docks generated bitter industrial disputes and considerable media interest such management action was quite rare. But, as Brown and colleagues (1998) point out, recognition is not an all or nothing matter. In their detailed case studies they show that some firms that have formally derecognized their unions, in practice make use of them informally. By contrast, other firms that provide apparently substantial recognition rights have, in practice, 'narrowed the scope of bargaining so that there has been a measure of implicit or partial derecognition' (Brown et al. 1998: 28).

Union decline turns mainly on the inability of unions to achieve recognition in newer workplaces, reflecting, for example, Thatcherite views among some managers and the growth of investment from overseas. In 1980 around three-fifths of establishments both under ten years old and over ten years old recognized unions. But over the next two decades unions found it progressively harder to organize new workplaces. By 1998 just over a quarter of workplaces under ten years of age recognized a trade union, only half the corresponding figure for older workplaces.

In 1980 1-employee-in-4 was in a closed shop, but the legislative onslaught against trade unions in the 1980s meant that by 1990 very few workplaces still had such an arrangement. There was a distinct shift away from the closed shop towards simple recognition. After careful statistical analysis, Millward *et al.* (2000) conclude that, 'the decline in the closed shop and strong management endorsement of membership were the main reasons for the fall in mean union density in unionized workplaces between 1984 and 1990'. But the picture is 'quite different' for the period 1990 to 1998 when 'employees appeared to have lost their appetite for unionism'. In a nutshell, in the 1980s unions lost the support of the state and managers, whereas in the 1990s 'they also lost the support of many employees' (Millward *et al.* 2000: 151–2).

An important advantage to the individual employee of belonging to a union is the wage premium compared with equivalent non-members. This premium was approximately constant at around 10 per cent in the 1980s but is at most half that now. Partly as a consequence of such lower returns to membership there has been a large rise in the fraction of the workforce that has never been a union member, up from a quarter in 1983 to a half in 2001. In their dealings with individual employees it is less that extant members are quitting but more that unions cannot get individuals to join in the first place. Another facet of declining overall membership is the ebbing of density where unions are recognized. This may reflect disenchantment with unions but some individuals would probably join if a union were to be recognized in their workplace. Younger employees are much less likely to belong to a union than older workers and this gap in membership rates by age has grown dramatically recently. This is a worrying trend from unions' viewpoint because such non-membership is prone to persist across generations. Therefore union membership in future turns on getting recognized in newer workplaces and attracting younger employees into membership – a difficult task if they or their parents have never experienced membership and if the benefits of membership are demonstrably, or perceived to be, below those two decades ago.

Unions' structures and policies

It is plausible that unions' own structures and policies compounded the problems of a hostile state, antagonism from employers and the growth of individualism. Structural issues include moves to decentralization, the nature of mergers and multi-unionism. Policy areas cover the manner in which unions interact with members and potential members, employers and the state.

In the 1950s and 1960s unions like the TGWU, AEU and ASLEF took a strategic decision to decentralize such that lay activists – shop stewards – became responsible for collecting dues and members. But this shop steward role was shortly submerged by their collective bargaining function. Such decentralization made for uneven bargaining outcomes, which was divisive, and implied a loss of national voice. It may also have weakened employers associations. Many employers recognized unions by default – it was the norm of their group – but once the employers association fragmented, many employers no longer felt bound by such norms.

Mergers among unions boost the concentration of membership. In 1980 the ten unions with 250,000+ members accounted for 60 per cent of membership. But 20 years later 11 unions with over a quarter of a million members accounted for three-quarters of (smaller aggregate) membership. The bulk of mergers were aimed at raising market share – shuffling members around – rather than generating scale economies which would release extra resources for servicing and organizing. Indeed many mergers are simply a reaction to the loss of members and income. For example, this is the rationale for the Graphic, Paper and Media Union joining forces with AMICUS recently.

Multi-unionism (i.e. more than one union in the workplace) was an important feature of our industrial relations scene. For example, in 1980, 41 per cent of establishments employing 2,000 people or more had three to five unions present and a further 38 per cent had six or more. Although there were only a few such plants they accounted for a large fraction of total employment. Evidence suggested that when such multi-unionism goes hand-in-hand with fragmented bargaining, rather than single table bargaining, productivity growth is lower and financial performance and the strike record worse than in similar workplaces with just one union.

Unions' policies towards members and potential members sometimes raised a question mark over their desire to make the best of the hostile environment they faced. Consider some examples. First, recruitment campaigns are costly, the more so with a mobile workforce, smaller workplaces and growing employer opposition. The balance of expenditure between such campaigns and infill recruitment to sign up free riders was seldom a strategic decision, more a piecemeal *ad hoc* response to the crumbling away of the organizing cadres of the old communist party. Second, the concerns of female members – family friendly matters and rights for part-timers – seldom had a high priority. As Frances O'Grady, now Deputy General Secretary of the TUC, put it: unions were 'male, pale and stale'. Third, unions generally seemed oblivious to the rapid growth in 'never' members and the fact that such a state is likely to persist over a lifetime. The organizing academy and Unions21 are welcome, but belated, initiatives to sign up younger workers. Fourth, what were unions selling? For example, attempts to sell insurance and holidays – memorably described as 'arcade unionism' – were never likely to flourish, not least because other organizations like the AA already provided such services efficiently. And such activities hardly provide a strong incentive for a worker to show enduring loyalty to the union.

Many unions also took a long time to come to terms with their reduced status when treating with employers. Even though some unions had championed decentralization as a way of boosting membership, when decentralized bargaining was proposed by the employer – reflecting changes in work organization, new forms of corporate structure and more intense product market competition – it was frequently opposed by union leaders. In some spectacular instances – TVAM and News International for example – such opposition resulted in derecognition although this was quite rare. Multinational firms investing in the UK in cars and electronics normally favoured recognizing just a single union, sometimes with a no-strike clause such that any impasse in negotiations would be decided by arbitration. The union movement as a whole was hostile to such single union deals and even expelled the electricians union (EETPU) from the TUC for engaging in them. This whole episode, coming on top of the defeat of the miners, did considerable damage to unions' image and anyway was fruitless – virtually all recognitions in the last decade have been of a single union.

It was in their dealings with the state in the 1980s that the union movement demonstrated its most acerbic behaviour. For example, unions opposed virtually every successive tranche of industrial relations legislation despite the fact that the Thatcher government had a clear mandate and many of its proposals were supported by the public. Who now remembers those Wembley conferences to oppose the 1982 and 1984 Acts designed to constrain strike activity and promote democracy in union elections and prior to industrial action? Specific unions also challenged the power of the state. Set-piece battles were lost in the steel and coal industries. And guerrilla warfare in teaching and the civil service was a catalyst for major alterations in the organization and delivery of these services. Unions seemed not to realize, until it was too late, the fragility of their situation. Once the state withdrew its support for their activities, and many employers followed on the coat-tails of the state, union membership unravelled very quickly and their bargaining agenda became hugely constrained. Even though the union movement got its act together in the 1990s under the leadership of John Monks, General Secretary of the TUC, it was too late to stem, let alone reverse, the sustained loss of members.

The future: structures, resources and context

Disciplinary approaches

In the first part of the book, four authors discuss the chances of union resurgence or demise from their four disciplinary perspectives. Some disciplines, for example, economics, have long directed their attention to the analysis of trade unions. However, the mainly descriptive institutionalist perspective has been the dominant method of study in UK industrial relations, while other approaches, for example, those derived from organizational behaviour, which would appear to be inherently suited to the study of the union as organization, have hardly been applied at all. Studies of behaviour on the shop floor involving negotiation, for example, are reduced to statistical observations of their outcomes or descriptions of their processes, but seldom tested against behavioural theories. Other newer approaches, for example, network analysis, are conspicuous by their absence. Many prominent industrial relations scholars have struggled for years in an attempt to develop an industrial relations theory *per se* without much success – although the debate has been revived in a recent volume (Kaufman 2004a). It is not the aim of this volume to join in this debate, but instead to see what we can predict about the future by the application of distinctive social science theories.

Gospel, in his overview, adopts a historical-institutionalist standpoint – the dominant paradigm in UK academic industrial relations – emphasizing the importance of both history and institutions but playing down the relevance of theory. While he revisits the Webbs' predictions on the future of trade unions, a main thrust of his chapter is that the fortunes of unions have been, and will continue to be, profoundly influenced by markets and firm pressures. For a long time, these pressures worked broadly in favour of unions but, increasingly since 1980, the tide has turned. More intense competition in product markets and the trend towards offshoring will constitute an obstacle to unions in their attempts to further regulate the market.

Regarding firms, the Webbs and their institutionalist friends had a view about the importance of firm structures, control systems and strategies, and later on Clegg described how employers' associations and company management shaped the collective bargaining process. Ensuing trends towards smaller firms and workplaces, more multinationals, decentralization and the increase in management intensity have combined with the market scenario to make life even harder for the unions. Gospel sees no reason why these trends should not continue, providing little incentive for firms to engage with unions, but possibly giving scope for an increase in joint consultation. New EU legislation on information and consultation may provide unions with a new role. Unions will be replaced by other forms of regulation and employment relations will become increasingly juridified. Internationalism, seemingly the next stage of the Webbs' market extension idea, shows no real sign of taking off. Gospel concludes that, although we should not exaggerate the present downward trends, the future for trade unions in the twenty-first century is bleak. Resurgence 0, demise 1.

Willman takes a rather different approach: one which bemoans the lack of theory in UK academic work on trade unions in favour of institutional description and fact finding. He therefore takes organization theory – much of which stems from the US – and applies it to the union sector as a whole, at organization- or firm-level, and at establishment-level, thus extending Gospel's observations on markets and firms to the union sector. He concludes that the very structure of the union movement in the UK makes any resurgence very unlikely. At the ecology level, births and deaths concentrate diminishing resources into a few large diversified organizations, and no new organizations are emerging to capture large chunks of the resource base – members – especially in the private service sector. At the level of union organization, Willman notes that it is surprising that principal-agent theory has not been applied to the structure of UK unions when examining the relation between administration and representation. He notes that the consolidatory and impoverished conglomerate is a risk-averse model that is ill-equipped to push forward major change. His third level of analysis is that of the establishment, where he notes yet again the lack of theoretical work on, for example, co-operation or conflict.

Willman's conclusions are as follows. Any theory that attempts to explain growth/decline in union representation must consider the question of choice in voice regime; unions must increasingly compete with other channels in this forum, and their continuing relevance will depend on their successes here; a check on mergers to maintain competition is necessary; there is a need to acquire resources from members/employers; unions need to lobby government more and more to regulate the employment relationship; and unions should concentrate on the large non-union voice sector. Resurgence 0, demise 2.

On a rather reserved note for an academic of his persuasion, Kelly poses the question: why are trade unions not growing in what would appear to be a favourable climate? Aspects of the business cycle, workforce composition, and policies of the unions, state and employers all appear to be more favourable since 1997. Kelly uses social movement theory – or mobilization theory – at two levels of analysis to explain the apparent contradiction. Collective action frames and collective organization do not emerge spontane-ously; they must be constructed by leaders at local and national level. At the macro level, the 'opportunity structure' of unions – i.e. a focus on unions' political action – is relevant to any resurgence. At the micro level, the necessary feelings of injustice have not emerged amongst union members, workers' perceptions of management–employee relations have improved, and only a small minority of non-union employees believe that a trade union would make a difference at their workplaces. At the macro level, it would appear that unions' influence over New Labour's policies since 1997 is not as great as many would have thought – union recognition and the national minimum wage being the result of prior union–party negotiations – and, according to Kelly, post-1997, the union influence has been even more modest. Using Tarrow's four-fold classification of variables that might contribute to successful collective action, Kelly finds very few favourable conditions for such action to emerge. He concludes with three scenarios that would have to come about in order for union revitalization to happen: a concentration on organizing those with a strong sense of injustice and an antagonism towards management; a vigorous campaign against certain government policies to increase the public's view of union effectiveness; and the hope that any future Labour majority would be greatly reduced, thus creating more instability and possibly more opportunity for unions. Resurgence ½, demise 2½.

Economists of all hues have long turned their attention to matters such as the rationale for unions, the impact of unions on wages, employment and productivity, and unions' impact on equity and justice at work. Today, evidence suggests that unions have only a modest impact on wage levels, labour productivity, and financial performance but rather more in the area of employment, which grows, on average, 3 per cent more slowly in a union workplace than a non-union one. As regards fairness, the union influence is still significant. They narrow the distribution of earnings. For example, without unions, the gender wage gap would be 3 per cent wider. They also cut accidents and promote equal opportunities and family-friendly working practices. In his chapter, Metcalf outlines the conditions that will dictate the future of unions. He concludes that the unions' prospects for revival centre mainly around where the new jobs are and unions' own structures and policies. Whilst public sector employment grew between 1998 and 2004, it is most likely that this growth will slow significantly in coming years. There is no evidence of growth in jobs in utilities or transport, and thus no reason to believe that the unionized sector will expand disproportionately. On the contrary, what is likely to happen is the continued growth of jobs in the private service sector, currently only 15 per cent unionized. Union leaders therefore have a difficult decision to make: do they simply continue to service their existing members who are covered by collective bargaining – some 5.4 million – or do they turn their attentions to organizing? And organizing here requires further thought: do unions pursue either those 3.3 million who are free riders, i.e. who are covered by collective agreements but do not pay union dues, or do they chase the 14 million employees who are neither union members nor covered by collective bargaining? As a final sobering thought, given the current rate of closures and the current 'appetite' for union membership, Metcalf suggests that the private sector is heading for a unionization rate of around 12 per cent. Resurgence ½, demise 3½.

Challenges

Whereas the first part of the book makes predictions about the future role of unions, and especially outlines courses of action or circumstances that would be favourable to any possible resurgence, the second part examines specific challenges faced by trade unions which, if overcome, might help shift the balance more to the 'resurgence' column. Bach and Givan, in their chapter on unions' responses to public–private partnerships in the National Health

Service, outline a situation where the theoretical propositions described in the first part of the book can easily be applied to help us understand the apparent lack of success of public sector trade unions in whipping up much enthusiasm amongst its membership to oppose new policies such as the private finance initiative. Since the introduction of compulsory competitive tendering in 1983, there has been a steady contracting-out of ancillary labour in the NHS. A two-tier workforce has resulted, with contracted-out employees receiving only limited protection from TUPE Regulations. Bach and Givan identify two challenges faced by health service unions: the need to articulate a coherent national policy to influence government reforms, and the need to ensure effective union representation at workplace level to shape the implementation of the new agenda. They find that the unions' policies and organization are out of touch with Labour's vision of public provision, and this is not helped by the not totally negative experiences of union members involved in PFI schemes. Thus, the conditions of mobilization theory have not been met, in that there is no universal antagonism to management – a survey of AMICUS-AEEU members indicated that the majority of members in PFI schemes were favourably disposed towards their new employers – and no coherent collective action – especially with the cleavage between the professional and general unions.

Further, the fact that unions' structures have not changed to accommodate workplace change – i.e. a continued centralized union structure with an increased demand for local presence – is resonant with organization theory's predictions of decline being endogenous. Add in the economist's worry about unions' effect on firm performance and the historian's concerns about increasing outsourcing, and it all adds up to a rather bleak picture in the public sector. Yet, of course, public sector union membership remains, at least for the time being, the bedrock of the union movement, and with successes such as the Retention of Employment Model, where ancillary workers in three new hospitals were allowed to be seconded to the private sector while remaining on NHS terms and conditions – a significant improvement for those employees – it is not hard to see why. Bach and Givan conclude that there is still much to be done by the unions to persuade the government that the union movement has a vision for the future of public service provision, as well as to convince management that it is ready to move away from the conventional, sometimes adversarial, industrial relations that have characterized the past.

Sticking with the public sector, Marsden and Belfield offer us an interesting and optimistic – from the unions' point of view – case study of a new role for trade unions: that of the provision of procedural fairness in pay decisions in the teaching profession. Whilst it is not true to say that, in the past, unions have never been involved in procedural justice questions – for example, the content and procedures of discipline and grievance policies have long been subject of local bargaining – it is fair to say that the demise of collective bargaining in teaching and the increase in managerial discretion resulting from the imposition of performance related pay will oftentimes result in perceptions of unfair treatment by teachers. This new source of dissatisfaction at work and any resulting demotivation can offer new opportunities for unions – indeed, a sense of injustice and the infringement of procedural rights is a prerequisite, albeit not the only one, of Kelly's mobilization theory. Marsden and Belfield outline three areas in which teaching unions can intervene in the administration of performance related pay systems in order to ensure optimal positive impact. They find from their nationally representative survey of school teachers that procedural justice issues, for example the processes of goal setting and appraisal, are indeed of great importance to teachers, and that teachers believe unions to be the best providers of services to meet this demand, namely informing employers about the most appropriate forms of incentives in teaching; conveying employees' views about the practicalities of applying performance measurement to their jobs; and working to ensure the fair operation of any PRP schemes by management. Moreover, the unions' negotiation and representational activities have impacted significantly on the way in which the new pay systems are operated – for example, the teachers' workload agreement was the first to be reached between the DfES and the teachers' unions (except the NUT) since collective bargaining for teachers was dropped in 1991. This is a good example of a union both servicing its existing members in an effective way, and taking advantage of the conditions necessary for organizing as well – thus achieving the dual challenge set out by Metcalf.

Not only moving from centralized to decentralized structures, but even venturing into the ether will prove to be the saviour of the union movement, according to Richard Freeman. In our second optimistic piece, he argues that trade unions are changing from 'institutions of the Webbs' to 'institutions of the web', which will improve their effectiveness and revive their role as the key worker organization in capitalism. Despite the fact that, in 2004, nearly half of UK citizens were non-web-users, Freeman concludes from his content analysis of UK and US union websites and review of union innovations that the unions' increasing use of cyberspace will increase their chances of resurgence. Most important here is the fact that, before the Internet, it was difficult and expensive for unions to provide information to workers outside the organized sector, and to organize workers in small workplaces. The provision of such information will increase workers' perception of the value of unions and hence augment membership. Kleiner, in his US chapter, cites the example of an organizing campaign at the University of Minnesota that was conducted completely online.

Freeman describes six other innovative uses of the Internet: the provision of information on global labour issues which may hasten the Webbs' vision of the international stage of development; the creation of online campaigns including building networks of activists; the significance of unions' websites during industrial action, for example, the official union and rank and file websites set up during the UK firefighters' strike of 2002; the provision of online learning; the strengthening of union reps' expertise; and the trend towards open source union designs, something yet to explode onto the UK scene but arguably the major innovation in structural change, involving a break with the tradition of organizing by occupation or industry. Of course, the real challenge here, as Freeman notes, is how to link offline and online activities, meaning that at some point real people have to get together in the real world. Freeman concludes that unions are not being slow to adapt to technological opportunities; on the contrary, the opportunity to provide new resources to workers through the Internet has been the source of the sort of creativity necessary to provide a new spurt in union activity, and history tells us that we need spurts of activity for any resurgence.

Returning to the pessimism – from the unions' viewpoint – that underlies most of the contributions to this book, Robert Taylor asks whether unions can ever again enjoy an effective future as public policy advocates, with influence and authority over the way in which government behaves. He takes us through a catalogue of union successes (and some failures) in the political sphere, from their adoption of the cause of temperance in the nineteenth century to their securing of legal immunities from Parliament and the formation of the forerunner of the Labour Party. But with no wish to become corporatist partners in the modern state, at least until the post-war years there was still not much interest in tripartism. It was not until the last years of the twentieth century that the unions came to realize they lacked the strength to remedy their own vulnerability. As the result of a traditional unwillingness to press for legal rights and statutory regulation, the unions suffered from the crippling experience of the Thatcher years, with its concomitant emphasis on the individualization – over collectivism – of society, and called instead for the introduction of the sorts of rights that existed in most of the rest of the EU. This ambivalent attitude of the unions towards legal regulation, and its reliance on voluntarism in the past, has resulted today, Taylor says, in a situation where it is hard to envisage any obvious public role for trade unions that would involve their incorporation into any form of social partnership at a higher level than, say, the Low Pay Commission or ACAS – unless the UK were to move towards a European social market model. With the emphasis on labour market flexibility, unions will be tolerated by government and employers only as long as they prove their value, for example by providing better training, or by playing a part in the quest for efficiency.

But, at the same time, many reforms and societal changes would seem to bring opportunities for unions to modify their roles. The Information and Consultation Directive, according to Taylor, will provide the opportunity for revival of unions at company and sector level. High performance workplaces will require trade unions, where they are recognized, to become more involved in the creation of a more competitive economy. Demographic changes – an older workforce, the rise of women's participation, the need for elder and child care – present opportunities for unions to take an active role in, for example, discussions on pension plans and to form strategic alliances with a whole host of partners. But the question remains: what added value, over and above any statutory protection, can unions provide for their stakeholders?

What about the view from abroad?

We have the benefit of two contributions from countries traditionally depicted as falling at opposite ends of the regulation continuum: from the free market-based US model and from the more regulated (for the time being) German experience. Which of these has most relevance for the future trajectory of British unions?

On the other side of the pond, Kleiner notes that only 12 per cent of the workforce in the US are union members, and only 8 per cent in the private sector. In order to test whether Britain will follow this extreme example of demise, he examines the incentives for unionization and the costs of violating labour laws in both countries. Union avoidance techniques are more common in the US, where the union wage differential is approaching 25 per cent, than in the UK, where it is less than 10 per cent; incentives to remain union-free are therefore much higher in the US, and the costs of violating labour laws is lower, thus ensuring that the level of union density in Britain remains substantially higher than that in the US. Additionally, high performance workplaces are providing voice to workers in non-union environments in the US, often with financial incentives; and US unions are spending less money on recruitment drives. But, in spite of the decline in density, American unions have maintained their level of political contributions – indeed, they are the largest contributor to the Democratic Party's funds – and thus maintain a strong influence in American politics, driven mostly by public sector union involvement. US unions now concentrate more on lobbying members of congress and legislators rather than collective bargaining.

Kleiner then details some of the methods used by unions in both countries to halt the decline in density: union/management partnership in the UK; innovative use of the Internet in both; associate memberships in the US to familiarize new workers with the benefits of union membership (a major challenge for UK unions, we know, from previous essays in this series (for example, Freeman and Diamond 2003 on young workers; Bewley and Fernie 2003 on women)); and financial influence in the US pension system. But he concedes that, without a more favourable public policy environment for unions in the US, there is little chance that the current downward tilt will be halted.

Schnabel documents the substantial fall in union density in Germany; structural effects, macroeconomic factors, the transition process in post-communist eastern Germany and union policies all playing their parts. With union density now approaching 20 per cent, Schnabel points out that it is now high time for German unions to reverse the negative trend if they still wish to play the role they have occupied in the corporatist system. Changes in the German system of collective bargaining, such as the introduction of opening clauses – involving the flexible use of working time – in collective agreements, all illustrate the tendency to decentralization. But whilst there are similarities between the German and British situation, he warns that we should not speak of a convergence between the two. The legal framework for collective bargaining in Germany remains intact. The challenge for German unions lies with the increase in workplace bargaining and the relationship between the unions and works councils – now the 'pivotal institution' of the German system. Schnabel concludes that, whilst, like Britain, perdition may be more likely than resurgence, we should not hasten to consign the German trade unions to the archive of industrial relations history. These two authors, then, whilst noting some important differences from the British system, see no real possibility of any resurgence for the union movement in their respective countries, and indeed point to the likelihood of further decline.

Conclusions

The editors of a recent book on the topic of unions across the world in the twenty-first century (Verma and Kochan 2004: 4) ask whether the continued existence of the institution of the trade union is 'vital to the working of a fair and just society, or just plain old nostalgia' – whipped up by the ageing white men who constitute both the union hierarchy and the IR academic community. In order to answer this question, we can invoke George Woodcock's 1960s question: 'what are we here for?', the answer to which is to aid both efficiency and equity in the workplace. With regard to efficiency, there is today no difference in productivity or financial performance between workplaces that recognize a union and those that do not. This means two things: first, that the alleged adverse effects of union presence have now been attenuated, but also second, that if we are to believe the 'unions as a part of high commitment management' rhetoric espoused by, for example, the TUC, we should expect to start to see a positive relationship between unionization and firm performance. But do we? Research on the impact of partnership arrangements on workplace performance is only in its infancy (and the unequal nature of the relationship in many cases precludes the full participation of the employee representatives) and the jury is still out concerning management–union partnerships and their impact on efficiency.

Regarding fairness, the increase in wage inequality since 1979 can be attributed in some degree to the decline in the unions' influence. But 'although the unions' sword of justice may be a little blunter and corroded, it has not been sheathed for good' (Metcalf, this volume). Unions narrow the pay differential between women and men, black and white workers, manual and non-manual workers, and those with health problems and those without. There remain, however, several other areas of fairness which exercise workers – fair and just treatment by line managers, freedom from sexual and racial harassment, a certain degree of autonomy in our work to name but three. A recent report finds that, although we are working fewer hours, getting better pay, and are not so worried about our jobs, we are more concerned than ever about the lack of control we have in our daily tasks and the growing pressure caused by excessive workloads (Green and Tsitsianis 2004). Although some unions' bargaining agenda have now expanded to include issues such as work–life balance, it is not at all clear what role the unions will play in bringing about a fairer workplace in these terms, and especially where competition from institutions emphasizing the individual – such as the growth in statutory protection, agencies such as the CAB, and firms' own internal procedures – is high. Why should a low paid care assistant fork out for union dues when the only body that has helped her get a wage increase is the Low Pay Commission? Why should a banker be a member when the firm's internal procedures allow not only for her grievances to be heard but also for them to be heard in the context of a wider involvement in the work process? Why should a young worker rely on a union to take up his and his fellow workers' cases when men dressed as Spiderman on bridges, holding up traffic in the rush hour, get more media attention? Detailed analysis of questions like these by the trade unions, coupled with appropriate responses, will contribute importantly to their future.

The chapters in this book have concentrated on three major aspects: what is the most suitable organizational form for unions to deliver their objectives; to what end should they direct their resources in order to maximize impact; and what are the likely contextual factors that will shape their activity. Unions seem to have some difficulties in recognizing that the world of work has changed, and are therefore using structures and tactics more suited to the 1970s. At the macro level, the continued emphasis on mergers and acquisitions seems to run counter to the emphasis on decentralization in all other spheres of work. Do workers really want to join a large group, representing many different occupations, or would they prefer to identify with a smaller, dedicated body? A possible merger of AMICUS and the T&G, or Natfhe and the AUT, for example, might appear to open up economies of scale, but may cloud the objectives of constituent groups. At the workplace level, union structures seem to have remained obstinately hierarchical in the face of increased flexibility. One-quarter of unionized sites have no workplace representative. Half of non-members in unionized sites have never been asked to join. And union activity is taking place more and more in free time. It takes a certain type of individual to get excited by the terms 'regional council' and 'composite motion' – and these sorts of leisure activity certainly cannot compete with a night in with the Playstation. Yet observations of this type are not new – see, for example, Goldstein (1952) – and still the unions find it a challenge to alter their organizational structures, widen their bargaining agenda and get the right balance of resources dedicated to local level activity.

The question of the direction of unions' resources is one that has attracted much attention, mainly in the form of the servicing versus organizing – either at the workplace, or labour market, level – debate. Many commentators have noted the need for unions to reach out to those hitherto uncovered groups – for example, the low paid (Wills 2004), the young (Machin 2004), and non-standard workers (Heery *et al.* 2004). The dilemma that unions face is not knowing whether the investment in organizing now, to the detriment of service provision to their existing members, will pay off in the future. Of course, a union's biggest resource is its membership base – the members *are* the union, so theoretically it should be worth it, but this will in turn depend on how members contribute to union activity. However, as Willman (2004) notes, the trend towards the pursuit of scale (i.e. mergers) encourages centralization of resource provision that moves activities from the volunteer to the employee – and thus raises rather than reduces costs. More innovative tactics include coalition building with other interest groups and international links, both of which are in their early stages here.

The final factor concerns the various contextual impacts touched upon in the first part of the book – economic, political/legal, employer policies – that will shape any future resurgence of trade unions. On the economic front, whilst global competition continues apace with uncertain consequences, low inflation and a high employment rate seem set to remain for the time being. The private service sector will continue to provide the most new jobs, at both ends of the skill ladder. Yet unions may find it difficult to make inroads in such rapidly-growing occupations as care home workers and security guards, where regulation in the form of the General Social Care Council and the Private Security Industry Act can be thought of as a substitute for union activity, for example in laying down minimum standards of training. At the higher end of the private service job market, where individuals exhibit strong job satisfaction, have a high degree of voice and feel confident with personal negotiations, the demand for a trade union is often non-existent. The economist, therefore, sees little prospect of resurgence in the private sector.

As far as employers' policies are concerned, it would appear highly unlikely that the UK will return to any form of industry level bargaining, the scope of bargaining is likely to continue to be narrowed, and direct communication with the workforce will be the norm. The only exception here is the representational arrangement involved in the EU Directive on Information and Consultation, which many writers hail as the saviour of the union movement. Private sector UK employers' attitudes to unions are likely to be neutral. The numbers of small workplaces will continue to grow, with the concomitant threat of authoritarian management practices, but the nature of new jobs in front-line customer service may attract a different type of human resource management tactic that emphasizes the worker satisfaction/customer satisfaction relationship. From the institutionalist perspective, then, the climate is not ripe for union resurgence.

As both Kleiner and Taylor note, per member expenditures on political activity has increased in both the US and UK, and here the four largest unions constitute 40 per cent of the total votes cast at the Labour Party conference. But what does this mean? The unions have lost their power and they are no longer seen as an inevitable institution of society. The language of 'fairness at work' and 'social partnership' which characterized Labour's first term seems to have faded from the Party's industrial relations programme. The idea of pushing the balance of power back towards the centre seems to have started and finished with the enactment of a national minimum wage and recognition legislation, which undoubtedly provided unions with opportunities and successes but whose honeymoon period now seems to be over. The whole raft of EU inspired legislation to be implemented over the next four years will provide an opportunity for trade unions to monitor, but perhaps less impetus for them to act. For the mobilization theorist, vigorous campaigning against government policies like the private finance initiative is vital to the resurgence process: given the public sector's own trade unions' lack of a coherent vision, this seems most unlikely.

Chapter 2

Markets, firms and unions

A historical-institutionalist perspective on the future of unions in Britain

Howard Gospel

Key points

- The historical-institutionalist perspective, associated with the Webbs, Commons, and some of their successors, saw the importance of macro-economic and macro-political factors as shaping the broad context within which trade unions operate. Nesting within this broad context, this perspective placed great emphasis on the nature of markets and the organization of firms as shaping many aspects of union behaviour.
- When markets and firms were largely unfavourable, in the nineteenth century, trade unionism was a minority phenomenon. When markets and firms were reasonably favourable over a long time from the 1910s to the 1970s, trade unions prospered, despite periodic setbacks. From the 1980s onwards, markets and firms have changed in ways that have made trade unionism again a minority phenomenon in the private sector.
- Private sector trade union density stood at less than 1-in-5 at the beginning of the twentieth century and it stands at less than 1-in-5 today. The years from the 1910s to the 1970s were years of major fluctuations, but in long-term perspective they may also be seen as a historic period of high union membership and power, in the context of a largely supportive macro-economic and macro-political context.
- In the past, there have been periodic upward waves of union revitalization and growth. A historical perspective makes us aware that such possibilities may occur in the future. However, overall, the market context and the nature of modern firms are particularly unpropitious for trade unions and collective bargaining. It seems likely that we have witnessed a major discontinuity. Overall, the prospects for the twenty-first century are bleak.

Introduction

In Anglo-Saxon countries, the study of trade unions has traditionally been dominated by the historical-institutionalist perspective. The origins of this tradition date back to the earliest writings on unions in what might be termed the 'classical' period (e.g. S. and B. Webb 1894, 1897; Commons 1909, 1918, 1919, 1924). Subsequently, the tradition dominated the study of British industrial relations in what might be seen as its academic 'heyday' between the late 1960s and the 1980s (Clegg and Flanders 1954; Turner 1962; Clegg *et al*. 1964; Phelps-Brown 1965, 1986; Clegg 1985, 1994; Bain 1970; Fox 1985). It is notable that most of these writers produced both historical and contemporary studies of unions and the former very much informed the latter. The tradition continues, though recently it has been challenged in its approach to the employment relationship by perspectives which are more orientated towards human resource management or which adopt primarily economic, sociological, or psychological perspectives.

The historical-institutionalist approach is posited on several assumptions. The first is that history matters. Put simply, history matters in that it is important to understand the broad context of change and continuity; the past shapes the present and the future, but allows for chance conjunctures and choice by individuals and groups. The second assumption is that institutions matter. Institutions include norms, rules, and organizations which shape the relationship between individuals in society. For many, the fact that institutions matter would seem a self-evident statement, and institutionalism is probably best understood in contrast to certain kinds of reductionism which can be found in some areas of economics and psychology. The third working assumption is that methods and data matter in the sense that one uses whatever is available, quantitative and qualitative, and the task of research is to integrate these into a historical-analytical narrative. The final assumption is that theory does not matter too much or matters only in that it should be empirically grounded and should be inductive rather than deductive.

This chapter focuses on a group of writers, primarily from the UK and to a lesser extent from the US. Above all, it draws on the Webbs, whose two classic works (1894 and 1897) contain analyses and predictions which it is instructive to revisit in the light of a century of trade union history. Their works had a major influence on later writers both in the classical period and in the heyday of industrial relations. The chapter relates primarily to trade unions in the British private sector. It is organized as follows. The next section sets out the main outlines of a particular historical-institutionalist perspective, as developed in the classical period and elaborated in the heyday of trade union studies. The following section then summarizes some of the main patterns in private sector trade unionism over the last century. This is followed by a section which presents an integrated narrative. Finally, the chapter draws conclusions and speculates about possible future trends.

The main empirical argument is that various aspects of trade unions have been profoundly shaped by pressures emanating from markets and firms. When the latter were largely unfavourable, in the nineteenth century, trade unionism was a minority phenomenon. When markets and firms were reasonably favourable over a long time from the 1910s to the 1970s, trade unions prospered, despite periodic setbacks. From the 1980s onwards, markets and firms have changed in ways that have made trade unionism again a minority phenomenon in the private sector.

A historical-institutionalist perspective

From the outset, certain qualifications must be stated. First, we chose a particular set of authors and stress certain of their writings. Second, the emphasis is on analysis which is more towards the economic rather than the sociological or political end of the historical-institutionalist spectrum. Third, we focus on ideas from the classical years and the heyday period of historical-institutionalist writing and not on later developments of the institutionalist tradition where unions have been less the focus of research. The aim is to outline interpretations from these two points in time so as to consider their usefulness in interpreting subsequent history and speculating about future trends.

A starting point common to all the historical-institutionalist writings is that, though labour is bought and sold in the market, it is not simply a commodity and cannot be analysed like other commodities. Nor is labour a simple resource within the firm akin to other resources and again it cannot be so analysed. Labour cannot be considered like other commodities or resources, not least because workers seek to control the supply of labour and effort and because the employment relationship is a particularly indeterminate and on-going exchange. This starting position is to be found in writings from earlier and different traditions (Marx 1867: vol. 1, ch. 6; Marshall 1890: book 5, ch. 2). However, it is central to the classical works of the Webbs in the UK (1897: 308, 319, 355, 572, 658) and Commons in the US (1909, 1924: 285). Of course, these authors were aware that in practice labour has been treated as a market commodity and a simple resource within the firm, at different points in time, in different contexts, and in different countries. A major object of research has been to understand these differences.

Given this starting point, there are three main sets of themes or propositions which we choose to distil from the historical-institutionalist literature and to use in this chapter.

First, in order to ensure that workers are not treated as a commodity within the market nor as a simple resource within the firm, trade unions will come into existence to regulate both market forces and managerial hierarchies. The purpose of unions is not to supersede the market or the firm, but rather to set constraints on them. In the words of the Webbs, they come into existence to establish a 'common rule' within a firm for a class of labour and throughout a market for a particular trade. Thus, 'the central position of trade unionism is the advantage of a common rule co-extensive with the trade or industry' (S. and B. Webb 1897: 279, 576, 715, 834). In practice, unions seek to establish a minimum rate of basic pay and working conditions for a class of labour and to put a floor under wage competition between firms.

For his part, Commons (1909: 65; 1934: v. I) used a similar analysis and stressed the 'competitive menace' which grew as markets extended. As stated in his classic 'American Shoemakers' article (1909: 64), the 'extension of markets' both created unions and drove their development. In particular, he argued that unions would seek to grow and regulate terms and conditions up to the limits of national product markets. In a similar vein, Ulman (1955: ch. 3) later reformulated this and argued that unions would seek to grow and establish the common rule up to the limits of national labour markets.

Using a slightly different terminology, Turner (1962: 242) argued that over time trade unions seek to extend membership to fill 'vacuums'. Such vacuums may be spatial or occupational. Spatially, unions tended to grow from local, to regional, to national. This follows the Webbs who had described 'local clubs irresistibly expanding into unions of national extent' and who wrote that 'the whole tendency of trade union history has been towards the national solidarity of each trade as a whole' (S. and B. Webb 1897: 72, 79). Occupationally, Turner again developed insights from the Webbs and provided a classic formulation of 'closed' and 'open' unions. Thus, some unions will organize one particular occupation and seek advantage in being exclusive and maintaining the wages bill of its members as a small proportion of the employer's total costs. By contrast, other unions will open up and recruit complementary or substitutable labour and then close down. Some other unions, who recruit workers less powerful in the labour market, will open up more generally or from the start will be based on organizing a wide spread of members. Such open unions seek advantage by being large and being able to use their larger resources to win both economic and political advantages (Turner 1962: IV, 2, V, 1).

The second theme or proposition in the writings of the historical-institutionalist tradition is that the main method of trade unionism is collective bargaining. Of course, writers in this tradition were aware of other forms of trade union activity. Following the Webbs typology, they were aware of the 'mutual insurance' side of trade unions namely the provision of unemployment, sickness, superannuation, and other off-the-job benefits. They were also aware that workers acting autonomously and informally via 'unilateral regulation' could control many aspects of their work. Equally, they were aware of unions' political activities which could win legislative and state benefits for workers. Though the Webbs themselves ultimately favoured what they called 'legal enactment', seeing it as more comprehensive and permanent

(S. and B. Webb 1987: part II, ch. 4), most writers in this tradition favoured collective bargaining as the main method whereby labour might be protected against market forces and from managerial arbitrariness.

A corollary for many of the writers in this tradition was that collective bargaining was not just the main, but also the best, method, in terms of both social justice and economic efficiency. The earliest, classic statement of this is to be found in the Webbs (1897: part III). Later writers in the heyday of industrial relations studies raised questions about the economic efficiency aspect of trade unions but usually not the social justice aspect.

The third set of themes or propositions in the writings of the historical-institutionalist tradition concerns the factors which are deemed to shape union membership, structure, and behaviour. These may be grouped into four areas. First, there is the macro-economic and macro-political context. Second, the composition and attitudes of the labour force are seen as important. Third, unions themselves can influence their own destinies, especially in choosing their structure and their policies. Fourth, markets and firms are seen as important. Here we briefly outline the various explanations, but then concentrate on the fourth set of factors which we suggest offer particularly useful insights at the present time.

(1) Writers in this tradition were fully aware that macro-economic trends affected the spread and fortune of unions. They drew attention to the business cycle, in particular levels of unemployment, price inflation, and real wages. They were also aware that broader trade and currency regimes worked through these factors to affect trade unions. At a later stage of the tradition, when data and techniques became available in the 1970s, business cycle explanations began to be formalized (Bain and Elsheikh 1976). However, a strength of the historical-institutionalist school was always to see that the macro-economic context was never a sufficient explanation, and writers always stressed that macro-economic factors were filtered through the specific institutions of particular market configurations, employer strategies, and union structures and policies.

Similarly, writers in this tradition were aware of the importance of macro-political factors. They saw that the state, in its role as legislator, manager of the economy, and employer, played a role in influencing union membership and behaviour. The Webbs (1897: part I, ch. 4 and Appendix 1) not only stressed legal enactment as a union method but also analysed how the law and government support underpinned union activity. However, influential later writers, close to this tradition, provided a reinterpretation of this history. They argued that, once unions and their methods had been made legal in the 1820s, 1870s, and the 1906 Trades Disputes Act, the main role of government was and, indeed, had been merely to maintain a minimalist legal framework which would provide basic employment protections and enable unions to act independently in pursuit of their objectives. The exaggeration of so-called 'voluntarism' in British industrial relations (Flanders 1974; Kahn-Freund

1972, 1977; Wedderburn 1972) led to a tendency to downplay the role of the state in influencing the fortunes of trade unions. Both the direct role of the state in terms of legislation and the more indirect role in terms of the political climate were more significant than the received wisdom in the area came to acknowledge. The advent of Mrs Thatcher in 1979 showed the shortcomings of an overemphasis on voluntarism.

(2) Writers in the historical-institutionalist tradition were also aware that the composition of the labour force was significant in shaping union membership and behaviour. Some sectors of the economy were more likely to be organized by unions than others. Thus, the craft sector was the first to be organized in Britain and indeed in most countries. But, ultimately, the belief was that, given the nature of the employment relationship and the desire by workers not to be treated as a market commodity or a simple resource, waves of unionization would spread to all sectors. For example, writing a quarter century after the first publication of their major works, it was with a sense of prophecy fulfilled that the Webbs referred to the 'spread of trade unionism to new fields – to women wage-earners, to the great army of agriculture labourers and general workers, to the clerks and teachers, to various kinds of technicians, and even to branches of the professions' (S. and B. Webb 1920 (eds): vi). In the 1970s, there was a similar keen interest in the growth of white collar unionism (Bain 1970). Thus, there was an assumption in the tradition of the long-term forward march of labour, in line with compositional shifts in the economy.

Some emphasis was placed in these writings on the attitudes and values of workers in shaping union membership and behaviour. As suggested, there was a belief that some workers might be more union-orientated than others. This was classically elaborated by Perlman (1949: 237–42) who identified a 'consciousness of the scarcity of opportunity' which would bring workers together. Overall, the belief among British writers was that strong collectivist tendencies were deeply embedded in British workers and these would always provide the basis for mobilization around grievances. Later, however, other authors in the tradition sounded a note of caution; they pointed to the historical coexistence of collectivism with strong traditions of individualism (Fox 1985) and later began to suggest that the balance between the two might be shifting irreversibly in the direction of the latter (Phelps-Brown 1990).

(3) Some (albeit relatively small) emphasis was placed on unions themselves and how they might influence their own membership, structure, and behaviour. Thus, the writers in this tradition were fully aware of the role of agency. The tradition saw how, at certain points in time, in circumstances not of their own making, national leaders made strategic choices about their own unions and sometimes choices which affected the whole union movement. In this way, different unions have responded differently to similar circumstances (Undy et al. 1981). Equally, at local level, generations of shop

stewards and lay activists could drive the organizing activities, bargaining strategies, and governance arrangements of unions, as happened during two world wars, in the 1940s–1950s, and again from the late 1960s–1970s. However, for the most part, the tradition avoided some of the charismatic 'great man' and heroic 'rank and file' type interpretations of union history.

(4) Finally, we turn to the role of markets and firms and the emphasis placed on them in this tradition as important factors shaping union membership and behaviour. Here there are important insights which can be further developed.

In terms of markets, it was explicit in much of the historical-institutionalist writing that unions came into existence to regulate the labour market. A belief was that membership coverage and the reach of activities would grow as product and labour markets extended. Thus the boundaries and the degree of competition in markets would have a major effect on unions. Unions would seek to extend to the limits of markets and to take wages out of competition between firms. In turn, their ability to do this would affect their power to engage successfully in collective bargaining. It would also affect the ability to attract and retain members. However, to revert to Commons' terminology (1909), as markets further extended, the 'competitive menace' would constitute a major constraint on unions, until they were able to re-regulate newly extended markets.

Important in the consideration of markets is the notion of the price elasticity of demand for labour. This idea was originally formulated by Marshall (1890: book 3, ch. 4) but was well known to the Webbs (1897: 643–57). It was also fundamental to the insights of other writers in this tradition (Commons 1909; Ulman 1955; Turner 1962; Phelps-Brown 1965, 1986). Put briefly, three factors determine the elasticity or sensitivity of employment to wage rises: employment is less reactive where the demand for the product or service is unaffected by cost increases; employment is less responsive where it is difficult to substitute other labour or capital; and employment is less sensitive where labour costs are a small proportion of total costs. Where demand elasticity is low, rises in labour costs can be passed on in prices without the demand for labour falling significantly. Where demand elasticity is high, this can be done less easily and the position of workers and their unions is relatively weaker. This concept usefully links the firm, the product market, and the labour market and it will be used below to analyse the changing fortunes of unions in Britain.

In terms of firms, the Webbs and others in this tradition had embryonic ideas that the structure, control systems, and strategies of firms were important. Hence the Webbs stressed what they saw as the significant move from 'small masters' to the internalization of activities within 'large modern corporations' (S. and B. Webb 1897: 691). Small artisanal firms had fitted well with craft-type unionism. Modern business firms posed both an opportunity to organize large numbers of members and a challenge for unions in that such firms could offer high wages and benefits and might depart from the common rule. There was also the suggestion in the Webbs that large organizations, such as the railway companies and the Post Office, with integrated operations and tight control systems, might encourage a new type of union structure which would parallel that of the enterprise (S. and B. Webb 1897: 582, 691, 776).

For his part, Commons had a sophisticated idea of how firms could externalize or internalize transactions. Thus, firms could out-source activities or internalize them in the firm. Out-sourcing put pressure on labour standards and led unions to seek to extend their boundaries; in-sourcing in large enterprises created opportunities for organizing but might also enhance the power of employers to resist unions (Commons 1909: 39–83; 1934: 1–9). Hoxie's study of US unions takes this further and refers to the 'tendency of unions to parallel the form of industrial organization' (Hoxie 1923; Carroll 1923: 416): thus smaller artisanal firms were associated with craft unions, such as the shoemakers; bigger firms in modern manufacturing industries were likely to beget industrial unions. However, these were early ideas.

Later writers in this tradition shared the view that the nature of firms and employer control strategies were important and developed a better perspective on company strategy and structure. Clegg (1976) argued that what shaped unions was collective bargaining and what shaped collective bargaining was employers.

> If variations in the dimensions of collective bargaining shape union behaviour, what causes the dimensions of collective bargaining to vary? In most instances the answer is that the structure and attitudes of employers' associations and company managements are the main direct influence.
>
> (Clegg 1976: 10)

Clegg's discussion then centred on the important strategic issue as to whether employers acted singly or collectively through employers' organizations. In addition, he showed an awareness that differences in firm-level organization might affect the behaviour of trade unions. Thus, he referred to the importance of company structure and managerial control systems and cited the contrasting examples of the then British Leyland, with fragmented structures and control systems, and the American auto companies, including their operations in Britain, with more unified structures and control. These differences, he suggested, shaped different bargaining arrangements and variations in union behaviour (Clegg 1976: 106–8). However, notions of how firms are organized (Chandler 1962, 1977, 1990; Williamson 1975) had not at that date and arguably have still not been integrated into the study of trade unions. This chapter attempts to integrate ideas about markets and firms with the development of trade unions.

Contours of British trade union history

This section provides broad stylized facts on the history of trade union membership, structure, and methods in the private sector in Britain. Tables 2.1–2.4 present summary statistics for key benchmark years (circa 1906, 1935, 1955, 1972 and 1998/2001), chosen as relatively 'normal' years, outside of war and major depressions, and years for which data exists.

As described in the historical-institutionalist perspective, trade union membership developed in waves – expansions occurring in the 1850s–1870s, 1890s–1910s, during the two world wars, and 1960s–1970s and contractions occurring in the mid-1870s–1880s, 1920s–1930s, and 1980s onwards. Unions came into existence early in craft sectors, such as engineering and shipbuilding, and spread spatially and occupationally in ways described by the Webbs, Turner, and Clegg. Other groups which established stability by the late nineteenth century were less skilled workers in cotton spinning and coal mining. The 1890s and the years around the First World War saw the organization of semi- and un-skilled workers and transport workers, especially railwaymen. The years around the Second World War saw the organization of workers in new mass manufacturing industries, such as motor vehicles. The next major surge of unionism occurred in the period from the late 1960s through the 1970s, with the topping-up of density in manufacturing, the extension of membership among white collar staff, a significant increase in female unionization, and a major expansion in the public sector. In the light of compositional change, the groups which at present constitute the next potential wave of union membership are workers in the expanding private services sector (see Tables 2.1 and 2.2).

The structure of trade unions has changed significantly over the course of the twentieth century. Overall, the number of unions has declined. In part, this is the result of the decline in new formations, the main peaks of which being the 1890s, 1910s, and the 1970s. In part, it is the result of mergers, the main peaks of which being the 1890s, 1918–24, 1944–8, and from the 1970s onwards (Waddington 1995: ch. 2). In the nineteenth century, the majority of mergers were horizontal within an occupation; in the twentieth century, most mergers have been vertical involving unions within the same industry; and in the late twentieth century, mergers have been diversifications involving both industrial and occupational expansion across industries and between blue and white collar unions. As a result, membership has become more concentrated, but more diverse within most private sector unions. In the terminology of Turner (1962: 242), unions have progressively opened up and, by the late twentieth century, most union members were in open unions which organize either broadly within a sector or across sectors. However, islands of closed unionism have survived. Mirroring these changes at workplace level, at the beginning of the twentieth century, most workplaces were characterized by multi-unionism, usually with two or more unions

Table 2.1 Employment, including self-employment, selected industries and dates, UK (000s)

Industry	1871	1901/6	1931/5	1955	1972	2001
Agriculture, forestry, fishery	1,818	1,457	1,383	692	432	389
Mining and quarrying	528	938	1,087	867	396	50
Construction	718	1,219	987	1,385	1,380	2,057
Manufacturing	4,349	5,742	6,335	8,153	7,866	4,448
Transport and communication	620	1,174	1,516	1,660	1,439	1,946
Energy and water	20	92	245	381	358	306
Retail, hotels, restaurants, and other related services	700	1,150	2,977	3,113	3,412	5,339
Financial, business, and related services	90	189	460	534	820	2,590
Public administration, health, education	200	533	1.248	2,657	4,178	7,172
All	11,628	16,932	19,585	21,913	22,961	27,798

Sources: For 1871, 1901 and 1931, figures are taken from the Department of Employment (1971). For 1906, 1935, 1955 and 1972, figures are taken from Bain and Price (1980). For 2001, the figures are from the Labour Force Survey (2002).

Note
For 1901/6 and 1931/5, figures are mainly for 1906 and 1935.

Table 2.2 Union density, selected industries and dates, UK (%)

Industry	1901/6	1931/5	1955	1972	2001
Agricultural, forestry, fishery	1	5	22	26	9
Mining and quarrying	61	60	93	87	25
Construction	25	24	42	33	19
Manufacturing	18	27	47	59	27
Transport and communication	17	61	86	79	42
Energy and water	13	22	73	88	53
Distribution and retailing	3	8	12	12	12
Financial services	2	18	31	37	27
Education	4	51	69	67	53
Health	15	32	41	49	45
Public administration	4	55	70	73	59
Private	18	30	41	46	19
Public	11	26	74	73	59
Male	17	31	55	59	30
Female	4	12	24	34	28
Blue collar	20	24	49	52	27
White collar	12	21	31	34	34
All	13	25	43	49	30

Sources: Bain and Price (1980: 37–78); Labour Force Survey (2001).

Note
For 1901/6 and 1931/5, figures are mainly for 1901 and 1931. For 1901/6, 1931/5, 1955 and 1972, figures are from Bain and Price (1980), as calculated by the author, with membership by industry re-distributed as required between private and public sector. The figures for education before 2001 also include local government; the figures for public administration before 2001 also include education. The figures for blue/white collar are for 1901, 1931, 1951, and 1971 and are from Bain and Price (1980); the figures for 2001 are as estimated by the author from the Labour Force Survey (2001) (*Labour Market Trends*, July 2002).

Table 2.3 Trade unions, numbers and type, selected dates

Date approx.	Number of unions	Number of members (000s) Males (%) White collar (%)	Members in top 10 unions (%)	Number of shop stewards (000s) Number per member	Trade union type. Ranked by approx. order of total union membership	Multi-unionism. Ranked by approx. order of number of workplaces. % where available
1906	1,282	2,210 90 6	37		craft industrial occupational general	adjacent multi-unionism competitive multi-unionism single-unionism
1935	1,049	4,867 84 23	49		industrial general craft occupational	adjacent multi-unionism competitive multi-unionism single-unionism
1955	704	9,741 80 24	56	200 49	general occupational industrial craft	competitive multi-unionism adjacent multi-unionism single-unionism
1972	454	11,359 74 36	62	300 38	general occupational industrial	competitive multi-unionism adjacent multi-unionism single-unionism
1998	224	7,155 53 74	70	145 49	general/ conglomerate occupational industrial	single-unionism 52% adjacent multi-unionism competitive multi-unionism

Sources: Number of unions and number of members are from Department of Employment (1971) and from the Certification Officer for 1972 and 1998. Male–female and blue–white collar are taken from Bain and Price (1980: 41–2) and are estimated from the Labour Force Survey (2001). Union concentration for 1910 and 1933 is calculated from Clegg (1985: 570). The figure for single-unionism is from WERS 1998 for workplaces with over ten employees. Figures for shop stewards are from Clegg (1979: 51–3) and WERS 1998 for workplaces with over 25 employees.

Note
Figures for white collar for 1998/2001 are estimated by the author from the Labour Force Survey (2001) (Labour Market Trends, July 2002). Union types are as follows: craft unions are unions such as the Engineers; occupational unions such as the Spinners and Teachers; industrial unions are the Miners and Railwaymen. Single-unionism is defined as a situation where there is only one union in a workplace; adjacent multi-unionism where there are two or more unions in a workplace, but where they organize different groups of workers; competitive multi-unionism where there are two or more unions in a workplace and where they organize the same groups of workers

Table 2.4 Methods of job regulation, strike propensity, and employment protection legislation, selected dates

Date approx.	Collective bargaining coverage, excluding statutory wage fixing (% of all employees)			Collective bargaining at multi-employer level (% of all employees)			Average annual number strikes per million union members	Average annual working days lost per thousand union members	Joint consultation coverage (% of employees)			Legal enactment/ statutory regulation
	All	Private	Public	All	Private	Public			All	Private	Public	
1906	15			12			190	1,800				low
1935	36			30			152	349				low
1955	55			51			261	473				low–medium
1972	70	66	78	43	25+		253	1,237	50	42	63	medium–high
1998	42	30	68	15	5	42	27	63	50	67	42	high

Sources: The figures for collective bargaining are from Milner (1995); Clegg (1985: 548–9); Cully et al. (1999: 108, 197, 228–9); Forth and Millward (2000: 18); the Labour Force Survey for 2001 (*Labour Market Trends*, July 2002: 353); and Brown (2003). The figures for joint consultation are from the WERS, as supplied by Alex Bryson, and are estimates for workplaces with more than 25 employees.

Notes

The figures for collective bargaining are the best approximation from various sources for the benchmark year. The figures for joint consultation are from the Workplace Employment Relations Survey (WERS), as supplied by John Forth and Alex Bryson, and are estimates for workplaces with more than ten employees. Strike figures are for 1905–9, 1935–9, 1955–9, 1970–4, and 1995–9. Legal enactment covers protective labour law and excludes trade union and collective bargaining law; the ranking denotes the volume of legislation and its importance.

organizing separate groups of workers (adjacent multi-unionism). By mid-century, multi-unionism was more complex, often also with two or more unions organizing the same workers (competitive multi-unionism). By the end of the twentieth century, the main form was single unionism (see Table 2.3).

Turning to union methods: (1) From the late nineteenth century, collective bargaining became the main method of trade unionism, as the Webbs suggested (1897: Part II, ch. 2). However, at the beginning of the twentieth century, it covered only around 15 per cent of the labour force. This rose through two world wars and reached a peak of about two thirds of the private sector labour force in the late 1970s. By the early 2000s, coverage had fallen to less than one third of private sector employees. Bargaining structure has also changed significantly. From the 1890s to the early 1970s, multiple-level bargaining (multi- and single-employer) dominated in Britain. From the 1970s, single-employer bargaining has come to dominate. (2) Unilateral regulation did not entirely die, contrary to the predictions of the Webbs (1897: Part II, ch. 13). It grew during the 1900s and 1910s and up to the 1980s. Over the longer term, however, it has either been subsumed in collective bargaining or been rolled back by management. The roll-back has been particularly significant from the 1980s onwards. (3) Mutual insurance has seen a long decline, again as predicted by the Webbs (1897: 171, 826). For the most part, recent attempts to provide off-the-job benefits in terms of financial and other services have not been very successful. However, unions still provide significant job-related benefits, especially legal advice. (4) Legal enactment in the form of protective labour law has grown steadily, as the Webbs desired (1897: Part II, ch. 5). At the end of the nineteenth century, legislation consisted of basic factory and mines regulations. Through the first half of the twentieth century, there was a slow build-up of social welfare (state pension and unemployment insurance) and of protections at work (trade boards, wages councils, and legislation for particular industries). An accelerated growth of regulation began in the 1960s, with legislation on contracts of employment, redundancy payments, equal pay, and unfair dismissal. Though Conservative governments of 1979–97 removed certain protections (wages councils) and diluted others (unfair dismissal), in practice, the rolling-back of the law was limited, and simultaneously new legislation was introduced (collective redundancies, transfer of undertakings), as a result of EU membership. Further extension has continued under Labour governments from 1997 onwards, with the introduction of a national minimum wage and various EU-inspired measures (see Table 2.4).

In this overview of methods, we refer finally to joint consultation, defined as voice at work via representative committees short of collective bargaining. With a few exceptions, joint consultation was little discussed by writers in the historical-institutionalist tradition (Clegg and Flanders 1954: ch. 6; Clegg 1960). Overall, joint consultation grew during periods of union strength (early 1890s, 1910–20, 1940s, 1970s) (Ramsay 1977; Ackers *et al.* 1992). In union settings, it grew particularly during the two world wars (Croucher 1982: 149–74). Subsequently in the 1950s and 1960s, consultation declined as unions demanded collective bargaining, and commentators increasingly came to dismiss it. Thus, quoting McCarthy, the Donovan Commission concluded that 'consultative committees cannot survive the development of effective shopfloor organization: either they must change their character and become essentially negotiating committees or they will be boycotted by shop stewards and fall into disuse' (Donovan Commission 1968: 27, 54; McCarthy 1967: 33). However, from the mid-1970s, there have been a number of developments. First, the law has mandated consultation with either a trade union or other representative groups in areas such as collective redundancies and transfer of undertakings. Second, joint consultation has increased in the private sector, with over a quarter of private sector workplaces having consultative committees by the end of the period and with around two-thirds of private sector employees being affected by such arrangements. Third, in situations where unions exist, they are now less bargained with than consulted. Thus, Millward *et al.* (2000: 138) have referred to 'hollowing out' of union bargaining and Terry (2003: 492–4) has referred to the growth of 'consultation-based unionism'. Fourth, there has been a significant growth of direct employee involvement at work in the form of workforce meetings, briefing groups, and problem-solving circles (Forth and Millward 2002: 3–7). Increasingly, therefore, unions have had to accept multi-channel representation and to take account of both joint consultation and direct employee involvement (see Table 2.4).

We single out one aspect of trade union action, namely conflict and cooperation with employers and government. Of course, conflict and cooperation are complex processes which are only in part chosen by trade unions. At the level of the economy, wartime significantly helped unions but begot contradictions: labour was strong and had grievances, but equally there were pressures for cooperation, and it is remarkable how cooperation largely prevailed. Outside of wartime, national attempts at cooperation were tried in the early and late 1920s and again under a series of incomes policies in the three decades after the Second World War. The latter attempts gave unions salience, but led to disputes which ultimately damaged them (Crouch 1979; Middlemas 1980). At industry and workplace level, periods of high conflict were the early 1890s, the 1900s–1910s, 1918–21, and the late 1960s–1970s. These coincided with periods of membership upswing and with low unemployment, rising prices, and threats to real wages. However, periods of downturn also resulted in major disputes, especially in the 1920s and 1980s (Knowles 1952; Durcan *et al.* 1983). Over the last two decades, strike activity has been at a historic low (see Table 2.4). In parallel, over the last decade, there has been talk of 'partnership' and some so-called 'partnership agreements' have been signed. Such discourse and activities have historical precedents, but little came of these in the past, and, at present, they indicate mainly an increasing concern with union security and a focus on the firm and its performance.

Finally, we refer to the relationship between trade unions and the state. As already suggested, in the area of individual labour law, there has been a long-term build-up of protective labour legislation. In the area of trade union and collective labour law, legislation of the 1820s, 1870s, and 1906 secured crucial immunities for unions under the law. Thereafter, periodically, judges intervened to develop new liabilities; in turn, the legislature intervened to take unions outside civil law. Notwithstanding hostile legislation in 1927, this pattern prevailed up to the 1970s, along with the growth of some auxiliary regulation intended to support collective bargaining (fair wages resolution, information disclosure). The two attempts by Labour in 1969 and the Conservatives in 1971–4 to constrain unions and create a new framework of collective labour law were undoubtedly failures. However, later legislation by Conservative governments 1979–97 worked much more as was intended and has significantly constrained union activity in the area of the closed shop, check-off, balloting, and strikes. This gainsays earlier suggestions that the possibilities for effective law in this area were highly limited (Wedderburn 1972; Weekes *et al.* 1975). It also suggests that historically so-called 'free' trade unions and collective bargaining were in practice very dependent on the law, as indeed the Webbs (though not necessarily others in this tradition) had always seen (S. and B. Webb 1897: Appendix 1). Of course, Labour governments since 1997 have not repealed Conservative legislation, but have introduced new law in areas such as union recognition and the right to information and consultation. Over the last quarter century, Britain has ceased to be one of the least regulated countries in terms of collective labour law.

A markets and firms interpretation

How useful in interpreting these major trends are the themes and propositions distilled from the historical-institutionalist perspective? We begin this section with markets and firms which we have argued have been seen as important contextual factors within this tradition. We then bring these together with the trade union story in a historical-analytical narrative.

In terms of markets, up to the First World War, product markets in Britain were open to international trade, but with much collusion in the form of market-sharing and price-fixing. During the First World War markets were closed to international competition; in the 1930s this was reinforced and collusive practices increased. This developed further during the Second World War. It was only from the 1970s that markets again became significantly more open, import penetration rose, and collusive practices were curtailed. In terms of financial markets, up to the First World War, high exchange rates based on the gold standard created a hard environment in which wage increases were constrained for all except a craft elite. This hard environment was eased during the First World War, but re-imposed with the return to gold 1925–31. With the departure from gold and the advent of managed exchange rates, there was less downward pressure on wages and cost increases could be accommodated via devaluation. However, over the last 20 years with high exchange rates, this is now more difficult. In terms of corporate finance, up to the First World War, funds came mainly from retained earnings, family owners, and relatively patient debt. Between the 1920s and 1970s, there was more resort to equity market finance and ownership became more dispersed. This was the classic period of the separation of ownership and control and of significant managerial autonomy from financial markets. Through the 1980s and 1990s, ownership has been re-concentrated in financial institutions and has become more international, and external financing has come to be via relatively shorter-term market-based debt (Gospel and Pendleton 2003). We will argue that these developments exert new pressures on the management of firms and on trade unions (see Table 2.5).

Table 2.5 Market characteristics, selected dates

Date approx.	Product markets Import + export/ income ratio % Degree of competition	Financial markets Ownership Source of external funds, by approx. rank order		Labour markets Elasticity of demand
		Family	Institutional	
1906	53 Open–collusive	83 Bank Equity	2	Medium
1935	39 Closed–collusive	38 Equity/Bank	8	Low
1955	46 Closed–collusive	26 Equity/Bank	26	Low
1972	51 Closed–collusive	26 Bank Bonds Equity	30	Medium–high
1998	68 Open–competitive	0 Bonds Bank Equity	75	High

Sources: Grassman (1980); Franks et al. (2004).
Notes
The imports + exports/income ratio uses GNP minus public expenditure in line with Grassman (1980) for 1905–14, 1935–44, 1955–64 and 1965–75. The figure for 1998–2001 is calculated by the author from the blue books. The figures for ownership are calculated by the author from the sample of UK firms in Franks et al. (2004), Table 2. Family denotes the percentage of companies where founding family shareholdings exceed 25 per cent of ordinary share capital; institutional is the percentage of companies where the largest shareholder is an institution. The degree of competition, source of external funds, and elasticity of demand are ranked by the author.

These factors shaped labour markets. Up to the 1920s (with the exception of the First World War), the price elasticity of demand for labour was medium to high for most of the labour force. In other words, rises in labour cost could not be easily passed on in prices without the demand for labour falling. This constituted a hard environment for trade unions, with the exception of those which organized small groups of skilled labour or workers protected from competition. The First World War temporarily changed this situation for all workers, though subsequently the 1920s were a particularly hard decade for unions. In the period from the 1930s to the 1970s, demand elasticity was lower in most sectors – in a situation where competition was restricted, it was possible to pass on labour cost increases. Unions could survive and later grow, both among the skilled and unskilled. The labour market situation began to change significantly in the 1970s and, over the last two decades, demand elasticity has risen such that there are fewer rents to be shared with labour. Unions representing workers who are less skilled and exposed to competitive pressures face a hard environment (see Table 2.5).

In terms of firms, a number of trends should be noted. (1) Large firms grew in size by employment over the twentieth century up to the 1970s. Thereafter, the size of big firms by employment has fallen and the proportion of total employment in medium and small firms has risen. In part this reflects trends towards de-diversification and the growth of outsourcing. In addition, over the last quarter century, average workplace size has fallen in many sectors. (2) British firms have become more multinational and more foreign multi-nationals are to be found among large UK firms. This has exposed the British economy both to new methods and to greater competition. (3) In the late nineteenth century, large firms were often relatively simple, single-plant and single-product enterprises (so-called S-form companies). Some were organized on unitary lines, with centralized and functional organization (U-form companies). From the 1920s through to the 1960s, in part reflecting periodic merger waves, many British firms came to be organized on loose holding-company lines (H-form companies). Since the 1970s, more strategically decentralized, multidivisional structures (M-form companies) have come to predominate. (4) Family management and weak managerial hierarchies persisted for a long time in Britain. However, slowly, through the postwar decades, more professional hierarchies of salaried managers developed and this growth accelerated from the 1960s onwards (Hannah 1983). (5) In terms of labour management, since the 1960s, there has been a growth of salaried managers internal within the firm, with a rise in the number and qualifications of personnel managers. This has been paralleled by a withdrawal of most large firms from membership of employers' organizations and by a growing capability and preference for managing industrial relations internally within the firm (see Table 2.6; Gospel 1992: ch. 7).

We now bring together the trends in markets and firms with the trends in trade unions in a chronological-analytical narrative. The summary argument

Table 2.6 Large firms' characteristics, top 100, all firms, selected dates (%)

Date approx.	Top 100 % of total labour force	Top 100 Type of large firm Unitary, Holding, Multidivisional			Top 100 Multinational	Top 100 Membership of employers' organization for collective bargaining
		U	H	M		
1906	8.5	60	40	0	11	45
1935	10.8	46	52	2	24	55
1955	21.3	24	63	13	44	50
1972	22.9	8	18	74	54	38
1998/2001	17.5	2	9	89	75	4

Sources: The Top 100 are drawn from a database constructed by Gospel and Fiedler (2004); Whittington and Mayer (2000).

Notes
The figures are calculated by the author from the Gospel and Fiedler database of the top 100 firms by employment for 1906, 1935, 1955, 1972, and 1992/5/8. The firms are from all sectors and include nationalized corporations and the Post Office. U-form are unitary, functional and centrally organized; H-form companies are holding companies; and M-form are multidivisional. The figures for 1955, 1972, and 1993 are from Whittington and Mayer (2000: 174). Employers' organizations are taken to be those which engage in collective bargaining; the figures therefore exclude membership of peak organizations. It is assumed that for 1906 none of the railway companies belonged to an organization which engaged in collective bargaining, but all the coal and iron and steel companies belonged to such an organization.

is that, nesting within a broader macro-economic and macro-political environment, trends in market forms and in the organization of firms worked in favour of trade unions for a long period, especially in the 1900s–1910s, the upswing from the inter-war depression, and the long post-war boom. Increasingly since the 1980s, trends have worked against trade unions and collective bargaining.

From the late nineteenth century, trade unions grew in major struggles, such as are chronicled in union histories, e.g. the advances of the years before the First World War. However, this meant they also grew when several factors were supportive, for certain groups of skilled workers. There were major compositional changes working in favour of unions – the move from agriculture to mining and transport and to manufacturing. Up to the First World War, unions grew in a situation where, though product markets were relatively open, Britain was still the price leader in many industries and had captive empire markets to which it exported. Moreover, competition was tempered by collusive practices within many areas of the domestic economy. Financial market pressures were muted in a context where firms were often family owned and where external borrowings were small. In this context, the elasticity of demand for labour was reasonably favourable for more skilled workers, and costs could be passed on in prices without too adverse an effect on employment. Managers, who were often also owners, might have preferred traditional paternalistic dealings with their labour forces, but this was becoming increasingly difficult in larger firms and many employers came to terms with trade unions, crucially recognizing and dealing with them through employers' organizations from the 1890s onwards. The latter gave employers strength in numbers and also served to put a floor under wage cutting in an industry.

During the First World War, union membership greatly expanded and collective bargaining and unilateral regulation grew at workplace level. The growth in membership and bargaining was encouraged by government support and wartime circumstances – unions were seen to be essential for production, showed they could behave responsibly, and were able to benefit from the reduction of market forces. However, national bargaining also grew because of strong employer preferences for bargaining at that level (Gospel 1992: 79–84). Within a period of 20 years, as the Webbs described, trade unionism and collective bargaining became significant phenomena.

These developments affected union structure and governance. In line with the Webbs' analysis, by the late nineteenth century, national unions had emerged for many broad occupational groups and larger unions had developed complex forms of representative structure and bureaucracies of full- and part-time officers. Over the period up to 1920, there was a tendency towards the centralization of governance, but also counter-tendencies, especially during the 1900s and 1910s. The extension of product and labour markets lay behind these developments. A wave of mergers in 1918–24, in large part prompted by the need to deal with employers nationally, led to a significant increase in union concentration and the creation of some of the biggest UK unions, especially in the form of the two general unions. Union structure was largely set for the next half century.

In the recession of the 1920s, with contracting market demand, rising unemployment, but also falling prices and steadying real wages, union membership fell. In these circumstances, employers used the opportunity to roll back workplace gains in industries such as engineering and shipbuilding. In coal and cotton, faced with particularly severe international competition subsequent on the return to the gold standard, employers forced major adjustments. However, it is significant that during the inter-war years, for the most part employers did not seek to eliminate unions but rather to assert managerial prerogatives at the workplace level and to restrict bargaining to multi-employer level. During the 1930s, toleration of unions is to be seen in the context of growing protection in product markets and collusion in many sectors. This created a situation where the elasticity of demand for labour was relatively low and where unions could survive better than they had in the previous decade.

From the mid-1930s recovery onwards, membership picked up and grew through the Second World War, again with very significant government support. However, during the 1950s and early 1960s, overall density stagnated, in part reflecting compositional change – the decline of well-organized industries such as cotton, railways, mining, and shipbuilding. Subsequently, from the late 1960s, density grew strongly, with a topping-up of membership in manufacturing and significant extensions among white collar and female workers. This was in a context of low unemployment, accelerating price inflation, and perceived threats to real wages. Shopfloor bargaining prolifer-ated, accompanied by a growth in the number of shop stewards and in small, fragmented strikes. This was the period as classically analysed by the Donovan Commission (1968). It was also a period when a particular configuration of markets and firms favoured these developments. Product markets were still relatively protected and collusive; loosely-coordinated and weakly managed firms often still relied on employers' organizations even though these were increasingly ineffective. However, the 1970s were a turning-point. In part at government prompting, but more because of the pressure of increasing competition, employers began to deal with this unarticulated system of industrial relations. The development of new strategies internal to the firm was facilitated by changes in corporate structure (the move towards multidivisional forms of organization), changes in managerial hierarchies (the growth of more professional internal management), and the departure from external employers' organizations (Gospel 1992: ch. 7).

The decline in union density through the 1980s and 1990s is due to a number of factors and is analysed in more detail elsewhere in this volume. Some are the result of changes in the composition of the labour force, in particular the decline of mining, manufacturing, and utilities. However, density has fallen within most sectors and a compositional explanation alone will not suffice. Some of the fall is a result of the changed macro-economic context – more than a decade of high unemployment, less rapid price increases, and rising real wages. Some is the result of the changing macro-political context since the advent of the Thatcher government, associated with major defeats for unions such as the miners and printers and the introduction of legal constraints. However, decline has also differed between sectors and in particular there is a striking contrast between the private and the public sectors, with density in the former having fallen to around 19 per cent, while in the latter it stands at 59 per cent.

There are a number of significant differences between the public and private sectors. The latter operates in a context of increasingly competitive markets. In this situation, the elasticity of demand for labour is high, especially in the case of lesser-skilled workers – it is no longer easy to pass on cost increases in prices and, in the case of many less skilled jobs, technological and organi-zational changes have made it easier to substitute capital or overseas labour for domestic labour. Employment is therefore more sensitive to wage rises and unions confront a harder environment. Simultaneously, new financial market pressures on firms have increased. At the economy level, with high exchange rates and constraints on devaluation, the macro-economic context can less easily accommodate wage increases above the level of productivity. At the firm level, corporate ownership has been re-concentrated in financial institutions, many of them foreign-owned, which can more closely monitor performance and which are more demanding. Moreover, external finance is increasingly in the form of short-term bonds and debts and an active market in mergers puts pressure on firms to maximize shareholder value (Gospel and Pendleton 2003). There have also been significant changes in firm structure. The growth of more decentralized multidivisional forms of organization, a reduction in the size of companies and workplaces, and the development of outsourcing pose problems for unions: such developments put pressure on managers to minimize cost increases, while simultaneously increasing the costs for unions of organizing and servicing members. These pressures have further hardened the environment in which private sector unions operate.

Taking these circumstances together, relative bargaining power has shifted away from unions: employees are less likely to gain significant wage and other benefits from union membership; employers are less likely to accommodate trade union rent seeking; and unions find it more difficult to recruit and service members.

We conclude by relating this historical story briefly to three areas – union structure, union governance, and the balance of union methods. Changes in union structure can in part be related to the changing nature of markets and firms. As described above, up to the late-nineteenth century there existed a large number of unions, restricted to particular localities and narrow occupations. This reflected local product and labour markets and small craft-based firms. By the time the Webbs were writing in the 1890s, national unionism had developed, to the limits of national product and labour markets. However, there was a legacy of a multiplicity of unions and different types of unions. The mergers of the 1910s and 1920s and the growth of the general unions were in large part driven by the need to bargain at an industry level with national employers' organizations and later by the advent of a harsher market environment. Turner (1962: 242) described the situation mid-century as one where a few small islands of closed unionism persisted in a sea of large general and industrial unions. This continued up into the 1980s. Since then conglomerate mergers have been a consequence of the membership squeeze. Today the islands of closed unions are smaller and persist in a few market niches (train drivers, airline pilots); a few middling open sectoral unions survive (shop workers, communication workers); but the scene is increasingly dominated by a small number of large conglomerate unions. In a more competitive market environment and confronting more professional and diversified firms which will only deal with unions at decentralized levels, open unions feel they can best survive by becoming ever more conglomerate. Alongside this in the 1980s and 1990s, at employer prompting, within the firm there has been a move from multi-unionism to single-unionism or at least to single-table bargaining.

Changes in trade union governance can also in part be related to market and firm pressures. In the late-nineteenth century, there was a tendency towards the centralization and bureaucratization of unions, as classically analysed by the Webbs (S. and B. Webb 1897: Part I). This reflected the extension of unions to the limits of national markets and the opening up of unions into new occupational areas. It was also a response to firms choosing to bargain with unions through regional and later national employers' organizations and to the need to create parallel bureaucracies. From the 1900s, these trends were taken further, though subject to periodic challenges and the assertion of local autonomy, especially before, during, and immediately after the First World War. From the 1920s, there was a shift of relative power towards the national union. At mid-century, Turner (1962) discerned a pattern of development through three stages: from 'primitive democracies' based on direct participation which survived only in a few small closed unions; to 'elitist aristocratic' governance where a section of more skilled workers ran unions which had opened up and grown in size (the Engineers); to 'popular bossdoms' in large open unions where members willingly accepted rule by a cadre of full-time officers (the general unions). Later, in the context of shopfloor bargaining, the 1960s and 1970s saw the growth of new autonomy in the 'domestic union' as represented by shop stewards. From the 1980s onwards, there have been contradictory trends. On the one hand, initial high unemployment reduced local autonomy and national leaderships sought to exert more control so as not to fall foul of new labour laws. The number of shop stewards per member, which had risen in the 1960s and 1970s, fell and they are arguably now more dependent on the national union for advice. On the other hand, the law has vested more power in union members at the local level (Undy and Martin 1984). Also important, employer preference for dealing with unions at company or workplace level has further encouraged local autonomy.

Finally, we turn to the balance of union methods. The long-term decline of mutual insurance can be explained by the costs of provision and the advent of substitutes as provided by the state, firms, and markets, with which unions could not compete. Unilateral regulation has fluctuated over time, tending to grow as circumstances encouraged membership growth, especially reflecting soft product markets and weak managerial control systems. The long-term roll back in recent years reflects greater market pressure on companies and stronger managerial control systems which exist in modern firms. Collective bargaining therefore remains the main method of trade unionism. However, in the present open and competitive market context, it has ceased to be about the establishment of a common rule for a trade or industry but takes place at company or workplace level and is concerned with the trade-off of pay for performance. Decentralized bargaining of this kind reflects market pressures and managerial preferences. Moreover, in recent years, bargaining has come more and more to shade into consultation. Again, market pressures and firm control systems have played an important part in driving the decentralization and hollowing out of collective bargaining. One implication is that, with the shrinking in the coverage and content of collective bargaining, more and more workers must look to legal enactment for protection. For their part also, unions themselves have slowly and reluctantly had to look more and more to legal enactment as a method.

Conclusions and future prospects for British trade unions

What does this historical-institutionalist tradition and a markets and firms perspective tell us about future trends and developments? In the introduction, we outlined three sets of themes or propositions, concerning the purpose of unions and their extension to new areas, the centrality of collective bargaining, and the role of determining factors, especially markets and firms. Here we take these in reverse order, moving from shaping factors, to methods and processes, and to union membership and behaviour.

The historical-institutionalist tradition always saw institutional forces nesting within two broad contexts. In terms of the macro-political context, we have suggested that at least from Taff Vale to Mrs Thatcher the role of the state was largely supportive of trade unions. In a more marketized economy and where union strength has already shrunk, governments are likely to be less concerned about private sector unions and less likely to offer benefits than at any time throughout the twentieth century. The EU offers some hope for British unions, but with upper limits which may soon be reached. In terms of the macro-economic context, it seems likely that liberalizing trade and hard currency regimes will continue. Even when unemployment is low, recent years have shown that a rise in trade union membership can no longer be predicted. However, a return to rapidly rising prices and falling real wages might stimulate membership as in the past. But this in turn needs to be put in the context of other developments.

The nature and degree of competition in particular markets will be significant in the future as they were in the past. The boundaries of markets are determined by two main sets of factors – the first technological (transportation, communications), the second political (tariffs, laws on monopoly and restrictive practices). Technological changes are a necessary condition for the extension of markets and tend to be irreversible. In the future, continuing developments in information, communication, and transportation technologies are likely to lead to further market extension. The political aspect of market extension is more problematic. However, barring any major abnormal developments or macro-economic collapse, it seems likely that product markets will continue to extend and will become more competitive (so-called 'globalization'). For similar reasons, it seems likely that financial markets will become more competitive and owners of capital more international and more demanding. Labour markets have been slower to internationalize than other markets, but there are new trends in terms of international migration and so-called 'off-shoring'. Given this combination of product and labour markets, the elasticity of demand for labour is likely to remain high, especially for less skilled workers, and firms will be constrained in passing on labour cost increases in price rises. In the case of many service industries which are less open to international competition (transport, retailing, leisure), less skilled workers are often substitutable and labour costs constitute a high proportion of total costs. Skilled workers are better placed, but they have seen strong wage growth and have less incentive to join unions.

In terms of firms, some big companies (supermarkets, banks) may continue to grow in employment, but the trend towards the downsizing of the average big firm is likely to continue, and medium and small firms will constitute a higher proportion of total employment. Similarly, workplaces are likely to become smaller. The shrinking of big firms reflects a continuing search for external rather than internal economies of scale. The trend towards the internationalization of big firms is also likely to continue. In terms of structure, firms seem likely to continue to use variants of the multidivisional form, and even looser network forms of organization may grow, though simultaneously with tighter central target setting and performance monitoring. All these factors put major constraints on unions, raise the costs of recruiting and servicing members, and reduce the rents they can exact.

In these circumstances, there is little incentive for firms to engage in collective bargaining unless the costs of avoiding it are too high or it can provide them with compensating benefits. Where collective bargaining does take place, it will be constrained, both in terms of levels and issues. It seems highly unlikely that British employers will revert to employers' organizations and multi-employer bargaining. Unions will therefore bargain at the level of the company and even more at the level of the plant, largely according to employer preferences. In terms of issues, the trend over the last quarter century has been towards a narrowing of the scope of bargaining and, unless product and labour market conditions change, the scope of bargaining does not seem set to expand. However, unions may be consulted on more issues and, indeed, on issues on which they were in the past seldom able to bargain. The corollary of this will be that joint consultation, both with and without unions, is likely to increase, especially under the impact of EU-inspired regulations.

The introduction of information and consultation committees in the UK may be important (Gospel and Willman 2003). Here there are opportunities for both employers and unions. Employers may use such committees to exclude or expel unions; they may use them to strengthen existing bargaining and consultative arrangements which involve unions; or, more likely, they may let trade unions search for a role in servicing such committees. For their part, unions may be able to use such committees to infill membership and to broaden the scope of issues in which they are involved. Whatever happens

with forms of indirect representation, it is likely that forms of direct participation will increase, not least in unionized workplaces, and unions will have
to learn to operate with these.

On other methods, there will be contradictory trends. The long-term
decline of unilateral regulation will continue in most sectors and
occupations, surviving only in a few and in limited form. It will come to be
confined to what the Webbs (1897: 571) predicted would be 'the nooks
and crannies of the industrial world', in particular now in areas of the
public sector where competitive forces are weak. Limited mutual insurance
will be provided by unions, mainly in areas such as legal assistance. In turn,
this will reflect the continuing juridification of the employment relationship
(Supiot 1999): though the volume of EU directives may decelerate, there
will be much for the courts to interpret. Workers and unions will look
more to state institutions.

In these circumstances, there are a number of possible future choices and
scenarios for trade unions. The easiest prediction is that the number of unions
will continue to decline and there will be a further growth of large
conglomerate unions. However, we should remember the Webbs' caution
that the 'One Big Union' is unlikely to emerge (S. and B. Webb 1897: 139)
and Turner's suggestion that islands of closed unionism will survive in a sea
of open general unions. The existence of conglomerate unions may lead to
problems, with some possibility of breakaways and de-mergers. The big
question is whether conglomerate unions can effectively service existing
members and organize the vacuums in the service sector. Given the largely
ad hoc manner of their creation, no one union seems particularly well placed
for this, and, given the counter pressures described above, gains will be small.

The tradition of writings to which we have referred would suggest that
unions will seek to extend their boundaries as markets extend, in an attempt
to re-assert something like the common rule. Over many years, there has
been speculation about the growth of international unionism. Indeed,
internationalization would seem to be the next stage in terms of Commons'
market extension thesis. As on most of these matters, the Webbs had a view:
they argued that international unionism would be checked by 'racial
differences', to which they also added, in a more politically correct manner,
'differences in legal position, in political status, in industrial methods, and in
the economic situation' (S. and B. Webb 1897: 81, 863–72). However, despite
assertions to the contrary, international unionism has to date remained
embryonic, even within the new economic and political boundaries of the
EU (Waterman and Wills 2001; Hyman 2001). By contrast, some writers
have detected a tendency in the reverse direction: under pressure from markets
and firms, there may be a move towards a more and more enterprise-
orientated unionism; under the umbrella of ever larger formal union
structures, unions will do more of what they do at the plant or company
level and members will increasingly identify with the union at that level

(Brown 2003; Benson and Gospel 2004). The possible advent of works councils may accelerate this

The main challenge for private sector unions at the present time is to infill membership where they already have some presence and to organize members in the growing service industries. In the past, there have been periodic upward waves of growth which have done just this. A historical perspective should make us aware that such possibilities may be seized in the future. It should also make us beware of exaggerating present downward trends. However, overall, the market context and the nature of modern firms are particularly unpropitious for trade unions and collective bargaining. It seems likely that we have witnessed a major discontinuity. At the beginning of the twentieth century, trade unions were a minority phenomenon. By the end of the twentieth century, they are again a minority phenomenon in the private sector. The prospects for the twenty-first century are bleak.

Acknowledgements

I would like to thank the following for help with sections of this chapter: Peter Ackers, Stephen Bach, Alex Bryson, Andy Charlwood, Colin Crouch, Richard Croucher, John Edmonds, Tony Edwards, Sue Fernie, John Forth, Sean Glynn, Gregory Jackson, David Metcalf, John Pencavel, Paul Ryan, Mari Sako and Roger Undy.

Chapter 3

Circling the wagons

Endogeneity in union decline

Paul Willman

Key points

- Unions are frequently considered as idiosyncratic organizational forms, but the literature on organizations might help us understand decline.
- Unions have declined in numbers, members and membership density and they are deteriorating financially.
- Responses to this decline have reinforced it, as a shrinking number of conglomerates fights over a declining membership base.
- This affects the ability of unions to deliver voice at the workplace.
- Some of the causes of union decline are now endogenous.

Introduction

Arguably, one of the more curious features of academic work on trade unions in the UK has been its failure to develop or indeed use theory. First remarked on by Bain and Clegg (1974), reaffirmed subsequently by both Winchester (1983) and Kelly (1998), the revealed preference is for fact finding, institutional description and research agendas driven by government policy. As Kelly (1998: 21–3) himself notes, where hypothesis testing has taken place it has tended to be based on *ad hoc* reasoning about trends or correlations rather than attempts to falsify theory. He goes on to remark that this approach has led to major gaps in our understanding of what has happened to UK unions since 1980 and in our ability to predict what will happen in the twenty-first century.

Of course, the truth of the proposition depends how one defines theory and which literature is being targeted. Some would contend that there is a theory of trade unionism under collective bargaining in Clegg (1976), others that there is a form of institutional economic theory embedded in Turner (1962). That a great deal of work on UK unions is descriptive and that more theory is needed are both relatively uncontentious.

One particularly clear divide is between the institutional tradition in UK industrial relations on the one hand and the closely linked disciplines of organizational theory and behaviour on the other. Despite frequently focusing on similar phenomena, these traditions are not additive. For example, a recently republished and highly regarded industrial relations textbook in the UK contains a chapter on pay which makes no reference to the literature on motivation and rewards, a chapter on individualism and collectivism which does not mention the literature on teams and a chapter on the employment relationship which refers neither to psychological contract literature nor to transaction cost economics (Edwards 2003).

The organizational theory and behaviour literatures have largely developed in the study of business organizations at several levels from the behaviour and dispositions of individuals to the structure and conduct of firms. Although industrial relations institutions may be thought to exist within and between firms and although, as we shall see, scholars from the organizational literatures have occasionally used unions as research sites, dialogue between the fields has been very limited.

It may be unkind to remark that this appears to be a local difficulty, in two senses. First, the tradition so criticized as atheoretical is the 'discipline' of industrial relations rather than the study of trade unions *per se*. Disciplinary work in psychology, sociology and economics has tested theory on data of interest to industrial relations scholars. As I try to show in what follows, this work has taken place at the ecological level, looking at the union sector as a whole, at the structural level, looking at the organization of unions, and at the establishment level, looking at their internal operation and interactions with employers. It does not sum to a general organizational theory of trade unions, but it does represent the main disciplines drawn on by organizational theory. Second, much of this work both originates outside the UK and uses non-UK data; a substantial proportion is from the USA.

At the root of this estrangement between organizational theory and the study of trade unions is the extent to which unions are conceived of as highly distinctive forms of organization to which generalizations from the field of organizational theory cannot readily be applied. Taking this view, the highly idiographic research tradition in the UK has tended to generate studies within which any conceptual development is immune to the influences of theories primarily developed in the context of imperatively co-ordinated firms (e.g. Turner 1962; Undy *et al.* 1981; Undy *et al.* 1996). This tendency may be reinforced by the extent of paradigm competition within organizational theory itself (Donaldson 1995). There is a variety of organizational theories rather than an integrated paradigm for organizational analysis and it may not be immediately clear which of the set might yield the best results were it extended to the study of unions (Pfeffer 1997).

In this chapter, I try to make the case for such an extension. The case is mostly pragmatic; analysing unions as a population of organizations with certain structural characteristics and behavioural attributes may help us assess their prospects. Three levels of analysis are used. First, organizational theory contains powerful tools for the analysis of organizational founding and death; these operate at the ecological level, enabling analysis of the union sector as a whole. Second, it also contains tools for the analysis of organizational structure and effectiveness. These typically operate at the organizational or firm level and I will extend them to unions below. Third, it also contains tools for the analysis of behaviour in work organizations; these may yield considerable purchase on those factors at establishment level which influence union presence and behaviour.

The structure is as follows. The second section looks at the size and structure of the union sector as a whole attempting to make some broad judgements about its condition. The third section takes the individual union as the unit of analysis, seeking to isolate some trends in the organization of the largest unions and looking at the implications. The fourth section has a more micro-level focus, looking at union organization within establishments. Finally, the fifth section offers some broad conclusions about the future of unions in the UK.

I shall argue throughout that the state of the union sector in the UK itself inhibits its recovery. The pattern of births and deaths, the predominant structural form adopted by the principal incumbents, and the role of unions in influencing behaviour in establishments are linked into a pattern of retrenchment which implies that revitalization – which I operationalize here to mean substantially improved membership performance – is highly unlikely. Exogenous factors such as sectoral shifts in employment and changes in government policy have rightly been accorded causal primacy in the explanation of union decline. I argue that the response to these exogenous shocks has in practice rendered the causes of continued decline endogenous.

Ecology

Two of the classic studies in the field of organizational ecology focus on the founding and mortality respectively of American unions from 1836–1985 (Hannan and Freeman 1987, 1988). They concentrate on union density, by which they mean the number of unions rather than, as is common in industrial relations research, the percentage of employees in the labour force who are union members. To avoid confusion, I will use the term 'number of unions' below. Their concern is to understand how the structure of the union population conceived in these terms exerts an independent effect on foundings and disbandments respectively. Two generic and chronological effects are central. As unions are founded and their numbers grow, processes of institutionalization generate legitimacy (creating positive externalities) for this particular organizational form which in turn reduces organizing costs;

the density dependence effect is positive. However, when population size is larger, competition between unions and attendant resource constraints generate mortality and the density dependence effect is negative (1987: 918).

Empirically, they discover that the number of unions does not vary closely with aggregate membership or union density as conventionally conceived. Rather, in the US, the number of national unions stabilized before the major burst of membership growth and indeed growth in the number of unions may have provoked that membership growth. The number of unions began to decline in advance of the decline in the number of members (1987: 912; 1988: 27). They also found that unions established by merger had lower disbandment propensities (1988: 42).

Before turning to the UK situation, it is worthwhile summarizing how the mechanisms interact. Within organizational ecology a population of organizational forms (unions) occupy a niche which is a set of resources (members). The organizations are founded, their numbers expand and then they cover the niche to the limit of available resources. Their numbers then stabilize and death rates come to exceed birth rates, leading eventually to concentration. The longevity of the population as a whole depends on its ability to keep out other competing forms of organization from the niche – this is termed 'competitive exclusion'. There is a rich texture of competition. It takes place between organizations in a population within a niche and *between* populations of organizations for the niche. It takes place *over* niche resources and between organizational products. In mature niches, this results in a fall in organizational numbers and an increase in organizational size (Hannan and Carrol 1992, 2000). The approach has some parallels with that of industrial economics (Geroski 2001) in seeing the union movement as a sector which approaches maturity, net entry of organizations in the growth phase yielding ultimately to net exit as the sector consolidates around a small number of large organizations.

The analysis has not been replicated for UK unions. Nonetheless, the central proposition – that the structure of the union movement might exert an independent effect on its prospects – is of interest. We look here at two aspects; first, the number of unions and, second, their membership and financial resources.

In the UK, there is a long history of decline in the number of unions (Buchanan 1981), which predates by decades the decline in membership beginning in 1979. Similarly, there is a long history of decline – at least since the mid-1950s – in financial resources such as reserves and solvency (Willman *et al.* 1993: 13) predating membership loss. In ecological terms, there are indications that resource constraints in this niche go back a long way. While one might not argue that the ecology of the union sector itself precipitated membership decline it may have a role in explaining why, as Kelly and Willman (2004: 1–3) note, union recovery did not take place in the apparently more favourable environmental conditions of the early 1990s.

Table 3.1 Union ecology and financial performance

Year	Membership (1990 = 100) (%)	Number (1990 = 100) (%)	Solvency (income/ expenditure)	Reserves (total funds/ expenditure)
1990	100	100	1.01	1.15
1991	96.7	95.7	1.04	1.11
1992	91.0	93.5	1.04	1.15
1993	88.3	88.9	1.02	1.14
1994[a]	83.9	82.7	1.02	0.98
1995	81.9	79.3	1.02	1.08
1996	80.9	75.9	1.05	1.13
1997	79.5	72.1	1.06	1.14
1998	80.0	69.3	1.05	1.15
1999–2000[b]	80.5	68.4	1.04	1.16
2000–1	79.3	63.8	1.04	1.18
2001–2	79.0	61.6	1.02	1.12
2002–3	78.9	61.0	1.01	1.08

Source: Certification Office returns.

Notes
a   Affected by an 18 month return from UNISON following formation through merger.
b   Move from calendar to fiscal year.

Table 3.1 presents data on membership, the number of unions and financial measures in the aggregate for the UK for the more recent period 1990–2003. Is there evidence of density dependent competition here? The continued decline of the membership figures implies that the ecological niche of unionization is itself narrowing but the decline in the number of unions by almost 40 per cent would, *ceteris paribus*, imply a diminution of competition. The dynamics of this decline are of interest. Of those unions listed by the Certification Office in 1990, 25.7 per cent disappeared through disbandment by 2001; a further 22.3 per cent, generally much larger ones and thus involving far more members, 'disappeared' through merger. Foundings across the period summed to 9.6 per cent of the 1990 total.

UK trade union membership is highly concentrated but there remain large numbers of relatively small unions. The largest unions in 2003 are the progeny by merger of the largest in 1980. New unions have formed but in this period none has grown to be large. Since many mergers have resulted in conglomerate unions with overlapping job territories (Willman 1996, 2004) it is possible that the fall in the number of unions has reduced congestion without reducing competition; by this is meant that although the number of choices a prospective member has of unions to join (or employers of unions to recognize) has declined, choice, and therefore competition, persists within a shrinking resource base (Geroski 2001).

Reduction in numbers has certainly not been associated with improvement in financial resources. Solvency, i.e. the margin of total income over total expenditure, averaged 1.032 across the period; the average for the period 1950–70 was 1.4 and that for the membership-loss decade of the 1980s was 1.09. Similarly, reserves, expressed as multiples of annual expenditure, are at historic lows averaging 1.12 across this period, compared with an average of 3.55 in the years from 1950–70 and 1.28 for the 1980s. The substantial volume of net exit from the union sector and the merger activity of the 1990s is not associated with improvements in resource availability and indeed the union movement which is seeking to revitalize itself in the early part of the twenty-first century is financially weaker on these measures than it has been for at least 50 years. From 1990–2000 the *nominal* increase in union total funds was 32 per cent which is substantially lower than the increase in the FTSE 100 (approximately 190 per cent) across the same period. Given that a large proportion of union funds are held in equities (Willman *et al.* 1993), the disparity in growth rates here raises the possibility that the observed very tight margins of income over expenditure are sustained by depleting the asset base. Subsequent falls in equity markets may be behind falls in reserves in 2001–3.

Union balance sheets do not summarize all union resources and one possibility is that there are countervailing forces at work by which much union activity is sustained not by application of union funds but by membership activism and employer subsidy. However, the evidence from successive WERS surveys covering the period to 1998 would suggest that the figures in Table 3.1 understate rather than exaggerate the resource depletion of the union sector in the last decade of the twentieth century since on available measures it seems that supplies of activism and subsidy have shrunk (Millward *et al.* 2000).

In summary, then, there is at least circumstantial evidence that the state of the union sector itself inhibits recovery. Competition may be the force reducing the number of unions without enhancing the resource position of remaining players. If the number of unions falls further, there may be legitimacy questions; the death rate might lead to questioning of the organizational form. Specifically, employers and employees who want voice may seek other means of providing it.

The ecology literature as a whole provides no grounds for seeing unions as distinctive forms of organization in that they seem to respond to ecological pressures in ways very similar to other forms of organization (Pfeffer 1997; Geroski 2001). Lessons from other organizational populations are not routinely quoted in attempts to predict what will happen to UK unions and those predictions tend to be based on very simple assumptions. But the patterns of mortality and the nature of survivors do tell us something. First, the pattern of births and the nature of most deaths (by merger or absorption) concentrates dwindling sector resources in a few large diversified organizations. Second, new organizations are not emerging to capture substantial parts of the resource base. In previous periods of rapid membership growth in the UK such as the 1880s and 1970s, variants of the organizational form, first general unions then white collar ones, emerged to capture substantial resources. This has not happened yet in, for example, the growing private services sector. Rather old forms have moved in by diversification. A corollary of this second point is that the future of unions debate is often not about organizational founding but about the revitalization of a small set of large organizations. In the next section, we look at the prospects.

Union organization

Some topics, such as union democracy, have attracted theory driven approaches. Others such as union effectiveness and performance have not. In the latter case, where organizational theory has been applied, the dominant approach has been Weberian, contingency-theoretic and quantitative. It is Weberian in seeing a central conflict between principles of democracy and rationality. It is contingency-theoretic in seeking to isolate a set of scale and environment dependent organizational parameters, and it is quantitative in seeking to measure and compare these across the union population. A seminal contribution is that of Child et al. (1973) which elaborates the interplay between two distinctive internal 'rationales' in unions of goal formation through representation and goal implementation through administration. In the original formulation, they may conflict but are not orthogonal by definition and their interaction is an empirical question. Nor is effectiveness reducible to efficiency; rather, the overall effectiveness of the union may depend on the interplay between administrative efficiency and representational effectiveness (1973: 78–9).

Although this original formulation is based on UK data, subsequent work has primarily been in the US. Jarley et al. (1997) use a national data set to establish that representative and administrative structures in US unions respond to different imperatives. Whereas the former relates to the internal resolution of the competing forces of centralization of decision making and encouragement of membership participation, the latter relates first to the ubiquitous contingency variable of scale and, second, to characteristics of the union's job territory, particularly complexity. Overall, there has emerged a substantial volume of work mapping and identifying key features of union organization, particularly the administrative systems of national unions, in which variance in particular in rationalization, centralization and innovation emerges in the national population (for a review, see Fiorito et al. 2001).

A rather different tradition dating back to Blau and Scott (1963) analyses unions as a species of mutual benefit non-profit organizations. Empirical work in this tradition emphasizes the distinctive *complexity* of trade union organizations. Again using US data, this time for the non-profit sector as a whole, Knoke (1990) finds unions use a wider range of incentives for members than other non-profits, embracing utilitarian, normative and social motivations; this correlates positively with participation measures but also with goal displacement where the incentive systems themselves become organizational objectives. He also establishes that unions are more likely than other forms of collective action organization to use all four of the included mobilization techniques – lobbying, publicity, involvement in (external) elections and demonstrations including strikes (Knoke 1990: 111, 119, 199). This in turn is associated with a greater need for co-ordination than in other forms of not-for-profit organization.

From both approaches, the emerging central organizational design consideration for unions is the need to balance centralization-autonomy in the administrative sphere with autocracy-democracy in the representative system within organizations of considerable scale and complexity. Focus on this design issue has arguably been hampered by the tendency to discuss representative issues in terms of the concept of democracy rather than the concept of governance (see Fiorito et al. 2001: 216). Use of the former concept has spawned a substantial literature but it is one to which concepts drawn from political science, rather than organizational theory, have been applied.

In consequence, the dominant paradigm in the study of corporate governance, principal-agent theory, has been applied sparingly to the study of UK unions. This is surprising since the interaction between multiple and dispersed principals (members) and powerful incumbent risk-averse agents (union leaders) might benefit from parallel work on firms. There are two clear US examples. A specific principal-agent model is used to discuss strike activity by Ashenfelter and Johnson (1969). They unlock some of the behavioural implications associated with acknowledgement of a separation between union members and their leaders in the negotiation of wage demands. This approach is generalized into a theory of union behaviour by Martin (1980). He suggests that in 'non-proprietary' unions – i.e. where members can exert no private property rights over union resources – monitoring of agent (union leader) behaviour by principals (members) is difficult to the point where considerable managerial discretion may be exercised (1980: 90–107). His analysis of the implications, which develops arguments reaching back to Ross (1948: 27), exactly parallels that on managerial discretion within firms (e.g. Williamson 1975).

The emergence of the conglomerate form among the large unions which dominate membership share in the UK make such parallels interesting. The central problem in agency theory is the monitoring and control of risk-averse agents by principals who suffer from adverse information asymmetry (Jensen and Meckling 1976). Dispersion of ownership and scale of organization exacerbate this problem, as does diversity of owner interest. In very large conglomerate unions, with many bargaining units and diverse memberships, the effective monitoring of leaders by members becomes more difficult.

However, arguably the stakes are quite low. In conglomerates, all of the membership incentives Knoke identifies as prevalent within unions operate on a decentralized basis. 'Utilitarian' needs (in effect union instrumentality), social and affiliation needs and identity or 'normative' needs are delivered by decentralized bargaining, local meetings and sectionalized structures rather than by the activities of a rather distant leadership. There is evidence that decoupling administrative centralization (for example of finances) from representative decentralization in the creation of interest, industry or sectional groupings both satisfies existing membership interests and attracts new groups (Undy *et al.* 1981; Willman and Morris 1995). Committed activists aside, the policies of leaders and the satisfaction of members' interests may be only loosely coupled in large unions. This would explain the radicalization of union leadership in the UK in 2000–1 without the radicalization of union behaviour; as US evidence would predict, representative and administrative processes respond to different influences.

The use of merger to generate conglomerates is consistent both with the risk aversion predicted by principal-agent theory and the decoupling of representation from administration discovered in the US contingency studies. First, the ecological evidence quoted above indicates the improved survival chances of merged unions. Merger is normally an activity managed and implemented centrally. Where it is absorption, common in the UK, it requires no ballot of the absorbing union (Willman 1996). It is thus a strategy likely to appeal to risk-averse leadership incumbents bent on organizational survival (Martin 1980). In fact, there is evidence from the US directly relating leader discretion to merger activity (Conant 1993). Where mergers are combined with representative decentralization, many members remain unaffected by it, but scale economies cannot then be derived. The outcome is often a portfolio of bargaining units diversified across industries and sectors with attractive revenue and risk properties, but with potentially difficult expenditure issues (Willman 2001). The case study illustrates one set of serial merger activities in the banking sector.

Case study: winning the war but losing the peace

The Bank Officers Guild (BOG) was formed in 1918 as the industry wide independent trade union for bank workers. Within a few years, the major banks had formed their own staff associations in response. BOG, which subsequently became the National Union of Bank Employees (NUBE), stressed industry wide, geographically based organization and independence from employers. The staff associations were company unions stressing professional status and domestic (in-company) activities. They were heavily subsidized by the banks and did not charge subscriptions for many years. In competition with them, NUBE remained financially a fragile organization.

For both NUBE and the staff associations the battle for collective bargaining was long, lasting until 1970 when national bargaining in the clearing banks was established. The problem for NUBE was that the national joint machinery

continued…

embraced the staff associations too. They were equally endowed with facilities, could sell insurance products and were cheaper to join than NUBE. In the 1970s their membership performance in banking post-recognition was better than that of NUBE, which remained one of the poorest unions in the TUC.

The fruits of recognition for NUBE were indeed bitter. Membership and finances deteriorated markedly in the five years after the establishment of national bargaining. It remained well behind the combined membership of the staff associations in the clearers. Fearing further incursions, the union registered under the Industrial Relations Act to protect itself from the staff associations and left the TUC only to have ASTMS – now free to compete – step in to absorb one of the staff associations. In response, NUBE decided to recruit outside its traditional industry heartland, moving into insurance and building societies in competition with ASTMS.

This proved a momentous decision. It was successful in membership terms. Union membership rose from 100,000 in 1975 to 175,000 by 1990. It was not successful in financial terms since the unions expenditure rose as fast as its revenue. There was a reason for this. NUBE snapped up staff associations in the finance sector but to do so it needed a sectional and company-based representative structure to accommodate new entrants, which proved expensive to service. This caused tension as the proportion of members in the clearing banks fell from over 75 per cent in 1970 to under 50 per cent in 1980. In 1977, the national machinery in the clearing banks collapsed leaving company-based bargaining conducted by company-based sections of the union the main negotiating activity. Recognizing these changes, NUBE became BIFU (Banking Insurance and Finance Union) in 1980. It operated with a powerful regional administrative structure responsible for recruitment and implementation of national policy together with a set of company-based negotiating committees.

Compared to other unions, BIFU had a good decade in the 1980s as membership grew; finances remained weak because of competition and an expensive structure. Toughening employer policies also radicalized the staff associations which became more collaborative with each other (to help cut costs) and more like unions – for example allowing for industrial action – thus reducing the differences between the traditional foes in terms both of structure and policy. Collapsing employment in the sector in the 1990s led to poor membership performance for BIFU and the staff associations. Collaboration emerged. The staff associations started to court TUC membership and competition on subscriptions with BIFU was stopped. Negotiations on merger began with BIFU again competing with ASTMS. Eventually agreement was reached and the staff associations and BIFU merged to form UNIFI in 1999.

The victory was Pyrrhic. The declared combined membership of UNIFI in 2000, the first year after merger, was 171,000 – lower than BIFU's in 1990. Total income was under 70 per cent of expenditure. Although the situation improved slightly, the union remained with revenue shortfalls for the next three years and the meagre asset base was depleted as the merger failed to yield major scale economies; in fact, the terms of the merger led to UNIFI being less administratively centralized than BIFU and more a loose affiliation of company unions.

Soon UNIFI, like many conglomerate unions of its size, found that for the structure it supported it was below minimum efficient scale. Its main TUC competitor, ASTMS, had failed to remain independent too and following a series of mergers ended up as part of the large conglomerate AMICUS. In August 2004, following relatively brief negotiations, UNIFI joined AMICUS as part of its now large financial services sectoral grouping. A key objective in the merger is to remove inter-union competition in order to target acquisition of the remaining independent staff associations in the sector.

Sources: Certification Office reports, Morris et al. (2001);
Willman et al. (1993)

Decoupling of representation and administration may be of significance for the future of UK unions. In the US, Fiorito et al. (2001) found that rationalization was not associated with organizing effectiveness. In the UK, Charlwood (2004a) found evidence of a positive relationship between organizing structures at local level and organizing effectiveness, but none between national level arrangements and organizing success. Kelly and Badigannavar's (2004) work also shows the role of essentially local factors in organizing success and failure. These considerations, taken together with the work of Heery et al. (2000) and the general lack of overall organizing success in the UK, may indicate that co-ordination of activity within conglomerates is difficult. If organizing success is more dependent on representative structures than administrative systems it will, under current organizational arrangements, remain a local matter.

Much of the UK literature on union effectiveness is on organizing effectiveness. However, the more systematic US work (Fiorito et al. 1993: 133) shows that members' perceptions of overall union effectiveness are defined primarily by their perceptions of *bargaining* effectiveness. In the UK, Charlwood (2004a) is able to show for non-union workers the importance of union instrumentality for willingness to join. It is probably true for the UK overall that member and potential member definitions of effectiveness relate to perceived bargaining effectiveness. Two points may be made. First, overall, the union wage premium has declined across the 1990s (see Metcalf, this volume). Second, given the decentralization of bargaining, attributions of effectiveness are likely to focus on local rather than national representation.

The essentially consolidatory and impoverished conglomerate may be less a mobilization tool than a defensive and risk-averse accommodation poorly equipped to mount an assault on the growing non-union sector. On the one hand, administrative centralization allows managerial discretion over surpluses and economies of scale in the deployment of the fixed costs base. On the other, representative decentralization both allows current membership needs to be satisfied locally and attracts absorption candidates concerned about the maintenance of autonomy within a safe haven. It sets clear limits on the scope for post-merger cost savings. Taken together, the combination of resource centralization and activity decentralization cements the separation of principal and agent interests.

The structure contains many of the ingredients for extreme risk-aversion predicted by organizational portfolio theory (Donaldson 1999). It is in the interest neither of members nor leaders to accept risky bargaining units for entry or to deplete resources through organizing. In the absence of proprietary interest, there is no strong driver for change emerging from poor financial or membership performance. The prime remedy for poor performance is merger or absorption. As the case study shows, this tends to be a reactive process in which the original goals of the union (in this case industry organization) are displaced by the accommodations necessary for survival. The logical end point is a single conglomerate structure experiencing no competition for resources but, arguably, with intractable problems of internal co-ordination.

Representation

Studies of shop floor organization and bargaining are arguably among the great strengths of the UK industrial relations tradition and they often contain rich institutional detail revealing how unions deal with complex combinations of co-operation and antagonism within the employment relationship (for reviews, see Edwards 1988, 2000). But they have not, by and large, tested or generated theory about co-operation, conflict or the employment relationship. So, as Kelly notes, we have few tests of behavioural theories of negotiation in industrial relations field settings (1998: 17); there have been many in other contexts. Sociologists and organizational theorists may use industrial relations contexts as field settings for micro-level research (e.g. Friedman and Podolny 1992) but there seems to have been a fairly deep intellectual chasm between these theory-driven tourists and the institutionalist natives.

What threatens this divide is the contraction of coverage of collective bargaining institutions and the expansion of management-initiated voice mechanisms whose study is the natural territory of organizational behaviour scholars. An institutionalist approach tends to deal with this expansion by documenting it and the corresponding contraction in union coverage. However, where those concerned to focus on expanding non-union forms of representation can with some success attempt theoretical explanations of their growth, there is a clear danger that the institutionalist position will die with the institutions it has mapped.

Two recent approaches are illustrative. Hammer (2000) examines the theoretical and empirical foundations for different forms of non-union representation embracing both the psychological processes determining employee behaviour and the macro-level organizational forces which determine the effects of non-union representational forms. Her conclusions point to the importance of employer policy and practice in defining representational effectiveness. In a more general analysis, Kaufman and Levine (2000: 153) use transaction cost economics to examine the benefits of different forms of employee representation. They decompose the efficiency effects of employee representation into three: improved co-ordination, improved employee motivation and reduction in supervisory moral hazard.

The importance of these approaches is both theoretical and empirical. They offer the prospect of explaining why employers and employees may choose different forms of voice mechanism under varying circumstances. And, empirically, they offer the chance to explain the most significant development in employment relations across the last part of the twentieth century: the decline in union voice.

Neither study focuses on the 'voice' position in the UK. This is depicted in Figures 3.1a and 3.1b. The figure indicates the decline in voice arrangements which involve unions at establishment level and the sharp increase in non-union forms between 1984 and 1998. The probability of union only voice at the end of the period is approximately one-third that at the beginning. The probability of non-union only voice has increased 2.5 times (Bryson *et al.* 2004). The key point to make here is that the voice business itself is in good shape covering over 80 per cent of the employer market throughout the period, but unions are to a decreasing extent seen as the preferred providers of it.

We know from survey evidence both in the UK and US that employees want representation (Freeman and Rogers 1999; Diamond and Freeman 2001). The kind of representation they want gives involvement and influence particularly over pay, ensures due process and equity, balances independence from management with acceptability to it and does not cost employees much. We can deduce from Figures 3.1a and 3.1b that *employers* want voice; they increasingly 'make' it themselves in the absence of unions. We also know from WERS data that both unionized and non-unionized employers are more positive towards unions when they are seen both positively to impact performance and to assist in consulting with employees (Bryson *et al.* 2004: 145–6). Across the period of union decline since 1979, consultation arrangements have stood up better than collective bargaining (Gospel and

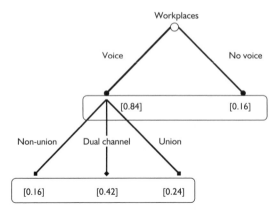

Figure 3.1a Unconditional probabilities of regime choice in 1984 (Source: WERS 1984)

Note
It was not possible to determine the precise nature of the voice in 2 per cent of cases.

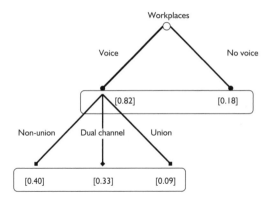

Figure 3.1b Unconditional probabilities of regime choice in 1998 (Source: WERS 1998)

Willman 2003). In short, in both markets unions are seen as 'solution goods' – i.e. one of several routes to the achievement of a desired organizational outcome.

As solutions, unions in the UK have become problematic. There is evidence of the 'hollowing out' of union representation, organization and membership density within unionized establishments. There is evidence of a reduction in the scope of collective bargaining. Both in the population of potential members and potential establishments there is a growing cohort of employers and employees who have never experienced unionization (Bryson and Gomez 2005). But there has been little derecognition of unions in old establishments. Moreover, new establishments which have chosen the non-union route have also chosen to install voice mechanisms. Although the market for what unions traditionally provide is in good shape, the traditional providers themselves are not.

A theory of growth or decline in union representation thus needs to explain employer and employee choice of voice regime. Given that most establishments have voice regimes, the theory needs to explain how unions succeed or fail in satisfying the demands of these two 'markets' for voice, which unions have traditionally dominated but in which they are losing substantial market share. It would contrast with those theories which see the factors determining union density, size or structure as exogenous – lying in macro-economic influences on employment or the sectoral composition of the workforce, with unions depicted as passive. Rather, an organizational theory would focus on how unions adapt to environmental change. It would indicate how trade unions generate and deliver benefits for two broad sets of stakeholder interests which are greater than those available through another form of voice regime. It ought to explain performance variations between unions and, given that most unions contain multiple bargaining units, within unions.

Indeed, one can sketch some of the policy changes unions could make better to satisfy the demands of both markets. Involvement and consultation are demanded by both markets but unions remain primarily focused on bargaining rights. Performance improvements are not routinely factored in to union policy decisions, but are positively viewed by members and employers. Organizational campaigns to recruit in new establishments or industries yield fewer benefits to existing members and employers than focusing on representational effectiveness within organized workplaces. Mergers between unions generate no obvious benefits, financial or otherwise, to existing stakeholders.

Conclusions

This chapter has tried to develop the theme that the current organizational form of UK trade unionism at sector, union and establishment level is inimical to union revitalization and thus that the current state of the union movement in the UK has itself become problematic. Put another way, unions in decline have made endogenous some of the motors for further decline and this may in part explain their inability to take advantage of ostensibly more advantageous conditions for union growth which emerged in the late 1990s. Further, it has suggested that sectoral, organizational and establishment level sources of decline are related. It has done so by deploying approaches not in common use to discuss UK unions, so the second objective has been to explore the usefulness of such an endeavour.

The chapter thus concludes by seeking to ask and answer several broad questions about the future of UK unions, using insights from organizational theory and analysis. The first is broadly ecological, the second structural and the remaining questions relate directly to union behaviour.

The first question is: what will define the size and population of the union sector? The overall size of the sector will be defined by the ability of unions to efficiently supply voice regimes for employers and members in competition with other mechanisms of voice provision. The number of unions will depend on the dynamics of inter-union competition in both employer and membership markets. Since competition for merger partners is an important part of that competition, it is likely that the number of unions will continue to decline but probably at a lower rate than the rate of membership concentration. Since founding rates are low and new unions show little sign of rapid growth, it is likely that the current incumbents will dominate the sector for the foreseeable future.

What will determine the structure of unions operating in the union sector? Membership is dominated by a few large players operating conglomerate structures in which the common organizational tension between administrative centralization and representative decentralization is acute. The merger process which has generated this set of structures has not eradicated inter-union competition. Nor has it generated the resource benefits following from economies of scale. In many sectors, employers and employees have a choice of union voice provider. Competition seems likely further to debilitate the union sector. The complete eradication of competition through further merger would create large problems of internal co-ordination and a loss of choice. In the short term, there appear to be powerful isomorphic pressures towards conglomeration as a defensive tactic.

What resources will unions deploy? The key resource a financially extremely fragile sector can deploy is the ability to acquire resources from employers and members in the form of recognition and facilities on the one hand and membership and participation on the other. As Kelly has noted (1998), the future of unionism is essentially a mobilization question.

What behaviours will unions engage in? Increasingly, unions will need to find a role in the governance of employment contracts which generates benefits for both employers and employees, although not necessarily in equal measure for both parties. This role can be secured both directly by engaging with the two parties and by lobbying government increasingly to regulate the employment relationship. The role is likely to diversify away from bargaining representation in at least two directions: first, towards consultation where employers are more receptive and legislation more favourable and, second, towards advice and insurance services selectively targeted within a diverse membership base. There is a large non-union voice sector which is probably a better focus for union energies than the smaller no-voice sector.

Will all of this work to restore union membership and influence to higher levels? Unions rose to high membership and influence levels in the institutional context of national wage bargaining and employer collusion to take labour costs out of competition. Neither firm performance benefits nor individual services were prominent in union policy concerns, nor was there large scale support for establishment level activity. They collectively rose to even higher membership levels and greater political influence under conditions of probably unprecedented shop floor bargaining power as national arrangements collapsed. Again, neither firm performance benefits nor individual services were prominent in policy concerns, nor were shop floor organizations highly dependent on the union. UK unions have contracted rapidly as their traditional strongholds collapsed and firms have sought to develop voice regimes without union involvement. Still, neither firm performance benefits nor individual services have been prominent in policy concerns and the capability to regenerate hollowed out shop floor organizations is still absent.

The rate at which employer preference for union voice has declined implies, in ecological terms, a legitimacy question in the private sector. Unions have declined so far that their ability to deliver voice is in doubt. If it continues even for a short period at the rate seen from 1984–98 then unionization will disappear as a private sector phenomenon. Employer choice is under-theorized in industrial relations but is probably the dominant influence on voice regimes in firms. In short, UK unions may not be on the road to perdition but they are probably in the twilight zone.

Chapter 4

Social movement theory and union revitalization in Britain

John Kelly

Key points

- Conditions for union recovery in Britain appear to have been very favourable in recent years but membership and density were no higher in 2003 than in 1997.
- Social movement theory throws a great deal of light on this puzzle by showing that whilst employees' sense of injustice and antagonism to management increased throughout the 1980s, they seem to have peaked in the early 1990s.
- At the macro-level, unions have been unable to exercise substantial influence over government, because of Labour's large parliamentary majorities and its ability to withstand divisions and rebellions within its own ranks.

Introduction: if conditions for union growth have become more favourable then why aren't unions growing?

Conventional economic and institutional theory suggests conditions for union revitalization in Britain are better now than for many years. But although decline in union membership – one facet of revitalization – came to a halt in 1998, unions have not yet returned to growth (Behrens *et al.* 2004). Even if we make some allowance for time lags in union responsiveness to changed conditions, these numbers are a puzzle for social scientists, and a disappointment for many union leaders. The principal aim of this chapter is to use social movement theory to try and understand why British union membership has not risen between 1997, when it stood at 7.80 million, and 2003, when it was 7.74 million (Certification Office). In addition I shall discuss the conditions under which unions might begin to recover their membership and influence. I begin by describing the economic and institutional reasoning that might lead us to expect a recent recovery in union membership and density. I then set out the main tenets of social movement theory, at both micro- and macro-levels, and in the next two sections use them to examine and interpret the relevant evidence. The final section of the chapter uses the theory to explore the determinants of these attitudes and to indicate the conditions under which union membership might recover.

Existing approaches to union growth

According to the introduction to this volume, union growth is a function of five factors: the business cycle, workforce composition and the policies of the unions, the state and employer. There are different ways of measuring the business cycle but levels and movements in unemployment, employment, prices and nominal wages are the four indicators used most frequently by labour economists. The majority of recent studies have shown changes in union membership and density to be inversely related to the first of these variables (unemployment) but directly related to the remaining three (Schnabel 2003). On recent evidence therefore business cycle effects have cut two ways: falling unemployment and rising employment should have encouraged union membership growth, but low inflation and steady increases in nominal wages should have had the reverse effect (see Table 4.1).

Workforce composition effects, measured by variations in density rates among different groups of workers, are far less important today compared to the 1970s. For example, in autumn 2002, union density was 29 per cent for men and the same for women. Turning to the policies of the main actors, and starting with unions, survey data of union structure and activity shows a significant increase in the level of resources devoted to organizing and recruit-

Table 4.1 Unemployment, employment, prices and nominal wages in Britain, 1992–2003

Year	Unemployment (%)	Population in employment aged 15–64 (000s)	Consumer price index	Nominal gross wages (whole economy)
			(% annual change)	
1992	9.8	25,275	4.2	5.8
1993	10.0	25,099	2.5	3.7
1994	9.2	25,307	2.0	2.9
1995	8.5	25,609	2.7	3.8
1996	8.0	25,955	2.5	3.7
1997	6.9	26,415	1.8	4.4
1998	6.2	26,773	1.6	5.1
1999	5.9	27,139	1.3	4.3
2000	5.4	27,515	0.8	5.0
2001	5.0	27,803	1.2	5.6
2002	5.1	27,961	1.3	3.6
2003	5.0	n/a	1.9	4.5

Sources: Unemployment: OECD (2004a), Statistical Annex, Table A; Employment, prices and nominal wages: European Commission (2003), Statistical Annex.

ment since the mid-1990s. In 1997 for example the TUC announced it was to open an Organizing Academy, which would train around 20–5 organizers each year (Heery *et al.* 2003). Measuring changes in union organizing resources is not straightforward and there are those who maintain that the current level of expenditure on organizing falls well below that required to return the movement back to growth (O'Grady and Nowak 2004). State policy overall has become more favourable to unions since 1997, measured in particular by the enactment of the union recognition provisions of the Employment Relations Act 1999 and by the willingness of government to include unions in deliberations over the national minimum wage. Again whilst there is debate about the problems and complexity of the law, it is clear that the costs to employers of avoiding union recognition are now higher as a result of the Act (Smith and Morton 2001). Consequently, and finally, employers appear to have become less hostile to union recognition post-1997. For example, cases of union derecognition, already in decline from 1992, had almost disappeared by 1997 (Gall and McKay 1999). At the same time the number of new recognition agreements rose from an average of 100 per year in the years 1995–8 to 483 per year during the period 1999–2002 (Gall 2004: 251). On the other hand, it is also true that a small but growing number of recognition cases are finding their way to the Central Arbitration Committee, an indication that employer resistance may be hardening even if it is not yet widespread (see Moore 2004).

Clearly it is difficult to weigh each of these variables and derive any exact predictions. In the case of the business cycle for example it would be possible to derive entirely conflicting predictions about the future trajectory of union membership. Nonetheless it would seem reasonable to argue that on balance they have become more favourable to union growth than at any time since the late 1970s. Yet the fact is that union membership in January 2003 was almost identical to the figure recorded six years earlier. Given the employment growth over these years, union density therefore declined, from 30.8 per cent in 1997 to 29.0 per cent in 2002 (see Chapter 1).

There are however two caveats that could be offered in relation to this evidence and which could serve to portray trends in union membership in a slightly more favourable light. First, these numbers refer only to *aggregate* trends and therefore make no distinctions *among* unions. If we look at membership trends for individual unions we find that in the period 1992–5, between one-quarter and one-third of TUC unions recorded membership growth each year (net of membership acquisition through mergers or transfers of engagements), while the majority were in decline. By the most recent five-year period – 1999 to 2004 – this situation had changed significantly and a majority of unions were recording growth most years (see Figure 4.1). This fact is not apparent from the aggregate figures because the scale of growth among the expanding unions since the mid-1990s has been just about matched by membership losses amongst declining unions.[1]

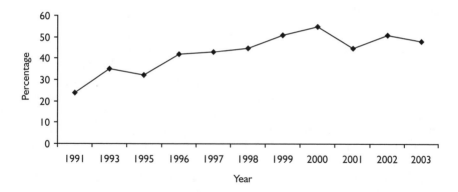

Figure 4.1   TUC unions reporting membership growth, 1991–2003 (percentage) (Source: TUC Directory, various years)

A second caveat turns on the distinction between stocks and flows of membership. Union organizing is a strategy to increase the rate of membership inflow but one could argue it is not necessarily designed to influence outflow, caused for example by employment contraction or inadequate servicing of union members. Measuring the success of organizing by reference to the stock of membership conflates these two flows and may therefore underestimate the impact of organizing on membership. Aggregate membership figures also fail to capture the composition of membership: a union may fail to increase its overall membership but still succeed in raising the proportion of women, ethnic minority or young workers among its ranks as a result of organizing activity. For example, former steel union ISTC (Iron and Steel Trades Confederation, now Community) has devoted substantial resources to organizing from the mid-1990s but has still experienced a sharp fall in membership from around 50,000 in 1995 to just 30,000 in 2003 (TUC Directory, various years). Judged by aggregate figures, its commitment to union organizing appears to have been a failure, but judged by membership composition it has been far more successful. A union that was once composed almost entirely of steel workers, an industry in steep employment decline, has been transformed through organizing into a union with over 60 per cent of its membership from outside the steel industry (Pass 2004).

So it is important to get beneath aggregate figures and differentiate the fortunes of individual unions, to disentangle stocks and flows of membership and to examine the composition as well as the volume of membership. But whilst these procedures are valuable correctives to a simple focus on aggregate stocks of membership, we cannot escape having to explain the big puzzle: why haven't unions and density grown in the relatively favourable conditions of recent years? To deal with that issue we turn to social movement theory.

Social movement theory

Social movement theory (sometimes referred to as mobilization theory) can be divided into two branches, covering the micro- and macro-levels of analysis respectively. The former focuses on the beliefs that an individual must hold in order for him/her to participate in collective action, such as joining a union; the latter is concerned with the structural conditions that are conducive to collective action by subordinate groups. Following an exposition of both branches of social movement theory, I then explain the potential significance of each for the puzzle of union membership trends in Britain before proceeding to look at relevant evidence.

According to the micro-level of analysis, it is not simply dissatisfaction at work which triggers unionization, but a sense of injustice, a breach of legal or collective agreement rights or of widely shared social values (Kelly 1998). Such rights could be either procedural – the right to a fair hearing on a disciplinary charge for instance – or substantive – such as the right to a certain rate of overtime pay. In order to generate support for unionism in a non-union workplace, such grievances must be felt by substantial numbers of workers. Workers with a shared sense of grievance are more likely to feel their grievance is legitimate and are more likely to develop a sense of group identity. Workers with a strong sense of group identity will also have a greater capacity to withstand managerial pressure against the formation of a union. Before getting to that stage, however, workers must either attribute blame for their problems to an agency, normally the employer or the government, or must feel the employer or government is liable for solving them. Attributions for injustice focused on impersonal forces such as 'the market' or 'global competition' are disabling (regardless of their validity) because they fail to provide a target for collective action. For example, Javeline (2003) found that Russian workers who believed the government was to blame for non-payment of wages were far more likely to engage in collective protest than workers who believed it was the result of 'economic forces'. Finally people must have a sense of agency (or efficacy), i.e. the belief that collective organization and action can make a difference. In the US literature on union membership, perceived union instrumentality, the belief that the union will be effective, is one of the best predictors of whether a worker will vote for or against a union in a certification election (Clark 2001).

These sets of beliefs, known as 'collective action frames' (Klandermans 1997: 17), are necessary but not sufficient for workers to join unions. There must also be a collective organization that can provide the resources necessary for such action; a balance of power favourable to such action; an opportunity structure, i.e. channels through which demands can be placed, such as bargaining structures; and minimal costs, e.g. state or employer repression, associated with collective organization and activity (Kelly 1998; Tilly 1978). Neither collective action frames nor collective organization emerge spontaneously from everyday social interaction: both must be constructed and reproduced by leaderships, typically small numbers of highly motivated activists, operating at both local and national levels. It is union activists who help construct a sense of injustice and focus worker attributions (blame) onto the employer, at the same time trying to encourage group identity and cohesion in the face of employer opposition to union presence or activity (Kelly 1998: 34–6).

The macro-level of social movement theorizing focuses on the link between the opportunity structure and the incidence of collective action. For most social movement theorists the 'opportunity structure' of interest has comprised the executive and legislative branches of the state. Translated into the world of trade unionism, this approach entails a focus on union political action and it is relevant to union revitalization in two ways. From the standpoint of union membership, it can be argued that union effectiveness (or instrumentality) can be demonstrated either through economic power in the labour market or through the exercise of political power in relation to the state. Union political influence in turn could impact on membership either because unions secure the passage of legislation which facilitates organizing – as in the case of the ERA (1999) – or because such influence convinces non-members that unions are effective.

But there is a second reason for examining the political role of unions and that turns on the nature of 'union revitalization'. Much of the literature on this topic within the 'liberal market economies' of the UK, USA, Canada and Australasia equates union revitalization with membership growth. But it is clear from the activities of union movements elsewhere in Europe that union revitalization can occur on dimensions other than membership. Unions can be assessed on their bargaining power, on their political power and on their institutional vitality, their capacity to recognize and respond to changes in their environment (Behrens *et al.* 2004). If union performance was highly correlated across these dimensions then a focus on membership alone would be sufficient to gauge union revitalization. In fact, the experience of a number of countries shows they are not. The Spanish trade union movement, for example, has exercised a significant degree of political power in recent years despite a density level below 20 per cent (Hamann and Kelly 2004). The 'collective action' so frequently discussed by social movement theorists need not consist therefore solely of strike action against employers, but might also embrace political action in relation to the state.

According to Tarrow (1994) the likelihood of such action depends on four variables: the degree of openness of the political decision-making structure, the instability of political alignments, the availability of influential allies and divisions among the ruling elite. The openness of decision-making structures can vary because of changes in political regimes or, more relevant in the case of Britain, because of changes in government. Shifting political alignments are especially significant when a government is formed by a coalition of parties or when the governing party rules as a minority administration.

Influential allies can be found either inside the state system, for example the House of Commons Select Committees, or within civil society where examples might include social movements dealing with issues of discrimination or welfare rights. Finally, social movements are more likely to pursue collective action and to be successful where there are divisions among the ruling elite, for example between different factions within the governing party (as with the Conservatives 1992–7 over European integration) or between different state ministries, e.g. between labour and finance ministries. To these four variables one should add a fifth and that is the attributes of union leadership. Political instability, opportunity structures and elite divisions will only be exploited by a union movement if its leadership is willing and able to mobilize union members for collective action.

It should be clear from this discussion that some of the variables identified in social movement theory are similar to those found in conventional theory: at the micro-level, the strategies of unions and employers clearly make a difference to the propensity of workers to unionize; and at the macro-level many commentators have argued for the importance of legislation in influencing union density levels (e.g. Freeman and Pelletier 1990). Social movement theory, however, focuses at the micro-level on the beliefs of individual workers shaping their willingness to unionize, an emphasis that is rather different from the strategic focus of conventional theorizing. At the macro-level of analysis, social movement theory goes beyond a focus on legislation and refers to the state as a political system embracing the executive, the legislature and political parties.

Micro-level evidence: muted discontent, tolerable employers, weak and quiescent unions

Central to social movement analysis at the micro-level is the concept of injustice. Unfortunately there is very little valid and reliable data on employee perceptions of injustice at the workplace so we are obliged to use a number of indirect measures in order to obtain some insight into what may have been occurring over the past 20 years or so. The annual British Social Attitudes survey, first conducted in 1983 and repeated every year since, is the only time-series data set of employee attitudes. For most years between 1983 and 2002 we have data on employee beliefs about pay inequalities and pay levels, about voice at work and about job insecurity (see Figure 4.2 and Table 4.2).

Broadly speaking, what this evidence suggests is the following: overall employee discontent about their own level of pay has hardly changed at all over the past 20 years. A little under half the workforce in 1984 thought their pay was unreasonable and the figure for 2001 was almost identical. The lack of change in recent years may reflect low price inflation and modest real wage growth, but appears curiously unaffected by the substantial rise in

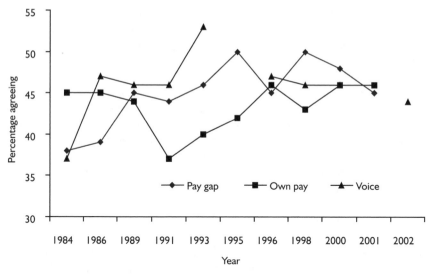

Figure 4.2 British attitudes to pay and participation, 1984–2002 (Source: Jowell *et al.*, *British Social Attitudes*, various years)

Notes
Pay gap: % who believe the gap between high and low incomes is too large at their own place of work.
Own pay: % who believe their own pay is unreasonable.
Voice: % dissatisfied with their say in decision-making at work.
Data only available for the years shown.

Table 4.2 An index of job insecurity in Britain, 1984–96 *

1984	1986	1989	1991	1993	1995	1996
−0.07	0.37	0.96	1.16	−0.37	0.22	0.35

Source: Bryson and McKay 1997.

Notes
* A 6-item scale anchored by −10 (high insecurity) and +8 (high security). Data only available for the years shown.

rates of profit and profit shares in national income since the early 1980s (Kelly and Hamann 2005). Employee concern about pay inequality rose from the 1980s but peaked in the mid–late 1990s and has since declined a little. Concern about lack of voice at work also rose from the early 1980s, peaked in the early 1990s and that too has since declined. Finally there is job insecurity where a composite measure based on questions about the perceived probability and costs of losing one's job shows both cyclical and secular trends. Between 1983 and 1996 perceived insecurity closely tracked the unemployment rate, falling between 1986 and 1990, rising in the early 1990s but falling again after 1993 as unemployment once again began to decline. However, it is also true that the recent level of employee insecurity remains significantly higher than the levels recorded in the early 1980s. Moreover disaggregation by occupational group shows some interesting shifts over time: insecurity amongst white collar workers, for example in financial services, rose more quickly in the late 1980s and early 1990s compared to manual workers (Burchell 2002: 68; and see also Heery and Salmon 2000).

This type of evidence on discontent is not easy to interpret, especially in a tightening labour market. It may be the case, for instance, that discontent remains as high as in previous years but is now more quickly resolved through quitting and labour-market mobility and therefore does not show through in attitude surveys. We also know that the link between these types of general attitudes and specific behaviours such as joining a union is indirect and mediated by a number of variables: perceived costs and benefits, social norms and personal controllability of behavioural outcomes. It is therefore important to try and corroborate this type of attitudinal data with behavioural evidence and there are three main sources available to us. Probably the best source is the number of employment complaints reported to Citizens Advice Bureaux, because the CABs are free to everyone and widely available throughout the country (see Figure 4.3). CAB complaints peaked in 1992–3 at almost 900,000 but have since dropped below 600,000: the 2002–3 level was 37 per cent below that of the early 1990s peak despite an 11 per cent rise in the number of employees over the same period (see Table 4.1). On the other hand, the number of applications to employment tribunals, claiming violation of legal rights, trebled between 1990 and 2003. This evidence appears to be suggestive of a steep rise in discontent but as Dickens and Hall (2003: 134) point out, the data is problematic because of the difficulty in disentangling the impact

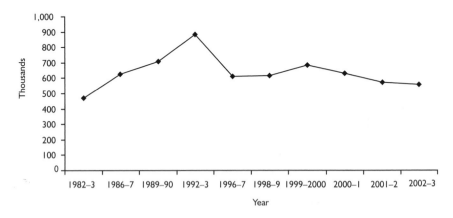

Figure 4.3 Numbers of work-related complaints reported to Citizens Advice Bureaux, selected years, 1982–2003 (Source: National Association of Citizens Advice Bureaux, Annual Reports)

of discontent from the effect of new legal rights and increased employee coverage for existing rights.

Finally, there is labour-market evidence on the probabilities of men becoming unemployed in Britain over the past 20 years and the impact of unemployment spells on earnings. This data usefully separates two components of job insecurity – the probability of job loss and the costs of job loss – whereas some of the attitudinal data conflates these aspects. According to Nickell *et al.* (2002) the probability of British men becoming unemployed was no higher in 2001 than 20 years previously: it rose sharply between 1979 and 1983, declined and then rose again from 1989 and fell once more after 1993 back to the level of the late 1970s. For less skilled workers, however, this cyclical effect has been superimposed on an upward secular trend as demand for unskilled labour has declined. There is also an upward trend in the cost of job loss, measured by the long-term (five year) drop in earnings on re-entering employment. From an average of 7.8 per cent in the period 1982–6 this rose to 15.5 per cent for 1992–7 (Nickell *et al.* 2002: 16).

Perhaps the best way of summing up this disparate set of data is to say that the general level of employee discontent did seem to increase from the early 1980s through into the 1990s but there has been no further significant increase during the past ten years or so and indeed there may even have been some reduction. To put the matter differently, employee discontent during the past five years appears somewhat muted compared to the 1980s and early 1990s. Other things being equal this evidence poses a problem for unions, but it is one that union leaderships could overcome provided they are willing and able successfully to attribute blame for employee problems onto the employer.

As with employees' sense of injustice, we are again obliged to use an imperfect measure for employee propensity to blame the employer for their workplace problems. The BSA survey series has data on a number of related measures, such as worker perceptions of management–employee relations in general and management-employee relations at their own workplace (see Figure 4.4). As with worker discontent, the BSA data show a modest rise in critical attitudes to management from 1983 through to around 1995 followed by an equally modest decline up to the present. In other words these data are consistent with the evidence on employee discontent, showing a rise and fall over the past 20 years with a peak in the early–mid-1990s.

Finally we turn to evidence on employee beliefs about union instrumentality because even aggrieved employees with a sense of antagonism towards management will be unlikely to join a union unless they believe it can make a significant difference at their place of work (Charlwood 2002). Time-series data from BSA reported in an earlier study was quite discouraging for unions: in 1983 a mere 5 per cent of the population thought trade unions had 'too little power' but by 1998 the figure was 22 per cent, with most respondents believing unions had 'about the right amount of power' (Kelly 1998: 48–9). It is not entirely clear whether we should read this data as indicative of an

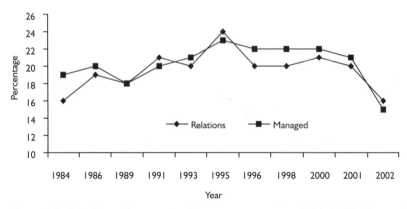

Figure 4.4 British employee attitudes to management, 1984–2002 (% employees agreeing) (Source: Jowell *et al.*, *British Social Attitudes*, various years)

Notes
Relations: % who would describe relations between management and other employees at their workplace as not very good or not at all good.
Managed: % who in general would say their workplace was not well managed.
Data only available for the years shown.

increased perception of union weakness (5 per cent up to 22 per cent) or focus on the fact that most respondents continue to believe unions have about the right amount of power. Nor is it clear what people understand by the 'right amount'. Fortunately the 1998 BSA survey asked a number of direct questions about union membership and effectiveness at the workplace. Of 646 non-union employees, 15 per cent said they would be 'very likely' to join a union if it was available at their workplace; a further 25 per cent thought they would be 'fairly likely' to join making 40 per cent in total. However, if we move from statements of behavioural intent to appraisals of union instrumentality, we find a rather different picture. Asked if unions would make a difference at work, only 17 per cent of these respondents thought they would do so (Bryson 1999).

If we look at evidence from WERS and elsewhere on the *actual* impact of unions, it is clear they do continue to make a significant difference to pay inequalities, equal opportunities policies, discipline and dismissal rates and employee voice. However, it also appears to be the case that the union impact on pay levels (union mark-up) has fallen significantly in recent years, especially for skilled, white Caucasian males (less so for low skilled, ethnic minorities and women) (Blanchflower and Bryson 2003; Metcalf, this volume). This econometric evidence on pay is consistent with the BSA social survey data on union effectiveness and raises a critical but neglected question: what factors influence employee perceptions of union instrumentality or power? There is hardly any evidence on this issue, but one piece of research, conducted many years ago, suggested that public perceptions of trade union power were highly correlated with three factors: the degree of approval of unions in public opinion, the level of strike activity and the individual's propensity to join unions (Edwards and Bain 1988). Theoretically this suggests that levels of strike activity may play an important role in supplying information to non-union employees about union effectiveness. In view of the fact that British strike frequency is now well below 200 per annum and there is little public evidence of trade union political influence (*pace* Spain or Italy for example), non-union employees face a serious problem in judging the likely effectiveness of unions at their place of work. Given the currently (2004) greater availability of the job 'exit' option because of relatively low unemployment, such uncertainty could seriously hinder successful union organizing.

To sum up this section then, social movement theory at the micro-level suggests British unions and their leaderships face a number of serious obstacles in raising their membership and influence despite the apparently more favourable conditions of the past ten years. Levels of employee discontent (a rough proxy for injustice) rose during the 1980s but seemed to have peaked in the early 1990s and have since stabilized or declined. Employee attitudes towards management (a proxy measure of employee willingness to blame management for their problems) seem slightly less critical in 2002 than in the early 1990s suggesting that employees may now be rather less likely to attribute workplace problems to their employer. Finally, worker perceptions of union effectiveness do not seem to be especially encouraging: for example, only a small minority of non-union employees believe union presence would make a difference at their workplace.

Macro-level evidence: strong and centralized government, weak unions

Both US and British evidence suggests employee beliefs about union instrumentality are likely to focus on the exercise of bargaining power in the labour market. It is unclear whether this tendency reflects the dominant locus of union activity in liberal market economies, but even if that is the case, it still leaves open the possibility that unions might influence employee perceptions of their effectiveness through the exercise of *political* power. This section first explores the political influence wielded by the union movement over government since 1997 and second uses Tarrow's macro-social movement theory (see above) to account for the obstacles confronting this facet of union revitalization.

How much influence have unions exercised over the 1997 and 2001 Labour governments?

Unions seek to exercise political influence over a wide range of issues, some of which are key priorities for the union movement, others less so. In order to assess this type of union influence there are three methodological issues that require clarification: first, we need to delineate and classify core, as distinct from peripheral, policy areas; second, we need to establish the outcomes of policy debates, a tricky exercise in complex areas such as employment law reform; and third, we need to disentangle union influence from other determinants of government policy. On the first issue, I propose to follow previous research and define three major areas in which unions in general seek to influence governments: wages and contractual conditions (including work time, for example); employment protection; and trade union influence (Hamann and Kelly 2003). What have British unions achieved in recent years under each of these headings?

During the 2001 general election, both TUC and union leaders produced lists of measures introduced by the first Labour government which had benefited working people and trade unions, citing in particular the National Minimum Wage and the unfair dismissal and union recognition provisions of the Employment Relations Act (1999) (Ludlam and Taylor 2003). All three measures were opposed in Parliament by the Conservative Party and their enactment appears consistent with the proposition that unions are able to exert political influence over a Labour government in the key areas of wages and conditions, employment protection and trade union rights. Closer examination of these and other issues, however, suggests a more complex story, in which union political influence may actually have declined since 1997 compared to the years prior to Labour's election.

Labour conferences voted for a statutory national minimum wage as long ago as 1986 (just one year after it became TUC policy), a commitment ratified in the Party's far-reaching policy reviews which began in 1987 and finished two years later. Subsequent debate inside the party turned on the mechanisms for determining, implementing and updating the appropriate wage level. By 1995 the party leadership had come round to the idea of a tripartite commission and that was duly created in July 1997 (Metcalf 1999: 172–3). Yet if the decision to proceed with a minimum wage constitutes evidence of union influence over the Labour *Party*, subsequent events suggested the balance of power between unions and the Labour *government* was a different matter. The Commission's final recommendation of £3.60 per hour was 12 per cent higher than the CBI proposal for £3.20 per hour but it was 22 per cent below the TUC conference policy figure of £4.60 per hour. The increase in 2001–2 was modest, closely tracking the rate of inflation and the growth of average earnings. Subsequent increases, at around 7 per cent per annum, were significantly higher.

Median income grew more quickly in 1997–2002 compared to the previous government, at 2.6 per cent per annum compared to 0.7 per cent in 1990–97. The rise in income inequality, which began in 1978, slowed after 1997, but has yet to go into reverse (Brewer *et al.* 2004). And whilst private sector employment rose 4.3 per cent 1997–2002 (an extra 944,000 jobs), public sector employment over the same period increased at an even faster rate of 6.9 per cent (an additional 344,000 jobs) (TUC 2003: 9).

Contracts of employment have proved to be a significant and contentious issue, particularly in the public sector. Union concern has focused on the reductions in terms and conditions of employment often associated with the transfer of employees to a private employer as part of a Private Finance Initiative (PFI). PFI has been opposed by successive Party and union conferences, particularly in 2002 and 2003, when both meetings unsuccessfully called for a moratorium on PFI pending an independent inquiry (Charlwood 2004b). Although the government ignored these resolutions, rightly calculating that the unions would not follow through their demands with any substantial campaigning, it did nonetheless offer one significant concession to union lobbying. In regulations governing the transfer of local government staff to a new employer under PFI it was stated that the terms and conditions of employment offered to new staff should be 'no less favourable' than those of their ex-public sector counterparts. And shortly before Labour's 2004 National Policy Forum, the government finally agreed that similar provisions would apply in the health and education sectors (BBC News Online 2004; Labour Research Department 2003).

Unions have exercised rather more influence over contractual conditions covered by European Directives, such as work-time and part-time workers' rights. This is because they have been able successfully to challenge the validity of national legislation through the European Court of Justice (ECJ). For example, the government's 1998 Working Time Regulations laid down a 13-week qualifying period for entitlement to 20 days paid annual leave but the ECJ upheld union objections and instructed the government to abolish the qualifying period (Hamann and Kelly 2003).

If we turn to employment protection, the TUC position since 1992 has been for employment rights, such as protection against unfair dismissal, to apply from the first day of an employment contract. In that same year Labour Party policy was for a qualifying period of six months rather than the prevailing periods of two years for full-time workers and five years for part-time workers. TUC lobbying through the 1990s failed to shift the Party towards its own policy. But worse than that, by 1997 the Party had backtracked towards a qualifying period of one year and this was the policy enacted in the ERA (1999) (Hay 1999: 112–13). Several years later the TUC was given another opportunity to pursue the issue of qualifying periods when the DTI carried out a review of the ERA, but once again it failed to make headway and the one year qualifying period was left intact (Department of Trade and Industry 2003). At the July 2004 National Policy Forum, meeting to discuss the next election manifesto, the major unions again tried to shift Labour policy but again they failed (Hall 2004).

Finally the Labour government enacted provisions for union recognition in the ERA, giving expression to its manifesto pledge to provide 'new statutory support for collective bargaining', first announced in 1983 and reiterated at subsequent elections in 1987, 1992 and 1997 albeit with very little detail (McCarthy 1999: 13). The provisions certainly met the TUC demand for a statutory mechanism to establish whether a union should be recognized and to enforce recognition in the face of employer reluctance. This was a considerable achievement in light of the high-profile lobbying conducted by the CBI to kill off legal recognition machinery in any form. Nonetheless it was also clear that most of the amendments introduced in the legislative process 'reflect the employers' preferences' (Wood and Godard 1999: 237). Furthermore, the government clearly signalled that the recognition law was not a device to re-establish union power. It did so by opting to maintain the framework of Conservative anti-union laws despite union pressure for repeal, and by reasserting its commitment to labour market flexibility. Further evidence of the limited capacity of unions to influence the Labour government emerged from the DTI review of the ERA, already referred to in connection with employment protection. The unions were particularly keen to repeal the exclusion of small firms (less than 21 employees) from the recognition provisions; to reduce or abolish the 40 per cent turnout requirement; and to restrict the freedom of employers to campaign against union organizing. The DTI Review concluded that no reforms were necessary in any of these areas and that the law was functioning adequately (Department of Trade and Industry 2003). Labour's July 2004 National Policy Forum took the same line on recognition law as it did on employment protection, rejecting union arguments that further reform was needed (Hall 2004).

Overall this evidence suggests two main conclusions about union political power. First, the government measures in which unions take most pride – the minimum wage, employment protection and union recognition – reflect the outcomes of union–Party negotiations from around 1987 through to 1996 rather than union influence over government since 1997. Second, although it is difficult and potentially misleading to sum up union–government relations in a few sentences, the degree of union influence over government employment and industrial relations policies since 1997 is sufficiently modest to suggest that unions have developed only a very limited capacity to influence government measures that touch on worker interests. In other words they have not yet demonstrated a degree of political effectiveness sufficient to overcome their limited bargaining effectiveness. It was therefore no surprise to see TUC General Secretary Brendan Barber complain in a widely-quoted speech in March 2004 about the 'low ebb of union-government relations' (TUC 2004).

Explaining political weakness

As noted earlier, Tarrow (1994) suggested four variables that encourage successful collective action by subordinate groups in relation to the state: increased openness of the political decision-making structure, unstable political alignments, the availability of influential allies and divisions among the ruling elite, and I look at each of these in turn in order to try and throw some light on the political weakness of British unions.

One way of measuring the openness of the state decision-making structure is by the number of contacts between subordinate groups and different branches of the state apparatus. Recent research by Marsh (2002) used TUC General Council Reports in order to chart trends in union–state contacts over time. This is far from being an ideal source as it reports only TUC contacts, not those of affiliated unions, and given the nature of the source, there is probably some upward bias in the reporting. But if we assume any such bias is constant over time, then it may provide a reasonably valid measure of trends (see Figure 4.5). What it suggests is that total contact increased significantly from 1997 and that actual meetings with ministers comprised a substantial share of such contact. In other words, and on this measure, the political opportunity structure did become increasingly open following Labour's first election victory. This conclusion is apparently reinforced by the appointment of union officials to a wide range of specific governmental task groups and commissions, most notably the Low Pay Commission (McIlroy 1998).

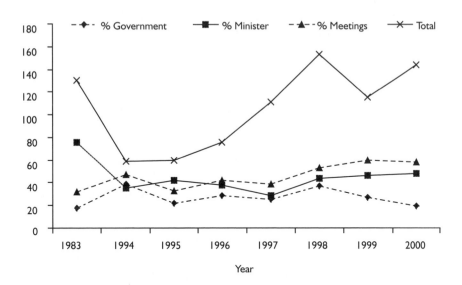

Figure 4.5 TUC-government contacts, 1983–2000 (Source: Marsh 2002: 148)

Notes
% government: % of all contacts initiated by government.
% minister: % of all meetings which were at ministerial level.
% meetings: % of all contact which took the form of meetings.
Total: total number of contacts between TUC and government.
Data only available for the years shown.

But if we turn from the *state* structure to the *Party* structure, then a very different, and more complex, picture emerges. Union influence inside the Labour Party was progressively reduced between 1992 and 1997 by cutting its share of votes at annual conference from approximately 90 per cent to 50 per cent and in leadership elections from 40 to 33 per cent. Unions were allocated just 30 seats on the 175-strong National Policy Forum (NPF), an advisory and discussion body created under Neil Kinnock's leadership in 1992 (McIlroy 1998: 544–5). After 1997 the NPF came to play a much greater role in the formulation of policy and its proposals are passed to a new Joint Policy Committee, chaired by the Prime Minister and without any union representation as such.[2] Once proposals are filtered through these two bodies they are then submitted to Labour Conference. According to Shaw (2004) this new structure has both centralized power in the hands of the Blair leadership and significantly reduced levels of intra-party dissent compared to the period 1970–90. This looser 'organizational integration' of unions into the Party was reinforced by a corresponding reduction in Party dependency on union finance. In 1992 the Labour Party obtained 66 per cent of its total income from unions; in 1997 it was 40 per cent and by 2002 it was just 33 per cent (Glover 2002).

Nonetheless unions continue to provide the bulk of the Party's *cash donations*, especially in election years (as compared to income from membership and commercial activities and payments in kind). In 2001, for example, Labour received a total of £11.96 million in donations of which 81 per cent (£9.68 million) came from the unions (calculated from figures in www. electoralcommission.gov.uk). The continuing dependency of the Labour Party on trade union finance coupled with the diminishing influence of unions inside the Party has created an acute and growing contradiction at the heart of the union–Party relationship. Tensions have expressed themselves in a variety of ways in recent months, including the disaffiliations of the Rail, Maritime and Transport Union and the Fire Brigades Union (in January and June 2004 respectively) and the concerted effort by the big four union leaders (from AMICUS, GMB, TGWU and UNISON) to wrest concessions from the Party leadership at the July 2004 National Policy Forum. Press reports suggested the unions had indeed been able to exploit Labour's continuing dependency on union finance and secure a number of substantial concessions. In particular, Party leaders promised legislation to bar employers counting Britain's eight public holidays as part of the statutory 20 day holiday entitlement of their employees. In fact this concession merely brings Britain into line with the rest of Europe (bar France and Sweden) and pre-empts a legal challenge to the European Court of Justice. On issues at the heart of the union agenda – PFI, renationalization of the railways, employment rights from the first day of employment and repeal of some of the Conservative anti-trade union laws – Party leaders made no concessions whatever (Hall 2004; Wintour 2004).

If we turn to the second of Tarrow's factors, however, there is little evidence of any significant instability in political alignments, indeed quite the reverse. Whereas the 1992–7 Conservative government began with a parliamentary majority of just 21 and ended with a majority of five, the 1997 Labour government secured a majority of 177 over its combined rivals and the 2001 government a majority of 165 (Pattie 2004: 17). The by-election record underlines the stability of recent years. The 1992–7 Conservative government faced 17 by-elections and lost eight of them; the 1997 and 2001 Labour governments by contrast have faced 23 by-elections but lost only two (www.bbc.co.uk/news 16 July 2004). The Blair governments have therefore been associated with a period of considerable parliamentary stability and one likely consequence has been to insulate the government from union pressure transmitted through parliamentary contacts and votes (see below). The strength of the government's position has been further reinforced by acute policy divisions between its two main opponents, the Conservatives and the Liberal Democrats.

Third, civil society in Britain affords the union movement many potential allies in its attempts to influence government. In June 2004, for example, a demonstration on pensions was jointly organized by the TUC and the National Pensioners' Convention and addressed by speakers from both organizations (www.tuc.org.uk/pensions). But recent research has shown that despite the presence of many potential allies in civil society, unions have built very few 'coalitions of protest' (as on pensions), especially when compared to their US counterparts in the AFL-CIO (Frege *et al.* 2004). Some 'coalitions of influence' have been built inside the state apparatus, through a number of parliamentary Select Committees, for example, but these bodies remain weak in the face of an executive that is both centralized and powerful (Richards and Smith 2004). On issues such as PFI and pension reform, they have not so far acquired 'influential allies' sufficient to make a substantial difference to government policy.

Finally, what of 'elite divisions', another potential source of leverage for unions? There are many ways of conceptualizing and measuring such divisions, but a focus on the legislature illustrates the difficulties unions have faced in recent years. In the House of Commons, divisions have become more frequent and more significant during Labour's second term compared to its first. Between 1997 and 2001 there were 97 rebellions against government whips by Labour MPs but in the first two years of the second term (June 2001– July 2003) the incidence of revolts more than doubled to 121. Among these were the votes on the Iraqi war in February and March 2003 when 121 and 139 MPs respectively refused to back the government, and the vote on foundation hospitals in July 2003 when there were 62 Labour rebels. Yet from the standpoint of union influence, the more significant point is that during its seven years in office (1997–2004) the Labour government has not suffered a single defeat in the House of Commons. Compare that record to the previous

Labour government of 1974–9 which was defeated on 42 occasions and to the 1992–7 Conservative government, defeated nine times (Cowley and Stuart 2003; www.election.demon.co.uk/defeats).

In summary, we can say that very few of the conditions necessary for groups such as trade unions to exercise political power have been present to a significant extent since 1997. While the state structure has become more open to union influence, measured by ministerial and other contacts, the Party structure has been progressively reconfigured in order to curb such influence. Labour's large parliamentary majorities and its perpetuation of a centralized executive have ensured a high degree of political stability, a correspondingly low degree of receptivity to 'coalitions of influence' and a relative absence of damaging divisions in its own ranks. Taken together these conditions help explain why union policy influence over New Labour has been so modest.

Discussion and conclusions

This chapter began by arguing that conditions for union recovery in Britain have been more favourable recently than for many years. Conventional theory might therefore have led us to expect union growth, but in fact membership and density were no higher in 2003 than they were in 1997. Social movement theory by contrast throws a great deal of light on this puzzle: it substantially increases our understanding of the modesty of union membership recovery since the mid-1990s and of the strict limits on the political influence wielded by the unions over the Labour governments of 1997 and 2001. Social movement analysis at the micro-level suggests that whilst levels of employee injustice and antagonism to management did indeed increase throughout the 1980s, they seem to have peaked in the early 1990s. In other words, the union organizing drives of the late 1990s were getting underway as the tide of employee discontent was already receding from the high-water mark of a few years previous. At the macro-level, social movement theory suggests unions have been unable to exercise substantial influence over government, despite the increased openness of the state structure. Labour's large parliamentary majorities in conjunction with a centralized executive have ensured a high degree of political stability and have been accompanied by an absence of damaging divisions and rebellions within its own ranks.

How can we explain these patterns of worker attitudes and union political influence? Within the framework of social movement theory, there are three lines of enquiry that would seem to hold out some promise. First, given the theoretical centrality of worker beliefs about union effectiveness, we need to know far more about the ways in which employees construct such beliefs and the information sources on which they rely. Second, these beliefs themselves may well be linked to broader world views, embracing both conservative and social democratic variants of neo-liberalism as well as more traditional socialist outlooks. This connection raises the question as to how far the rise of neo-liberal ideas has eroded the types of beliefs and values traditionally associated with union membership. Third, the role of national and local union leadership requires more investigation. For example, to what extent has the simultaneous promotion of partnership and organizing conveyed a clear message to non-union members about union effectiveness? Has the emergence of a group of general secretaries highly critical of 'New Labour' been helpful to worker perceptions of union influence? Or have their differences in approach to the Labour Party conveyed an image of division and ineffectiveness (see Charlwood 2004b)?

Finally, what implications does the theory have for the future of trade unions and in particular for the policies unions ought to pursue in order to revitalize themselves? There are three main points that flow from the arguments and evidence in this chapter. First, organizing needs to be targeted very carefully at those segments of the workforce with a relatively strong sense of injustice and some antagonism to management. This in itself, however, is unlikely to make a dramatic difference to union membership and density unless unions can find a way of visibly demonstrating their power. We conventionally think about union power in Britain in terms of bargaining outcomes and mobilization, but from April 2005 unions may also be able to exercise power through works councils, established under the Information and Consultation of Employees legislation. Second, if union leaders were to campaign more vigorously and publicly against particular government policies then given certain political conditions (see below) such activity could help increase public perceptions of union effectiveness. Third, the outcome of the general election could have a major impact on the potential for unions to exercise political power. The reduced Labour majority could help create less stable political alignments, more divisions in the legislature and therefore more opportunities for unions to exercise a significant degree of political influence.

Acknowledgements

Thanks to the following for helpful comments on an early draft of this chapter: Carola Frege, Gregor Gall, Kerstin Hamann, Ed Heery, David Metcalf and Paul Smith.

Notes

1   This time-series should be interpreted with some care because it does not actually comprise the same set of unions over time. Twenty-nine unions affiliated to the TUC for the first time between January 1990 and December 2003 whilst 32 unions disappeared through merger or absorption (TUC General Council Reports and TUC Directories, various years). However, recalculation of the figures omitting the newly affiliated unions produces almost exactly the same levels

and trends. For example, the 2003 and 2002 figures of 48 and 51 per cent would be 51 and 49 per cent respectively if all newly affiliated unions were excluded. Annual membership growth due to mergers or transfers of engagements has also been discounted in the calculations.

2   In addition to the Prime Minister, the JPC comprises eight ministers, eight members of Labour's National Executive Committee and three members of the NPF.

Chapter 5

Trade unions: resurgence or perdition?

An economic analysis

David Metcalf

Key points

- Economists have long been interested in unions. For much of the nine-teenth century economic thought tended to be hostile to combinations because, under the Wage Fund doctrine, unions could not alter the share of national income going to labour, so industrial action was needlessly disruptive. The Webbs and the US institutional economists suggested, instead, that unions could enhance both efficiency and equity by countering any exploitation of labour. In the twentieth century interest in the monopoly face of unions has flourished and there has been greater emphasis on union voice in, for example, contract negotiation and resources devoted to workplace safety.
- At its peak UK membership stood at 13 million in 1979 but lost 5.5 million in the subsequent two decades. Presently 29 per cent of employees belong to a union, 3-in-5 in the public sector but under 1-in-5 in the private sector. The sustained decline in membership in the 1980s and 1990s was a consequence of interactions among the composition of the workforce and jobs; the roles of the state, employ-ers and individual workers; and of unions own structures and policies.
- As a consequence of their decline unions now impact only modestly on pay, productivity, financial performance and investment. But the negative association between recognition and employment growth, even assuming it is not causal, will depress future membership if it continues. Unions are a force for fairness in the workplace: they narrow the pay distribution, boost family friendly policy and cut accidents.
- Presently there are around 3 million free-riders and 3 million employees who might join a union if one existed at their workplace. The challenge for the union movement is to organize these workers while still ser-vicing their existing 7 million members. On present evidence such a challenge seems too steep and calculations suggest that long run union density will be around 20 per cent, implying a rate of 12 per cent in the private sector, where perdition is more likely than resurgence.

For two centuries economists have discussed unions' impact on wages and resource allocation, their role in countering exploitation and their important voice function. Thus economists have a long history of analysing membership, impact and the future prospects of unions ('Classical and institutional economists, Marx and the Webbs'). Union membership declined by over 5 million in the two decades after the 1979 zenith of 13 million such that British unions presently cover just 3-employees-in-10. The future of British unions turns in large part on what they do – to economic efficiency, fairness and to industrial relations ('Impact of unions'). Any resurgence of unions depends on where the new jobs are, support from the state, interactions with employers and unions' own servicing and organizing policies ('Hereafter: resurgence or perdition?'). Summary and conclusions are presented in the fourth section, where it is shown that current organizing efforts are insufficient to offset membership losses and that unions are in the twilight zone.

Classical and institutional economists, Marx and the Webbs

Economists have long been interested in trade unions. In the nineteenth century the English classical economists discussed unions' impact on economic efficiency – what we now call the monopoly face or vested interest effect – and normally concluded that the adverse effects outweighed any benefits of union activity. At the end of the nineteenth century the Webbs in England and the institutional labour economists in the US fundamentally altered the debate, providing a rationale for unions via their focus on the unequal bargaining power of capital and labour. This element in the economic analysis of unions embraces, but is broader than, Flanders' later sword of justice effect which emphasizes equity, whereas the institutional economists also argued that economic efficiency might be better served by tempering the inequality in bargaining power experienced by labour. More recently interest in the differential strength of workers and employers has waned, but imperfections in employment contracts and internal firm governance – of which the need for collective voice is but one element – suggest an alternative rationale for unions. But it is probably fair to state that throughout the twentieth century mainstream economics, while recognizing the merits of the institutionalist and transactions cost arguments, continued to emphasize negative net union effects on resource allocation and economic efficiency. Though, as we shall see in the second section, any such outcomes are – at worst – very small presently in the UK and many will be counterbalanced by unions' favourable impact promoting fairness and due process in the labour market.

Adam Smith was hostile to the apprenticeship system, which he held raised craft pay by restricting the numbers entering the trade. But he also stated that combinations of workers were an important counterweight to employers' price- and wage-fixing cartels. Despite Adam Smith's caution classical economists tended to be anti-union on three interlocking grounds. First, while recognizing that a union might raise the pay of a particular occupation, it was held that combinations could not influence the share of national income going to wage earners. Under the Wage Fund doctrine – most strongly associated with McCulloch (1823) – the amount of national income going to labour at any one time was fixed. So strikes and industrial action were held to be pointless because they could not enhance the wage fund and so were needlessly disruptive. Second, in the unlikely event that the share of wages did rise as a consequence of union action, this would be at the expense of profit, thereby reducing the rate of capital accumulation: as Ricardo (1817: 136) put it, 'the motive for accumulation will diminish with every diminution of profit'. Third, as a final backstop against unions, any such boost in labour's share came up against Malthus' 'principle of population' such that higher wages would increase the supply of unskilled labour and drive down pay to starvation level. Cairnes (1874: 388) summed it all up nicely: 'Against these barriers [the theories of the wages fund, accumulation and population] trade unions must dash themselves in vain'.

But the classical economists did recognize that union activity could extract a wage premium for a sectional group. For example Senior (1841), the chairman of the Commission looking into the condition of the hand-loom weavers, argued that workers essential to the production process could successfully apply pressure to raise their own pay:

> A combination frequently succeeds in effecting its immediate purpose, when the inactivity of the workmen in combination, can produce the further effect of throwing out of employment other and more numerous sets of workpeople, or render useless a large amount of fixed capital.
>
> (Senior 1841: 32)

And J.S. Mill (1848) stated that unions could raise pay above the competitive level 'in trades where the workpeople are few in number, and collected in a small number of local centres' because such a pattern implied their organization would be effective.

Unions could also impact on employment. J.S. Mill set out the direct link between union effects on pay and jobs when he analysed the consequences of unionization of the entire labour force – higher pay leads to fewer jobs: 'But if they aimed at obtaining actually higher wages than the rate fixed by demand and supply ... this could only be accomplished by keeping part of their number permanently out of employment' (Mill 1848: 930). The indirect effect of union activity on employment was set out in the report into the hand-loom weavers. Hand-loom work was obsolete because of technical change but, according to the Commission, the weavers' spell of unemployment was lengthened as they were unable to switch to other sectors because of the exclusive behaviour of unions elsewhere: 'a portion of them [weavers] should transfer their own labour, or at least that of their children, to better paid occupations, but from these they are repelled by combinations'.

The Webbs also noted that

> if the workmen in any trade could, either by law or by an absolutely firm combination extending from one end of the kingdom to another, permanently restrict the numbers entering the trade, they might gradually force their employers to offer them higher wages.
>
> (Webb and Webb 1897: 712)

This reinforced many economists' hostility towards trade unions because, as the Webbs put it, economists assumed that 'the whole aim and purpose of Trade Unionism was to bring about this position of monopoly of a particular service ... plainly inimical to the interests of the community' (Webb and Webb 1897: 712).

Marshall (1892) was more balanced. The notions of the wage fund and the population principle were discredited by the time he wrote. He set out the ('Marshallian') conditions under which a wage premium was more likely: inelastic demand for the product; low elasticity of substitution between union labour and capital or other labour; labour costs a small fraction of total costs ('the importance of being unimportant'); and an inelastic supply of other factors. He argued that such a premium was more likely where there were monopoly profits (rents), but if labour gained at the expense of income due to capital (quasi rents) the rate of capital accumulation would slow. Crucially Marshall also recognized that unions might stop exploitation. As the Webbs put it 'unions generally can so arrange their bargaining with employers so as to remove the special disadvantages under which workmen would lie if bargaining with individuals without reserve' (Webb and Webb 1897: 652).

Concern with the monopoly face of unions continued throughout the twentieth century to the present day. Hicks (1931: 137) stated that 'very much the same motives which drive businessmen to form rings and cartels drive their employees to form unions'. And Friedman (1951: 206) wrote that: 'labor unions and enterprise monopolies are conceptually similar ... have similar effects ... [and] are undesirable'. More recently Pencavel (1991: 11) summarized economists' pre-occupation with the monopoly face rather vividly: 'unions are said to behave as monopolists, driving up the price of labor by fabricating or threatening a shortage through entry restrictions, coordinated malfeasance, or strike action'.

Nineteenth-century economists also analysed unions' mutual insurance policies against unemployment, sickness and accidents, pensions for retired members and death benefits (see Boyer 1988 for a full discussion). There was considerable interest in whether the motive for union-provided mutual insurance was a response to a demand from their members or an attempt by union officials to enhance worker solidarity. One key question was whether the existence of such insurance funds nurtured and intensified militancy or the reverse. Employers argued in the mid-nineteenth century that the funds were used to finance and prolong strike activity. But unions stated that their insurance role lessened strikes because workers and officials were cautious of depleting the insurance fund. The Webbs point out that by the end of the century employers 'had come to believe that the most militant unions were those without insurance benefits' (Webb and Webb 1897: 160). This was because the more militant unions were the ones seeking recognition and, consequently, they did not yet have accumulated benefit funds.

In the late nineteenth century and the first third of the twentieth century the monopoly face approach was countered by the Webbs (1897) in Great Britain and the institutional labour economists in the US centred on John R. Commons and the Wisconsin School which 'provides a substantially different and more positive theoretical perspective on unions ... the most compelling rationale ... to level the playing field and protect the underdog' (Kaufman 2004b: 389). It should be noted for the record, and in some mitigation of the classical perspective, that both Adam Smith and Alfred Marshall had earlier suggested that unequal bargaining power provided a rationale for unions.

Institutional economists agreed that unions' impact on efficiency was important and that the competitive model of the labour market was too narrow. They stated that other dimensions of union activity should also be examined including equity and justice in the workplace. At this time many wages were administered and workers had to take it or leave it; and asymmetric information, discrimination and employees' lack of resources all benefited the employer over the worker. Monopsony – company towns – and imperfect labour mobility implied that the employee would be paid less than s/he was worth to the firm. And a lack of jobs – high aggregate unemployment – put the workers at a further disadvantage. These perceived handicaps caused the institutional economists to espouse collective bargaining which they argued had both an economic function, equivalent to the monopoly face, and a political or governance function, analogous to the voice face.

Discussion of the economic effects of collective bargaining by institutional economists anticipated the modern literature (e.g. the second section) by over 70 years. Consider first the suggested advantages. Wages would be taken out of competition and the wage structure standardized across firms (what the Webbs called 'the device of the Common Rule' or 'standard rate'). This would, in turn, promote efficiency as firms competed on quality and service rather than on the basis of cost. The common rule was also held to protect 'good employers' because it inhibited undercutting by other firms. (As the Webbs noted, it also provided a barrier to entry to firms wishing to enter the sector.) Collective bargaining was further held to protect employees from overwork, to promote greater effort – a precursor of the efficiency wage arguments – and increase investment in human capital because labour turnover was reduced. It was also held to improve the workers' voice by introducing joint decision-making, worker participation and representation and due process into firms' governance structures. Familiar disadvantages included: monopoly wage effects; restrictions on labour supply; possible restrictive practices lowering productivity, profit and in the longer run investment and employment; externalities associated with secondary strike action; and worsening wage inequality because the (higher paid) craft workers were more likely to be covered by collective bargaining. Overall, the Webbs concluded that collective bargaining had a net positive effect, both in terms of voice and efficiency.

Marx, Engels and their twentieth-century disciples also had a lot to say about the role of unions. Marx and Engels agreed with the classical economists that the economic power of trade unions was modest. In 1845 Engels wrote:

> The history of these unions is a long series of defeats of the workingmen, interrupted by a few isolated victories. All these efforts naturally cannot alter the economic law according to which wages are determined by the relation between supply and demand in the labour market. Hence the unions remain powerless against all great forces which influence this relation.
>
> (Engels 1892: 216)

Two decades later Marx echoed these sentiments but suggested that unions were more successful at resisting wage cuts during recession than raising them when trade improved. Further, the long run immiseration of the workers also pointed, in both theory and practice, to a limited impact of unions on wages. It was, as Hyman (1971) notes, this very impotence of unions which would lead – in Marxist theory – to the overthrow of capitalism:

> Marx argued that collective organization, at first adopted merely as a means of defending wages, came to be pursued for its own sake; and that the ensuing conflict – 'a veritable civil war' – served to generate among workers a consciousness of class unity, transforming them from a class 'in itself' to a class 'for itself'.
>
> (Hyman 1971: 6)

In a nutshell, the limited economic achievements of their unions would lead workers to adopt political forms of action, and ultimately to challenge the whole structure of class domination directly. The successful unions of the 1870s and 1880s – rather inconvenient for the theory – were dismissed as 'an aristocratic minority of privileged workers'.

Socialist theory in the twentieth century inverted the Marxist analysis and, instead, focussed on why trade unionism inhibits the overthrow of capitalism. Hyman labels the three key theories as integration, oligarchy and incorporation, their most prominent exponents being Lenin, Michels and Trotsky respectively. Lenin argued in *What is to be Done?* that trade unions were simply sectional interests – mirroring the industrial and occupational divisions of capitalism rather than being a vehicle of class interest. Michels then added unions' need for organization and bureaucratic control which led to entrenched leadership. This 'oligarchic control was reinforced by mass apathy' (Hyman 1971: 15). And Trotsky asserted that such union leaders, having acquired authority over their members, become incorporated – used to assist capitalism in controlling the workers.

Core Marxist theory is refuted on both its economic and political counts. First, for much of the second half of the twentieth century unions did have an important impact on economic variables such as pay, productivity and profits (see 'Impact of unions' section). Second, capitalism has not been overthrown. But the later socialist thought has much greater relevancy for analysing unions. For example: sectional interests are reflected in the union pay premium; oligarchic control has been advanced as a factor in declining membership; and the debate about the merits or otherwise of partnerships between unions and employers (see 'Hereafter: resurgence or perdition?' section) are simply a modern version of the incorporation arguments.

From around 1870 and for most of the twentieth century, up to the Thatcher era, the share of labour in national income rose secularly, while that of capital gradually decayed correspondingly. Thus labour won the battle with capital, but without overturning capitalism. Given this switch in income shares away from profit towards pay most economists no longer pay much attention to the perceived inequality in bargaining power between capital and labour. So interest in this rationale for union activity has waned, and has been replaced by a new one which 'shifts attention from imperfections in the structure of markets to imperfections in employment contracts and internal firm governance' (Kaufman 2004b: 390). There are three main strands in this approach. First, unions replace individual voice with collective voice which enhances the supply of workplace public goods like safety or flexible working. Second, unions might boost productivity by lowering labour turnover, spoiling the quiet life of managers in monopolistic enterprises and 'expanding the breadth and depth of employee involvement'. Third, unions lower transactions costs and increase efficiency by providing agency services to workers and firms. For workers, the union provides information (for example on wages in competing plants), monitors the performance of the employer and communicates workers' preferences regarding personnel practices to the employer. The advantage of collective bargaining to the firm is that it signs one contract instead of hundreds of individual contracts (Freeman and Medoff 1984).

Economists have historically paid great attention to the objectives and impact of trade unions. Often such work has influenced union prospects and the ebb and flow of membership. For example, in the USA research by the institutional economists contributed to the passing of the 1935 National Labor Relations Act which played a central role in restoring union fortunes over the next quarter of a century. And in the UK the work of Hayek (1980: 58) and the Institute of Economic Affairs (1984) – 'There can be no salvation for Britain until the special privileges granted to the trade unions three-quarters of a century ago are ended' – provided the intellectual underpinning for the onslaught against unions by the Thatcher administration.

In what follows we adopt a pragmatic and empirical economist approach to the analysis of British unions. In recent years there has been a great deal of careful economic research on the impact of unions on efficiency, equity and employee relations – the very items which so exercised the classical and neoclassical economists. These are analysed next. Economic techniques can also be applied to the work of industrial relations scholars to set out the costs and benefits of, for example, organizing and servicing ('Hereafter: resurgence or perdition?' section). It might be noted in passing that virtually every issue examined in this chapter was carefully analysed over a century ago by the Webbs in *Industrial Democracy*, surely the most consequential book ever written on unions, who also found time to set up the LSE at this time!

Impact of unions

Forty years ago Alan Flanders, the most perceptive contemporary observer, suggested that unions have both a 'vested interest' and 'sword of justice' effect. The vested interest impact, similar to the monopoly face of unions set out by the classical economists and Richard Freeman, turns on unions' influence on pay, productivity, profits, investment and employment. The question is, essentially, what effect do unions have on workplace and firm performance? The sword of justice – vividly described by Flanders as unions' 'stirring music' – is more about fairness and due process including unions' impact on the pay distribution, accidents and family friendly policies. In addition unions affect employee relations through their bearing on the industrial relations climate and job satisfaction. These impact effects of unions profoundly influence their future and will be considered in turn.

Wage premium

If the presence of a union in a workplace or firm raises the pay level, unless productivity rises correspondingly, financial performance is likely to be worse. If the product market is uncompetitive this might imply a simple transfer from capital to labour with no efficiency effects, but it is more likely to lead to lower investment rates and economic senescence. In the 1970s and 1980s the evidence indicated that union members received a pay premium, but without the corresponding rise in productivity. If anything demarcations, unofficial industrial action and multi-unionism lowered productivity. Hence profitability in workplaces with union recognition was below that in non-union workplaces. But the world has moved on: what effect have the changes set out in Chapter 1 had on workplace performance?

One major reason for belonging to a union is, historically, union members have received a pay premium ('wage gap') over similar non-union members. There is a large literature on this topic, recently surveyed by Blanchflower and Bryson (2003: 203), who conclude that for the 1980s and the first part of the 1990s 'the consensus in the literature was that the mean [hourly] union wage gap was approximately 10 per cent'. But the outlawing of the closed shop in 1990, falling density where unions are recognized, more intense product market competition and the loss of 5 million members was bound eventually to result in a lower wage premium. Such evidence for 1993–2000 is set out in Table 5.1. Over the period as a whole the mark-up averaged 9.9

Table 5.1 Disaggregated estimates of the union wage premium, 1993–2000 (%)

	Wage gap average 1993–2000	Wage gap 1993	Wage gap 2000	Decline 1993–2000
All	9.9	14.2	6.3	7.9
Male	3.6	9.4	−1.4	10.8
Female	15.8	18.3	13.7	4.6
Age <40	10.0	15.8	4.4	11.4
Age >=40	9.4	11.6	7.3	4.3
White	9.9	13.9	6.0	7.9
Non-white	9.7	20.8	1.3	19.5
Public sector	13.5	11.0	6.6	4.4
Private sector	5.3	10.2	0.9	9.3
Manual worker	17.0	22.1	12.7	9.4
Non-manual worker	6.8	13.2	6.2	7.0
Manufacturing	4.2	11.0	−2.4	13.4
Non-manufacturing	11.3	15.1	8.0	7.1
High education	3.8	5.5	2.2	3.3
Medium education	10.0	15.5	4.9	10.6
Low education	13.0	17.4	8.3	9.1
Full-time	6.2	9.9	3.0	6.9
Part-time	16.0	19.0	13.4	5.6

Source: Blanchflower and Bryson (2003: Table 7) calculations using pooled UK Labour Force Surveys, 1993–2000, comprising 105,112 observations.

Notes
'High education' = at least a bachelor degree; 'Medium education' = some qualifications below degree level; 'Low education' = no qualifications. Sample is all sectors. Controls comprise 61 industry dummies, 18 region dummies, age, age squared, 40 highest qualification dummies, six workplace size dummies, usual hours, eight race dummies, gender dummy and a time trend.

per cent, but it halved from 14.2 per cent in 1993 to 6.3 per cent in 2000. The fall in the premium occurred for each sub-group. For example, the male premium declined by 10.8 points over the seven year period and the female by 4.6 points. Likewise the private sector union mark-up was trimmed 9.3 points and that in the public sector 4.4 points. A spate of recent studies confirm this decline in the premium. Machin (2001) is particularly informative. For men, the wage premium fell from 9 per cent in 1991 to zero in 1999, while for women it fell from 16 per cent to 10 per cent over the eight years. More importantly, there is now no (wage) benefit to joining a union and no cost to leaving. Machin summarizes his work:

> For men it used to pay to be in a union [in the early 1990s] and it used to pay to join a union, but by the end of the 1990s it does not. For women the answer is: it does still pay to be in a union, but not by as much as it used to, and it does not pay to newly join.
>
> (Machin 2001: 13)

A brief caveat is in order here. There are still some occupations and sectors where unions have sufficient clout to achieve a wage premium. Consider three examples from the public sector. On the London underground, tube drivers earn around £35,000 a year for a 35-hour work week, yielding twice the average hourly wage. In the fire service, the Fire Brigades Union has successfully resisted alterations in shift patterns and thereby maintained so-called stand-down (i.e. sleeping) time at night, significantly enhancing the true hourly wage of fire fighters. In the face of incompetent management, adversarial unionism by tube drivers and firemen has paid handsome dividends. Finally, the public finance initiative often results in inferior pay and conditions for workers in the new PFI schools, hospitals or prisons. So UNISON or other public sector unions can justifiably claim that they achieve a premium for their members in the traditional public sector workplaces.

Productivity

Unions can influence industrial relations and personnel management for good or ill. The union impact on things like apprenticeship and training methods, promotion policies, work organization, wage levels and payments systems and grievance procedures will feed through into productivity. It is impossible to determine a priori whether such a union effect will raise or lower the level of labour productivity. Indeed, it is likely that productivity-enhancing union effects and productivity-detracting effects occur simultaneously, so the net effect must be a matter of careful empirical investigation.

Four sets of reasons why union presence may lower labour productivity are noted: unions may be associated with restrictive work practices; industrial action may have an adverse impact; union firms may invest less than non-union firms; and if unions are associated with an adversarial style of industrial relations the consequent low trust and lack of cooperation between the parties may lower productivity. Equally there are five sets of reasons why labour productivity may be higher in the presence of unions: firms' responses to union relative wage effects may result in higher labour productivity, but this should not be interpreted as raising the welfare of society; unions may play a monitoring role on behalf of the employer; the familiar collective voice arguments may have favourable consequences; it is sometimes held that a union presence may make managers less lethargic; finally, as the Webbs argued, unions should stop exploitation of labour, resulting in improved productivity.

Union presence can influence the *level* of labour productivity for good or ill, so unionization can also be associated with differentiated *changes* in labour productivity. If any of the productivity-enhancing channels discussed above, like voice, are strengthened or if restrictive practices and the like which are harmful to labour productivity are weakened, union presence will be associated with improved performance relative to the non-union sector. These dynamic forces are obviously important because the manner in which union(s) interact with management or influence investment will vary over time. For example, if managerial practices become more effective or the industrial relations climate more cooperative in union firms, then union presence will be associated with faster growth than before. But it is most unlikely that heavily unionized workplaces or industries can have permanently higher or lower productivity growth than corresponding less- or non-unionized organizations. This would imply an ever-widening gap between the two groups, which is most implausible. Thus findings for the one decade should not, for example, be extrapolated to the next.

Links between the industrial relations regime in a company or workplace and its productivity performance have long been a matter of interest and debate in the UK. The state of play in the 1970s and 1980s was surveyed by Metcalf (1990b). The focus of the studies of that period was the manufacturing industry where

> the weight of the evidence suggests that around 1980 union presence was associated with lower levels of labour productivity, but that in the first half of the 1980s strongly unionized workplaces and industries had faster growth in labour productivity than their non-union counterparts.
> (Metcalf 1990b: 255)

For example Lord Scanlon, President of the Amalgamated Union of Engineering Workers (AUEW) in the 1970s, stated (in 1983) that wildcat strikes and other forms of disruption in the 1970s had robbed Britain of its place as a world centre for the car-making industry. The subsequent turnaround in the productivity performance of the highly-unionized manufacturing sector was examined by Metcalf (1990a). Britain went from being bottom of the league table of productivity growth in the G-7 countries in the 1960s and 1970s to top in the 1980s and near top in the 1990s. This was attributed to the interaction of more intense product market competition, higher levels of unemployment and the legislative onslaught against organized labour which altered management and labour practices in favour of higher productivity. Card and Freeman (2004) examined productivity in the whole economy, not just manufacturing. They state that the elimination of the previous negative union productivity gap in the 1980s and 1990s contributed a 4.3 percentage point gain in average productivity over this 20-year span. This is one-sixth of the difference in the growth rates between what they call 'pre-reform 1960–79' and 'post-reform 1979–99'.

Two questions remain. First, is there any longer any difference in productivity performance between workplaces which do and do not recognize a union? Second, do multi-union workplaces perform worse than single union workplaces and can any such disadvantages be offset if the separate unions bargain jointly? Pencavel (2004) investigates these issues. The results are clear-cut. There is no difference in the productivity performance of union compared with non-union workplaces. But multi-unionism with fragmented bargaining still puts the workplace at a disadvantage. Pencavel concludes:

> By the end of the 1990s, average union – non-union differences in labour productivity appear to be negligible. Where such differences emerge, they are in establishments where fragmented bargaining occurs. Such bargaining is unusual – only 7 per cent of workplaces in 1998 were characterized by fragmented bargaining. This allows the generalization that unionism may serve as an agent permitting employees to participate in shaping their work environment without productivity suffering.
>
> (Pencavel 2004: 219–20)

Financial performance

If unions raise the level of wages without similarly increasing productivity the resources underpinning the higher pay level have to come from somewhere. Such union wage gains might come from lower wages for non-union workers; or from consumers via higher product prices; or from the owners of capital via lower profits. Each of these routes is circumscribed by competition. Large wage differentials between similar union and non-union workers tend to be partially eroded by selective hiring, threat effects raising wages in the non-union sector and cost advantages enjoyed by non-union firms. Cost increases cannot easily be passed through to consumers in the form of higher prices unless a union has organized an entire industry or local market where exclusion of foreign and non-union competition is possible. And in many sectors competition in the product market will limit surplus profits as a source of wage gains. Any union gains from potential firm profits turn largely on the existence of above-normal profits resulting from market power, government regulation, returns from fixed capital and firm-specific advantages like location and R&D returns.

In the 1980s virtually all studies reported a negative association between union presence and financial performance. But as the impact of unions on pay levels and productivity is weaker now than it was 20 years ago it is plausible that the union effect on profitability will be similarly attenuated. Such a dilution is made even more likely by both the extensive privatization and deregulation and the more intense product market competition (partly caused by 'globalization') over the last two decades.

Some evidence is reported in Table 5.2 and confirms that there is now no association, on average, between financial performance and the presence or otherwise of a union. Nevertheless the 'average' lack of association masks some interesting findings once the sample is cut in other ways. First, Pencavel shows that where there are multiple unions which bargain separately – rather than round a single table – the workplace is 6 per cent less likely to have a lot better than average financial performance (as compared to a similar non-union workplace) and 5 per cent less likely to have simple better than average performance. This suggests that the adverse effects of multi-unionism reported in earlier studies remain in place. Second, Metcalf notes the crucial importance of the product market. Where there are five or fewer competitors, the work-place is 12 per cent less likely to have above average financial performance. By contrast where there are 6 or more competitors, union recognition is not significantly related to financial performance. This suggests any union effect is likely to be benign: where there are few competitors monopoly profits are more likely and unions can siphon-off some of that surplus, away from the owners of capital towards labour. Third, Wilkinson's results show that weak unions (below 50 per cent membership or coverage) have negative associations with performance while medium and strong unions have positive links. This hints that where a union is recognized it is – at least when considering financial performance – better to have an encompassing union rather than one where under half the workforce is unionized.

Investment in physical and human capital

Capital accumulation is the key to long run growth. Therefore the impact of unions on investment is a matter of great importance. The arguments typically refer to investment in new technology and process innovations, but could also be used to analyse any effect unions might have on investment in research and development; on product improvements through design, marketing, advertizing and after sales service; and on human capital. A further dimension concerns 'where to invest' which influences closure and relocation decisions, especially in multi-establishment organizations.

Table 5.2 Unions and financial performance: WERS98 evidence

Author	Sample	Indicator of financial performance	Indicator of union	Controls	Results
Pencavel (2004)	1,484 workplaces trading sector	5 categories	single (322) multi-joint (337) multi-separate (228)	% PT, female workplace size years at present location	Union workplaces (cf non-u) • 3% less likely to be a lot better than average • 2% less likely to be better than average Multi-u, fragmented bargaining (cf non-u) • 6% less likely to be a lot better than average • 5% less likely to be better than average
Metcalf (2003)	1,195 workplaces trading sector 25+ employees	better than average	recognition	HRM (9 variables) % female, skilled pay cf LLM workplace size industry	Union workplace (cf non-u) • 8% less likely to be above average • 12% less likely to be above average where 5 or fewer competitors (sig at 1%) • 7% more likely to be above average where 6+ competitors (non-sig)
Wilkinson (2000)	whole econ (1,843) trading (1,418) private trading (1,133) private trading with profit measure (718)	4 categories	recognition recognition by coverage bargaining level union strength	workplace size, age % PT, female HRM score ESOS incentive pay product mkt (9 variables) ind, region	76 coefficients reported, 72 non-sig • weak unions always − ve assoc • medium strong unions normally + ve assoc
Addison and Belfield (2000)	1,021 workplaces trading sector	better than average	recognition	workplace size, age % unskilled nat/internat mkt participation repres problem solving downward commun financial partic	no significant associations

The presence of a union in a workplace might inhibit investment either directly or indirectly in the rent-seeking model. The direct effect occurs if a union delays the installation of new machinery, perhaps because the union representatives are not content with associated organizational changes such as modifications to shift patterns or any required easing of skill demarcations. Further, inflexible work rules might mean that the investment is not used to its full capacity, effectively adding to the cost of installation. Indirect union effects may occur when a firm invests in a new project. Unionized workers may capture ('tax') some of the returns in the form of higher pay because, once the capital is installed or the R&D done, the process cannot easily be reversed thereby weakening the firm's bargaining position. This 'hold-up' reduces the profit incentive for new investment thereby depressing the overall investment rate. It is well known that the union may be able to appropriate rents accruing from monopoly power in the product market. The argument here is that, in addition, the union is able to capture quasi-rents from capital that represent some of the normal competitive return to capital. There is an offsetting force. In the traditional on-the-demand curve model a higher union wage stimulates investment because the firm substitutes away from expensive labour. In this case union activity raises investment (although the positive substitution effect might be attenuated by a negative scale effect), but recall that higher investment consequent on wage push does not necessarily raise social welfare.

As the rent seeking model predicts unions have a negative effect on investment but the traditional substitution approach predicts a positive impact the issue cannot be decided empirically: any impact of unions on capital accumulation is an empirical matter.

UK evidence concerning union effects on physical investment was surveyed in Metcalf (1993) and is mixed. Denny and Nickell (1991) get the most clear-cut union effects. Their sample is drawn from manufacturing industries and incorporates information on industrial relations variables from the Workplace Indutrial Relations Surveys (WIRS) 1 and 2. They find, for 1980–4 – before unions were tamed – that union recognition depressed investment, but that this adverse effect was offset (albeit never completely) as density rose. By implication, they point out that the worst possible situation is union recognition but with only a small fraction of the workforce being union members. Voice effects are also apparent – where many workers are covered by joint consultative councils (whether in union or non-union workplaces) investment rates are higher.

There has never been much evidence that union recognition hinders investment in plant and machinery. Despite the decline in unionization rates and the apparent shift to more cooperative relations with employers, the rate of growth of capital per worker (or per hour) did not accelerate in the 1980s and 1990s relative to that in West Germany or France (Card and Freeman 2004). This implies unions probably did not dampen investment in the earlier period.

Unions can also influence research and development spending, innovation (the output of R&D) and diffusion. Menzes-Filho and Van Reenen (2003) surveyed the recent studies but found no evidence of a union effect one way or the other. In particular, the negative raw correlation between union recognition and R&D expenditure occurs simply because unions are found in older firms and low-tech industries.

The presence of a union might also influence *investment in human capital* in the workplace over and above any more traditional effect on investment in physical capital or R&D. Recent evidence points to a positive impact of union presence on training investments. Green *et al.* (1999) used nationally representative samples to analyse both the incidence and intensity of training. Unionized establishments and workers are more likely to provide and receive training than their non-union counterparts. This union impact holds with even more force for the intensity of training. Consider, for example, non-manual workers. A unionized workplace provided nearly an extra day of training during the previous year (the sample average is 2.7 days so this is a large effect). Likewise unionized workers received an extra 0.34 hours of training in the previous week (sample average 1.3 hours). So union activity does not act to lower physical investment and gives a boost to investment in human capital.

Employment

Trade unions influence employment levels in a number of ways. At the micro (workplace) level unions might impact on the probability of closure and the rate of employment growth. At the macro (economy-wide) level if unions are militant in their pursuit of pay increases the NAIRU will have to be higher than if they are less militant. Further, various institutional arrangements have – at different times and by different authors – been suggested as influencing employment and unemployment, e.g. centralization of pay bargaining or the extent of cooperation between social partners.

The discussion here deals only with workplaces and focuses on associations between union recognition, workplace closure and employment growth, partly influenced by any union impact on pay, productivity, profits and investment. This is an important issue. If union activity does influence closure rates or employment growth such that union members disproportionately lose jobs and have a spell of unemployment, they lose seniority and they may only get inferior (lower wage) jobs when re-employed.

There is virtually no difference in raw closure rates between establishments which do and do not recognize a trade union. In the 1980s the annual closure rate was 2.5 per cent among workplaces which had no unions and 2.3 per cent where unions were recognized. The closure rate dropped in the 1990s to 1.9 per cent in non-union workplaces and 1.8 per cent in unionized establishments. Millward *et al.* (2001) undertook the most thorough study of unionization and closures and conclude as follows:

workplace closures during the period 1990–1998 were little affected by whether workplaces had union representation in 1990. In the private sector, workplace performance, market conditions, workforce composition and structural features of the workplace such as size and ownership were far more important.

In summary, there is no overall association between union recognition and the probability of a workplace closing.

Nevertheless union activity can certainly cause employment *levels* in union workplaces to either be higher or lower than that in corresponding non-union workplaces. In the most straightforward case, if unions extract a wage premium and employment is sensitive to the wage level then employment in unionized workplaces will be lower than it otherwise would be. Alternatively, unions may boost employment via restrictive practices covering demarcations on manning levels. But the debate about unions and employment is not about union influence on levels of employment but on *changes* in employment. In a nutshell it is asserted that unions dampen employment growth or magnify employment declines every year for many years (see, e.g. Blanchflower *et al.* 1991).

We now have a very careful study for the 1990s (Millward *et al.* 2001). Employment levels in workplaces with recognized unions declined by an average of 1.8 per cent p.a. between 1990 and 1998, whereas those without unions grew by an average of 1.4 per cent p.a. The annual rate of growth was therefore around 3 percentage points lower among workplaces with recognized unions (see Table 5.3). This differential need not be causal. It

Table 5.3 Employment change, % per year, private sector workplaces, 1990–8

	Change in employment % p.a.		
	All workplaces	Manufacturing	Services
Raw change			
Union recognition	–1.8	–0.7	–2.4
Non-union	1.4	1.5	1.4
Net union	–3.2	–2.2	–3.8
After including controls	–3.9	–3.4	–4.7
Plus allowing for survival probability	–4.4	–	–

Source: calculated from Bryson (2001c).

Notes
1　From WIRS panel 1990–8, 558 workplaces, employing 25+ employees in 1990 and 1998.
2　Controls are: workplace size; % non-manual; single independent workplace; region; sector; uses short-term contracts; no goods/service accounts for 25%+ sales; number of competitors; financial performance better than average; operating considerably below capacity.
3　The row allowing for the survival probability takes account of the fact that some workplaces ceased trading between 1990 and 1998.

may be, for example, simply that unions are more likely to be operating in decaying sectors and workplaces.

But the authors have no such doubts. They state unambiguously that: 'Unions reduce employment growth by 3–4 per cent p.a. in the private sector between 1990–1998' (Millward *et al.* 2001: 16). Further, there were

> big differences in unionized and non-unionized workplaces *within* industries ... This is very strong evidence that the effect of unions is not simply an industry effect, such as a decline in employment associated with traditional, heavily unionized industries ... the employment effect is still apparent once we account for workplace organizational and technical change, the concentration of unions in declining industries and the age of unionized workplaces ... the union effect arose through wage bargaining, or because union voice is less effective than non-union voice in communicating with management.
>
> (Millward et al. 2001: 16)

Millward *et al.* (2001: 16) go on to state: 'unions were still acting to depress workplace employment levels in the 1990s, as they had done in previous decades'. These are very strong sentiments. What Millward and his colleagues are saying is that union activity has caused employment growth (decline) in union workplaces to be 3 per cent p.a. lower (faster) than in non-union counterparts for the best part of two decades.

Frankly, I do not believe this association can be causal. Surely it is impossible that the wage premium has continued to rise since 1980 (the evidence suggests the opposite). Equally, any adverse union effects on productivity and profits were attenuated or eliminated by the end of the 1990s. Rather, the association may reflect a more sensitive union labour demand elasticity – consequent on more intense non-union competition – such that the employment penalty for any given wage premium has grown. In addition, unionized workplaces may have experienced more organizational change, often involving a cut in jobs, than their non-union counterparts. Nevertheless, the raw numbers themselves ought to be a cause for concern for trade unions. There is no getting away from the fact that while (except in manufacturing) closure rates are not different between union and non-union workplaces, employment declines faster/grows more slowly in union workplaces. Indeed, if the 3 per cent p.a. employment differential found for 1980–98 continues into the future it will compound the membership problems set out in the appendix which suggest a steady state union density of some 20 per cent.

Case study: unions wield the sword of justice

Throughout the twentieth century trade unions were an important force tempering the inequality in the distribution of pay. At the beginning of the century the Webbs emphasized the key role of the 'common rule' and 'rate for the job' in unions' wage policies. By the middle of the century Britain had a system of industry-wide regulation of industrial relations such that the same job had similar national minimum pay among all firms in the same industry. In the 1960s and 1970s, when the locus of collective bargaining gradually decentralized from industry to firm or workplace, shop steward combine committees sought to pursue this egalitarian role.

Since 1980 there have been profound changes to our system of industrial relations. The labour market has been deregulated as a consequence of the legislative onslaught against unions, more intense product market competition and, for much of the time, historically high levels of unemployment. The number of workers covered by collective bargaining has halved. Did unions still wield the sword of justice at the end of the century?

Detailed investigation for 1998 – the year of least intervention in wage-setting by the state for any time in the post-war period – using evidence from both workplaces and individuals shows that:

- unionized workplaces continue to make greater use of objective pay setting criteria such as job classification and tenure, and less use of subjective merit pay, than their non-union counterparts.
- although the move away from national bargaining to decentralized bargaining has caused pay dispersion to rise, workers in the organized sector have much lower pay dispersion than those in the unorganized sector. The standard deviation of log hourly pay, after controlling for the fact that workers and jobs are more similar in the union sector than they are among non-unionists, is 0.33 for union members and 0.44 for non-members.
- the national minimum wage came in 1999. Before then unions truncated the lower tail of the pay distribution. And today almost all union members are paid well above the minimum wage. Therefore the incidence of low pay is much lower in unionized workplaces and among union members than in the unorganized sector.
- putting all this together, if there were no unions the wage differential would be wider by the following amounts:

male–female	2.6%
white–black	1.4%
healthy–health problems	0.6%
non-manual–manual	3.1%

continued...

> Unions narrow the wage differential between women and men, blacks and whites, those with health problems and those without, and between manual and non-manual workers.
>
> Although unions' sword of justice may be a little blunter and corroded it has not been sheathed for good – unions remain a major egalitarian influence on the British labour market.

Sword of justice

Any impact of trade unions on economic performance is more muted than it was 20 years ago. But unions still wield the sword of justice in the workplace. Unions narrow the distribution of pay, promote equal opportunity and family friendly policies, lower the rate of industrial injuries, and handle grievances.

The *spread of pay* among unionized workers is smaller than the spread among their non-union counterparts (see Table 5.4 and the case study). This is because unions protect the pay of those on low earnings and because unionized workplaces make more use of objective criteria – seniority for example – in setting pay rather than subjective factors – like merit – preferred in non-union establishments. Unions also compress the pay structure between different groups in the labour market: women and men, blacks and whites, and those with health problems and the healthy. If there were no unions the gender pay gap would be 2.6 per cent wider and the race pay gap 1.4 per cent bigger. These are very substantial effects. When it was introduced in 1999, the national minimum wage impacted particularly on female pay – two-thirds of those affected were women – but it only narrowed the gender pay gap by a little under 1 per cent. The impact of unions on narrowing the gender pay gap is three times as strong as that of the national minimum wage.

Union recognition is associated with a much greater likelihood of the workplace having some form of *equal opportunity policy and an array of family friendly policies* designed to encourage female employment. These practices include parental leave, working from home, term only contracts, the possibility of switching from full- to part-time employment and job shares. Women in unionized workplaces are much better off in terms of career opportunities, flexible work arrangements and general support for family responsibilities than their counterparts in non-union workplaces (Bewley and Fernie 2003).

Such family friendly policies go hand-in-hand with better performing workplaces (Gray 2001). A private sector establishment with an array of family friendly policies has a greater likelihood of above average financial performance, labour productivity, product or service quality, and lower quit and absentee rates than a workplace without such practices. Even if the causal

Table 5.4 Impact of unionization on pay structure by gender, race, health and occupation, 1998

Group	Unionized %	Premium %	Without unions, wage structure would be wider by %
Male	33	0.0	
Female	31	8.7	2.6
White	32	3.9	
Non-white	32	8.4	1.4
Healthy	32	3.9	
Health problems	33	5.3	0.6
Non-manual	32	3.0	
Manual	32	12.9	3.1

Source: Metcalf *et al.* (2001) using Labour Force Survey, Autumn 1998.

Notes
1   Total sample size is 16,489.
2   Hourly pay premium associated with union membership estimated from regression equation with the following controls: age, marital status, qualifications, part-time worker, temporary worker, industry, occupation, region, public sector, workplace size and (as appropriate) gender, ethnicity and health.
3   In all the regressions but one the coefficient on unionization is significant at better than 1%. Further, in each pairwise comparison the premia are significantly different from one another at 5% or better.
4   The method by which the last column – how much wider the wage structure would be in a notional labour market without unions – is calculated, is fully detailed in the source.

mechanism behind such associations is unclear this evidence is surely something for unions to build on in their attempts to appeal simultaneously to management and workers.

Unions also cut *industrial accidents*. An accident in this context is where an employee has sustained any one of eight injuries during working hours over the last 12 months, including bone fractures, burns, amputations and any injury that results in immediate hospitalization for more than 24 hours. Unions tend to organize in workplaces where an accident is more likely to occur, but their presence lowers the rate by a quarter, compared with similar non-union plants (Litwin 2000). This favourable effect lowering accidents occurs because unions lobby for safety legislation and take industrial action locally to make the workplace safer. Many trade unions also provide health and safety courses. Further a union presence will tend to promote 'voice' over 'exit': where a union is recognized, employees with concerns about accidents are more likely to be listened to rather than labelled as a nuisance. This accident-reduction role of unions is rather neglected. They could, instead, worry less about deaths and injuries and agitate for a bigger compensating pay differential in dangerous sectors and occupations. The evidence (Sandy and Elliott 1996) suggests the reverse – such compensating wage differentials are lower where there are unions. Organized labour has chosen the socially responsible accident prevention strategy in preference to squeezing out a bit more pay in dangerous workplaces.

Effect on industrial relations climate

Union membership and recognition profoundly influence employee–management relations in the workplace, although this union impact has been less studied by economists than the corresponding union effect on efficiency and equity. In the UK three main discussions of unions' effect on industrial relations have been analysed. First, are union members more or less satisfied in their jobs than non-unionists? Second, how does union recognition influence the governance of the workplace – defined by factors like the climate of relations, trust and perceptions of managerial performance? Third, what do unions do to quit and absenteeism rates? These will be discussed in turn.

Surveys consistently report that women and older workers are more *satisfied in their jobs* than men and younger employees. In addition, union members are shown to be less satisfied than non-union members. This stylized fact – union members are not as content with their jobs than workers not in a union – is something of a puzzle because it appears to be inconsistent with another such fact, namely union members have lower quit rates than non-unionists. Surely if you are dissatisfied at work you will be more likely to quit?

Freeman and Medoff (1984) reconcile these apparently contradictory facts by highlighting the role of unions as a 'voice institution'. Their explanation 'differentiates between 'true' dissatisfaction, which leads workers to leave their jobs, and 'reported' or 'voiced' dissatisfaction which results from critical attitudes towards the workplace and a willingness to complain about problems'. In a nutshell, such voice 'operates by fanning discontent'. Bryson (2001b) and Clark (1996), using evidence from WERS and BHPS respectively, both confirm such fanning. Bryson, for example, states that 'unions highlight the shortcomings of management, a process that leads to more voluble complaining'.

Bender and Sloane (1998), using the BHPS, put forward an alternative explanation. They argue that it is not union recognition itself that ferments dissatisfaction. Rather, where a union is recognized collective bargaining takes place and workplaces with such bargaining have a worse climate of industrial relations than those with no bargaining – and the worse climate feeds through into reported job dissatisfaction. Recently, a third explanation has been advanced: given that unions address issues of worker dissatisfaction, there is a sorting process such that more dissatisfied workers will be attracted to union membership. Thus Bryson *et al.* (2003) conclude that lower satisfaction among union members flows from the demographic characteristics of employees who become union members and the characteristics of workplaces (size, region etc.) that employ them – unions themselves do not lower satisfaction in the job. These interesting studies confirm that union members are, on average, less satisfied with their job than non-members. Unfortunately they do not yet provide a consistent explanation for the evidence.

A union presence also influences workers' perceptions about the *governance* of their organization. This includes the climate of relations between management and employees, the trust employees have in their managers, and managerial performance. On average during the 1980s and 1990s evidence from the BHPS and WERS98 suggests that workplace governance is perceived as poorer among employees in workplaces with recognized unions, relative to their counterparts in non-union establishments (Bryson 2001a). The author suggests that better perceptions about governance in non-union workplaces may flow from the use of direct voice – briefing groups, team meetings and the like – rather than representative voice via the union, discussed above.

This 'average' finding is only part of the story. Once the decision is taken to recognize a union, governance is profoundly affected by the way the parties go about their business. First, governance is perceived to be better by workers when there is a balance of power between management and union in the workplace. Very strong or very weak unions detract from a good climate or high trust. Second, when the union is recognized it is better for management to support membership: recognition coupled with hostility to individual membership produces the worse outcomes. Third, unions are perceived to be more effective when workplace governance is good. Once the decision is taken to recognize a union it makes sense to encourage membership and ensure that the union is effective in representing employees. This suggests, for example, that partnership arrangements promoting cooperative employee relations are likely to yield superior governance to adversarial, fragmented relations.

In both the 1980s and 1990s union recognition is linked to a lower *quit rate*. This is consistent with the exit-voice model such that discontented union workers voice concerns through their union whereas similarly disaffected non-union employees have no choice but to exit their firm. Further, during the 1990s, union recognition went hand-in-hand with a higher *absenteeism* rate. This may reflect the fact that absenteeism rates and unionization are both much higher in the public than in the private sector: for example there has been much concern recently about absenteeism in the police and fire service which are both virtually 100 per cent unionized. As Addison and Belfield (2001) note, what is now needed is an investigation of the effect of lower quits in improving labour productivity and of absenteeism in reducing it.

Summary

A quarter of a century ago union recognition was associated with higher levels of pay and lower productivity, so consequently unionized firms and workplaces had lower profits. In the intervening years product, labour and financial markets have changed profoundly. More intense product market competition – globalization, privatization, compulsory competitive tendering etc. – put pressure on firms to ratchet down their costs. In the labour market, the legislative onslaught against collectivism coupled with (till recently) historically high levels of unemployment, restored managerial prerogatives. The roots of unions' traditional power – the closed shop and the strike threat – were reined back, almost castrating much of the labour movement in the process. In financial markets, exchange controls were axed and employee and firm interests were brought into closer alignment via profit sharing and employee share ownership schemes. This all emphasizes the 'cruel paradox' (Hirsch and Schumacher 2001) facing unions: in the long run success with the 'monopoly' face tends in turn to put organized labour and 'collective voice' out of business, such that now unions 'have less and less to offer individual workers' (Blanchard 2001: 295).

Not surprisingly, the presence of a union in a firm or workplace has a more modest impact now. The evidence in this section suggests that: the average union wage mark-up is low; unionized workplaces no longer have lower labour productivity than their non-union counterparts, except in the ever decreasing group of workplaces with multi-unionism; consequently financial performance is, on average, similar in union and non-union workplaces, although where the firm has some monopoly power a trade union can siphon-off some of the rent from capital to labour; but there is no evidence that such transfers lower investment rates in firms and workplaces with union recognition compared with similar non-union organizations – indeed investment in human capital is stronger in unionized workplaces.

There is, however, one acutely worrying economic outcome for unions. Other things being equal, employment in a unionized workplace grows some 3 per cent a year more slowly (or falls 3 per cent a year more quickly) than in a non-union workplace. Even though it is unlikely that union activity is itself the cause of this differential change in employment – which has now been in evidence for 20 years – if it persists into the future the implications for future membership levels are very serious.

Although the impact of trade unions on economic outcomes is tempered, their effect promoting fairness is still very much in evidence. Unions narrow the distribution of earnings, cut accidents and promote family friendly and equal opportunities policy. Similarly, union recognition continues to influence the industrial relations outcomes. The evidence suggests that a union presence is associated, on average, with weaker job satisfaction, perceptions of poorer workplace governance (defined by factors such as trust in management, and the climate of management–employee relations), lower quits and higher absenteeism.

This evidence suggests, broadly, that the individual employee now has less reason to belong to a union – s/he gets a much reduced wage premium. Equally the employer has less reason to oppose unions because they now have such modest effects on productivity and profits. The future of unions surely depends on what they do. Therefore the challenge for the union movement is now to show that they can deliver for workers without putting employers at a disadvantage and/or to deliver for employers without working to the disadvantage of the employees. Some mechanisms for such delivery, and the pitfalls, are discussed next.

Hereafter: resurgence or perdition?

What can unions do to achieve a sustained rise in membership? Broadly there are two routes to revival. Either employment in unionized sectors of the economy has to grow relative to non-union employment or unions must engage in more intense organizing activity and enhance their appeal to both employers and potential members.

Impact of differential changes in employment

It is unlikely that any boost in the aggregate number of jobs in the next decade will occur disproportionately in the unionized sector. In the public sector employment rose by 509,000 between 1998 and 2003. While the number of teachers, nurses and police has been rising – which has helped the teaching unions, the RCN and UNISON to boost membership – the speed of job creation in these sectors will slow significantly in the coming years. And in manufacturing, employment now is only a little over a third of its 1966 peak and jobs continue to go. Anyway, unions now find it just as difficult to get recognized in new manufacturing plants as in new private service workplaces. Similarly there is no suggestion of strong growth in jobs in utilities or transport. It is likely, instead, that the major share of any growth in employment will occur in private services with a present union density of 15 per cent.

Organizing and servicing

Alternatively, unions can invest more in organizing and servicing activity, which may yield a larger return presently than in the last two decades because the climate of opinion fostered by the state is no longer hostile to collective labour institutions. But the allocation of such servicing and organizing investment requires considerable skill. Consider Table 5.5: 36 per cent of employees are covered by a collective agreement on pay but over one-third of these (14 per cent) are free-riders, not members of a union. Looking at the information the other way round, a quarter (7 per cent) of total union members (29 per cent) are not covered by collective agreements for their pay. By far the majority of employees (57 per cent) are neither covered by a collective agreement nor a union member. The evidence in Table 5.5 provides remarkable food for thought for unions. Consider each cell in turn.

Table 5.5 Coverage of collective agreements on pay and conditions and union membership UK employees in employment, autumn 2003

| | Pay and conditions covered by collective agreement | | | | | |
	Yes		No		Total	
Union member						
Yes	5.5m	22%	1.6m	7%	7.1m	29%
No	3.3m	14%	14.0m	57%	17.3m	71%
Total	8.8m	36%	15.6m	64%	24.4m	100%

Source: Calculated from Kevin Brook, 'Trade union membership: an analysis of data from the autumn 2001 LFS', *Labour Market Trends*, July 2002: 343–54; 'Spotlight', *Labour Market Trends*, July 2003: 338, and *Labour Market Trends*, March 2004: 100; and details at www.dti.gov.uk/er/emar/trade.htm.

Example: 8.8 million employees (36%) are covered by collective bargaining. Of these 5.5 million (22%) are union members and 3.3 million (14%) are not union members.

Dilemma: a difficult choice for unions

Consider the following data, taken from Table 5.5, which sets out the number of employees who are or are not union members and corresponding information for those whose pay is set by collective bargaining.

| | | Pay set by collective bargaining | |
		Yes	No
Union	Yes	5.5m	1.6m
Member	No	3.3m	14.0m

Out of 8.8 million employees covered by collective bargaining only 5.5 million are union members, the other 3.3 million being free-riders. Looking at the information the other way round, nearly a quarter (1.6 million) of the 7.1 million union members are not covered by collective bargaining. Finally, 14 million out of 24.4 million employees are neither union members nor covered by collective bargaining.

Where should unions put their scarce resources if they are to flourish in the future? First, they need to continue to service the 5.5 million who have their pay set by collective bargaining and belong to a union. This involves providing services to individual union members such as promoting lifelong learning and representing members in employers' procedures. Some unions have adopted partnerships with employers – a more cooperative and less adversarial form of industrial relations – in order to better service their members. The bulk of these 5.5 million employees are in the public sector where the unions must deal with members' concerns such as a possible two-tier labour force in health consequent on the public finance initiative, the introduction of performance related pay in teaching, moves to decentralized bargaining in the post office or alterations in work arrangements in the essential fire service.

Second, absorbing the 3.3 million free-riders – 'in fill' recruitment – is a potentially attractive (cheap) way of boosting membership. The growth in free-riding runs parallel with the rise in 'never members', now equal to half the workforce, so union intervention at the recruitment stage is vital.

Third, unions must convince the 1.6 million employees who are members but not covered by collective agreement that continuing to belong to a union is worthwhile. These include some members signed up in organizing campaigns which have not yet reached fruition and workers in firms who have derecognized the union for pay bargaining but perhaps continue to recognize it for dealing with individual grievances.

Finally, unions must attempt to organize among the 14 million employees who are neither members nor have their pay set by collective bargaining. There is a delicate balancing act here because organizing expenditure represents a 'tax' on existing members. Between 2000 (when the new recognition law came into force) and 2002 unions organized around 170,000 workers a year into recognition agreements and some 100,000 of these are union members. This represented a 25-year high organizing figure. The problem for unions is that even this rate of organizing is inadequate to keep pace with new job creation, lost members from workplace closures, redundancies, extra free-riders and derecognitions. Unions echo the Red Queen in *Through the Looking Glass*: 'it takes all the running you can do, to keep in the same place' (Carroll 1872: 39).

First, unions must *continue to service the 5.5 million workers* (22 per cent) who have their pay set by collective bargaining and belong to a union. The majority are in the public sector. There are three main components of union activity to support workers in this cell – service to individuals, partnerships with employers and, in the public sector, maintaining terms and conditions. Activities on behalf of individual members form a major component of the tasks performed by union officers and shop stewards. These include promoting lifelong learning, advice on employment matters, representing members in employers' procedures and before courts and tribunals, and providing members with information about their company or organization.

Next, some unions have adopted partnerships with management to improve services. The bulk of such partnership agreements are signed between employers and unions where unions are already recognized – turning over a new leaf, e.g. at Blue Circle Cement and Tesco – rather than new recognitions in non-union companies, e.g. at Bristow Helicopters. There is no one model of partnership but there is agreement that 'management–trade union partnerships centre on a shift away from adversarial employment relationships and towards mutually cooperative and harmonious relationships, usually with the aim of improving organizational performance and competitiveness' (Oxenbridge and Brown 2002).

Finally, the majority of workers in this cell are in the public sector (or ex-public sector) where unions face a number of challenges. For example, in the health service the public finance initiative impacts on their capacity to influence patterns of service delivery, workloads, the composition of employment, governance structures and the exercise of union voice. In education, the civil service and the Inland Revenue in the last decade performance related pay (PRP) evolved from being a radical managerial innovation to part of standard organizational practice. Unions were often hostile to its introduction because they worried that PRP denied them their traditional role of monitoring standards of fairness in employer behaviour. And even where union density is very high – the fire service, prison service and post office – unions will only sustain such strong membership if they are able to deal with members' concerns over alterations to work practices and moves to decentralized bargaining.

Second, *absorbing the 3.3 million free-riders* (14 per cent of employees) – so-called 'in fill' recruitment – is a potentially attractive (cheap) method of boosting membership. Almost two-fifths of workers covered by collective agreements are not union members – a fraction some four times higher than the corresponding figure for free-riders in the US. The growth in free-riding runs parallel with the rise in the number of 'never members', so union intervention at the recruitment stage is important.

Some 1.6 million employees (7 per cent) are *union members but not covered by a collective agreement* on pay. They include members of some staff associations, some teachers and nurses whose pay is set by arbitration rather than collective agreements, some members signed up in organizing campaigns which have not yet reached fruition, workers who have switched jobs to a non-union firm but retained their membership, and workers in firms who have derecognized the union for pay bargaining but perhaps continue to recognize it for dealing with individual grievances. In the 1990s 1-private-sector-workplace-in-3 abandoned collective bargaining, but only a quarter of these formally derecognized the union. Unions face a hard task convincing such members that it remains worthwhile to continue to belong to the union.

Last but not least are the 14.0 million (57 per cent) of employees who are *neither members nor have their pay and conditions set by collective bargaining*. The bulk of these workers will never have been a union member. Unions must perform a delicate balancing act here: organizing expenditure on this group can be thought of as an investment for the future health of the union or as a 'tax' on existing members: 'Commitment to organizing still jostles uncomfortably with all the other demands on unions' efforts and resources'

(TUC 1999: 7). Around a fifth of these 14 million workers say that they either desire union representation or would be very likely to join a union if one were available (see Bryson *et al.* 2004). This suggests a 'representation gap' of some 2.8 million employees, a potentially rich pool of employees for unions to organize. However, in order to achieve recognition these employees need to be concentrated by firm or workplace or there will never be a union available to join. There are some interesting occupations involved here. Recently MSF-AMICUS signed up some 2,000 Church of England clergy who had no employment rights – their employer was held to be divine not earthly. And the GMB has had some success in recruiting lap dancers. Signing up the dancers nearly led to an inter-union dispute: the steel union ISTC also claimed jurisdiction because they worked with metal poles!

Recognition occurs voluntarily or, since 2000, via the law. Voluntary recognition stems either from true love (cooperation between capital and labour) or a marriage of convenience (a pragmatic second best). The legal route, inevitably associated with adversarial industrial relations, is a shotgun marriage, imposed on a reluctant employer by an arm of the state. Under the legal route, if a union can prove a majority of membership in the bargaining unit, then it gains recognition. If not, a ballot is held in which the union must win 50+ per cent of the votes cast in the ballot and must have at least 40 per cent of the workforce in the bargaining unit voting 'yes'. The direct effect of this law has been very modest – fewer than 25,000 workers have been covered by recognition orders since the law came into effect in 2000.

However, its indirect or shadow effect is larger (see Gall 2004 for some meticulous calculations). Over 1,500 voluntary agreements such as the marriage of convenience between Bristow Helicopters and BALPA and AMICUS – or partnerships like those at Virgin and EasyJet – were signed in the three years 2000–2 bringing almost half a million new workers under recognition. And there are many campaigns currently underway, covering perhaps another half a million potential members. Not all the 0.5 million workers in newly recognized workplaces became new union members. Some, for example, were already members – perhaps the vanguard of the recognition campaign – while others remained free-riders. Nevertheless it is something of a puzzle that such a high figure did not translate into a growth in union membership. The answer to the puzzle must be that depreciation among existing members is high and/or that very many of those newly covered by recognition agreements garner the benefits of recognition but choose not to join the union.

In the first half of the 1990s union organizing efforts resulted in fewer than 10,000 workers a year being newly covered by a recognition agreement. Once it became likely that a Labour government would be elected this figure rose to 40,000. And when the recognition provisions of the Employment Relations Act came into force in 2000 the gross inflow of newly covered workers averaged 170,000 a year for the three years 2000–2 (though this number contracted in 2003). Perhaps 100,000 of these will be union members. This annual 170,000 figure represents a 25-year organizing high but it is equivalent to only just over 1 per cent of the stock of uncovered workers (15.6 million). And with employment growing at around 0.2 million a year since 1990 it does not even keep pace with the extra jobs created. (And before the new recognition law, organizing yielded only 0.1 per cent of the unorganized stock.) This 170,000 coverage figure, or 100,000 gross annual inflow of union members, is almost certainly insufficient to offset the gross outflow of members from workplace closures and contractions, redundancies, extra free-riders and derecognitions. The appendix has a more formal discussion of the inflows and outflows to and from union membership. Even taking reasonably favourable assumptions, it suggests that in the longer term (i.e. in steady state) density is likely to stabilize at around 20 per cent, implying private sector density of some 12 per cent.

Summary and conclusions

It is not surprising that union membership crumbled away in the 1980s and 1990s. The climate was cold. The composition of jobs altered such that employment declined in unions' traditional heartlands of manufacturing and the public sector. The state did what it could to undermine collectivism through successive tranches of industrial relations legislation, privatization, contracting-out, the introduction of performance related pay for its own employees and subsidizing (despite no apparent market failure) profit sharing and employee share ownership schemes for private sector workers. In turn, employers responded to the signal sent by the state and were more likely to oppose unions, such that new recognition became difficult to achieve. Simultaneously many workers lost their taste for membership and the number of 'never members' doubled to half the workforce. Unions' own structures and policies – male, pale and stale – compounded their problems.

Unions do not flourish in adversity. In the 1950s and 1960s, with the post-war settlement and the growth of the welfare state, membership blossomed. In the 1970s, when that settlement disintegrated, unions were well dug in. They were the fifth estate of the realm and employees joined even if they disliked unions. In the 1980s and 1990s with the altered industrial structure and high unemployment unions needed support from employers and workers. By and large they did not get it, rather the reverse: the state and employers did their best to undermine collectivism and unions' own structures and policies compounded the haemorrhage of members. What had previously been conforming behaviour – to recognize or belong to a union – became deviant. This contrast between UK unions' experience in the 1980s and 1990s, compared with their successes in the 1960s and 1970s, closely resembles that of US unions in an earlier period. In the 1920s US unions appeared to be in terminal decline, yet in the 1930s and 1940s they flourished under the New Deal, protectionism and the wartime regime. Whether or not unions follow the road to perdition, or instead become resurgent, largely depends on two things. First, what they do to firm performance and fairness at work. Second, whether or not the intersection of what the unions see as the malevolent forces of the 1980s and 1990s continue over the next decade or so.

The monopoly face (vested interest) impact of unions is much less strong now than it was a quarter of a century ago. The nineteenth century classical economists would have less to rail against now. The roots of union power – the closed shop and the strike threat – are shut down and product market competition is more intense. The evidence suggests that now: the average union wage mark-up is low or zero; unionized workplaces no longer have lower labour productivity than their non-union counterparts; therefore financial performance is, on average, similar to that in non-union workplaces, although where the firm has some monopoly power a trade union can siphon-off some of the rent from capital to labour; but there is no evidence that such transfers lower investment rates in firms and workplaces with union recognition compared with similar non-union organizations – indeed investment in human capital is stronger in unionized workplaces. However, there remains one acutely worrying economic outcome from the union viewpoint. Employment in a unionized workplace grows some 3 per cent more slowly, or falls 3 per cent more quickly, than in a similar non-union workplace. Even though union activity is unlikely to be the cause of this differential growth in jobs, if it persists the implications for future membership levels are serious.

This evidence suggests that the employer now has less incentive to oppose unions because their impact on productivity and profits is so modest. Equally, the worker has less cause to belong to a union because s/he gets a much reduced wage premium. The challenge for the union movement is to demonstrate that they can come through for workers without putting employers at a disadvantage and/or deliver for employers while simultaneously looking after worker interests. Perhaps unions need to make more of what Alan Flanders called their 'stirring music': unions do continue to wield the sword of justice – they narrow the spread of earnings, cut accidents and promote family friendly and equal opportunity policy. Further, from around 1870 and for most of the twentieth century the share of profit in national income gradually declined, but this long run trend has reversed in the last two decades: this too suggests a role for unions in countering exploitation – a return to the rationale for unions set out by the Webbs.

It is unlikely that future employment in the more highly unionized segments of the economy – the public sector and utilities, for example – will grow more rapidly than jobs in private service where union density is below average. Therefore the future of unions turns, in part, on the thorny matter of balancing servicing and organizing activities. Unions have 7 million members, but 1.6

million of these are not covered by collective bargaining because, in many cases, the employer abandoned collective bargaining without formally derecognizing the union. Unions face a hard task convincing such members that it remains worthwhile to continue to belong to the union. Unions must also continue to service their 5.5 million members who are covered by collective bargaining, the majority of whom are in the public sector. Key tasks here include maintaining terms and conditions and providing services to individuals including advice on employment matters, promoting lifelong learning and representing members in employers' procedures and before labour courts.

There are 8.8 million workers covered by collective bargaining, but 3.3 million of these are free-riders. Absorbing such workers – in fill recruitment – is a potentially low cost route to boost membership. Finally, and much more difficult, are the 14 million employees who are neither members nor covered by collective bargaining. From 2000 to 2002 unions achieved a 25-year high in the annual numbers of this group being organized, but this figure still represented only 1 per cent per year of the total unorganized and was insufficient to offset the gross outflow of members from workplace closure and contractions, redundancies, new free-riders and derecognitions. And in 2003 the numbers newly organized by successful recognition campaigns fell sharply.

Since New Labour came to power in 1997 the hostile forces of the 1980s and 1990s have largely evaporated. Public sector employment is rising, the state is at worst neutral in its dealings with unions and has also established, for example, recognition machinery, a national minimum wage and various family friendly initiatives. Almost 3 million non-union workers say they would be likely to join if there was a union at their workplace. And the union movement generated a raft of initiatives aimed at their revitalization. Despite all this, membership is now the same as it was in 1997 and density has fallen 2 percentage points.

One plausible explanation for this paradox is as follows. When unions were powerful they pursued their 'monopoly face' in manufacturing, mining, utilities and the public sector and they largely ignored the significant groups of low paid workers who suffered the worst inequalities in power and conditions. Subsequently, that monopoly face has mostly disappeared so there is less incentive for such workers to belong to a union. Simultaneously state initiatives displaced many of the collective voice and sword of justice activities including promoting better grievance procedures, enhanced rights for part-time workers, limits on working time, better parental leave and the national minimum wage. In addition both the voice and monopoly faces of unions have been supplanted by the largely unremarked huge expansion in occupational licensing and certification, again a state initiative.

In the longer run, the passage of the EU Directive on Information and Consultation may be an important influence on unions' futures. It establishes, for the first time, permanent and general arrangements for information and consultation for all workers in the UK in organizations employing more than 50 employees and will cover three-quarters of the British labour force by 2007. The tough job for unions is to build on these schemes and to maintain and expand their role within them such that they are seen as the legitimate voice representing employees. Although evidence from France and Germany suggests that a union presence complements these arrangements and makes them more effective, union density remains low in those countries so perhaps, instead, this indirect voice institution crowds out a union voice.

Finally, it is worth re-emphasizing the numbers. For the first three years of the new millennium the organizing rate was at a 20-year high of some 150,000 workers a year newly recognized, of whom perhaps 100,000 are or become union members – approximately equal to 0.4 per cent of employees. Let the net depreciation of density from closures and lost appetite for membership be 2 per cent (in fact it was larger than this in the 1980s and 1990s). In such circumstances – remember the organizing figure is probably overgenerous and the depreciation rate understated – steady state union density is 20 per cent (= 0.4/2), implying private sector density of around 12 per cent. The future for private sector unionization is bleak indeed. Perdition is more likely than resurgence.

Acknowledgements

I acknowledge with thanks research assistance from Jian Wei Li and helpful discussions/comments from John Addison, Alex Bryson, Andy Charlwood, David Coats, Steve Dunn, Sue Fernie, John Gennard, Rafael Gomez, Howard Gospel, John Kelly and Leo Troy. 'Classical and institutional economists, Marx and the Webbs' draws freely on Kaufman (2004b, 2004c). Andrew Glyn kindly provided data on the distribution of income between pay and profits and was a source of guidance in their use, a notoriously difficult area.

A fuller version of this chapter, with a complete list of references, is available as WP1235e from http://cep.lse.ac.uk/people/cv/david_metcalf.pdf.

Appendix – stocks, flows and steady state union membership

Stocks and flows of union membership

Union membership is a function of changes in existing membership and investment in organizing activity. The following identity relates these flows to the membership stock:

$$\text{UNION}_t = \text{UNION}_{t-1} - r\,\text{UNION}_{t-1} + \text{NEW}_t$$

- UNION_t is the number of union members in a given year t.
- $-r$ is the rate of change of membership due to changes in employment in organized establishments. It can, in principle, be positive or negative, but it is likely to be negative reflecting the closure or contraction of union workplaces, the growth in the number of free-riders, and the fact that new establishments tend to be born 'non-union'.
- NEW is the number of new members obtained via new organization of workplaces (net of any members lost because of derecognitions). It should be recalled that this number is substantially lower than the number of workers newly covered by collective bargaining: approximately 60 per cent of newly covered employees become/are union members.

Consider an example:

- if there are 7 million union members in 2003;
- and employment in unionized workplaces falls 2 per cent 2003–4;
- and 150,000 workers are newly organized in 2003–4 of whom two-thirds are union members;
- then union membership in 2004 is:

= 7 million – 0.02 (7 million) + 150,000 (0.67)
= 6.96 million

On the basis of these reasonable assumptions, even the 2000–2 peak organizing effort in the last quarter century is insufficient to forestall a decline in membership.

Steady state union membership

The identity above can be manipulated to indicate the steady state rate of union density:

$$\text{UNION DENSITY} = \%\,\text{NEW} / (r + g)$$

- % NEW is workers newly organized who are union members as a percentage of the total number of employees;
- g is the growth rate of total employment;
- $(r + g)$ is the net rate of depreciation or appreciation of union density reflecting closures, lost appetite for membership etc.

Consider an example:

- Assume 150,000 workers p.a. are newly organized, of whom 100,000 are/become union members, approximately equal to 0.4 per cent of employees. This is the peak organizing rate since 1980.
- Assume the net depreciation of density is 2 per cent p.a. (it was more than this in the 1980s and 1990s).
- Then steady state union density is:

0.4 / 2 = 20%

For further details of the method and assumptions behind these calculations see e.g. Farber and Western (2001, 2002) and Freeman (1988).

Chapter 6

Union responses to public–private partnerships in the National Health Service

Stephen Bach and Rebecca Kolins Givan

Key points

- Public–private partnerships are the dominant method of procuring new assets in the NHS and have caused serious tensions between unions and government.
- The employee and patient experiences with privately financed hospitals vary widely.
- General public service unions whose members are now employed by private contractors have campaigned against private financing with limited success.
- Professional unions whose members are only indirectly affected by private sector involvement have remained pragmatic and have not taken a public stance for or against private financing of public services.
- The key determinants of both high quality patient care and effective employment relations are staff involvement throughout the procurement process, and a private sector partner which takes a constructive and open approach to employment relations.

The expansion of public–private partnerships (PPPs) in the public services has been a prominent cause of the sharp deterioration in the relationship between public service trade unions and the government, during the Labour government's second term in office. Underlying trade union concern about the direction of public service modernization was highlighted during the 2001 election campaign when the Labour manifesto signalled a substantial, but unspecified, expansion in the role of the private sector in the provision of public services (Bach 2002: 328). These tensions have been most visible in the health sector as the Labour government has shifted from the cautious, incremental changes that marked its first term in office, towards more radical structural reforms that include a central role for public–private partnerships and a revitalization of the internal market in the NHS. This reform agenda has been disconcerting for health service unions as they confront a dual challenge of articulating a coherent national *policy* response to influence government reforms and the need to ensure effective union *organization* and *representation* at workplace level to shape the implementation of this modernization agenda.

These challenges can be illustrated by the response of public service unions to the private finance initiative (PFI) which has become the dominant system of procuring new facilities (e.g. hospitals) using private capital and management. The experience of PFI is important for assessing the future prospects for public service trade unions because an increasing proportion of public services are being delivered by diverse forms of public–private partnership. We argue that health sector trade union policy and organization remains committed to a model of public service provision that is being abandoned by the Labour government and the experience of union members in PFI schemes is more varied than the majority of trade unions acknowledge.

Two implications flow from this analysis. First, public service unions face a major challenge; they have so far been unable to articulate a vision for the future of public services, and the role of trade unions within it, that is persuasive to New Labour. The absence of a common vision reinforces the limited influence of public service trade unions in shaping Labour government policy. Second, the structure and organization of public service trade unions remains substantially unaltered despite the radical changes in organizational structures and employment practice at workplace level. The historical emphasis on a highly centralized form of trade union organization that focuses on establishing national agreements with senior government officials is increasingly ineffective. In an era of increased local managerial flexibility, continuous reorganization and the proliferation of public and private sector employer units, an effective local presence is essential, reinforced by support from the centre. As Fairbrother (2002: 78) notes, however, most public service unions have been unable to reorganize themselves to take account of these altered circumstances.

This chapter examines the challenge posed by the private finance initiative (PFI) to union organization and membership. It uses data from interviews with national and regional union officials and trade union representatives and members in PFI hospitals in the National Health Service as well as interviews with members of private sector service providers and other private sector managers associated with PFI schemes, comprising 34 interviews in total. This data was supplemented by a review of national trade union policies, including materials associated with campaigns and congress resolutions. The chapter examines the evolution of private sector involvement in the National Health Service and union responses in the national political arena and at the workplace.

The challenge of PPPs: from CCT to PFI

The antecedents of the private finance initiative lie in the expansion of procurement from the private sector during the 1980s and 1990s. In the

NHS, the policy of compulsory competitive tendering was introduced from 1983 for catering, cleaning and laundry services. Although the majority of contracts remained in-house, competitive tendering enabled managers to alter employment practices, and undermine terms and conditions of employment and led to substantial reductions in the workforce (Bach 1990; Colling 1999). Since this period the scope of contracting-out has broadened and the majority of hospitals have utilized outside contractors to provide services such as maintenance, cleaning, laundry and catering.

Data from the Workplace Employee Relations Survey (WERS)[1] in 1998 confirm the extent of outsourcing in the NHS, which represents a continuation of earlier trends. Of the 148 health sector workplaces surveyed which were in the public sector, all of them contracted out one or more services. The data show the steady increase in contracting out throughout the NHS: 38 per cent of these workplaces were contracting out some services which had been performed by in-house employees five years earlier ($n = 99$). Of these 37 workplaces, 24 stated that some of the contract employees had previously been in-house employees. The transfer of employees to private contractors is an ongoing trend. Thirty-three workplaces stated a reason for out-sourcing this work in the previous 5 years, of which 11 gave compulsory competitive tendering (CCT) or other government regulations as one reason. This data, although based on relatively few observations, provides a detailed picture of forms of contracting-out, prior to the larger-scale private service provision central to PFI.

The experience of CCT highlighted a number of challenges for trade unions that have been accentuated by PFI. CCT resulted in changes to terms and conditions of employment and alterations in work organization, associated with the creation of a two-tier workforce. In cases where in-house provision was retained the obligation placed on senior managers to accept the lowest cost tender resulted in reductions in bonus schemes and hours worked and the introduction of local pay and conditions packages which reduced enhancements for working weekends and evenings (for example, Bach 1998: 570–1). Contracting-out often resulted in further adaptation to local labour market conditions with reductions in sick pay, holiday entitlement and basic pay rates (Colling 1999).

Although the Transfer of Undertakings (Protection of Employment) Regulations 1981 were gradually applied to contracted-out workers from the early 1990s, following a series of union wins at TUPE employment tribunals, this provided only limited protection. The terms and conditions of existing workers were protected when services were contracted out but TUPE excluded pension rights and provided no defence against subsequent changes for new starters (IRS 2003). Similar concerns have emerged under transfers associated with PFI and the reluctance of the Labour government to address the two-tier workforce in the NHS has soured the relationship between public service unions and the government.

UNISON and the GMB have secured national recognition agreements with major private contractors such as Serco and Sodexho. This has the potential advantage, in comparison to the complex national bargaining machinery in the NHS, of developing a direct relationship with a private contractor who has greater scope to be responsive to the immediate needs of the workforce. The disadvantage, however, is that the degree of recognition for pay bargaining purposes does not usually match recognition arrangements in the NHS. Trade unions also require local organization and expertise to influence pay and conditions at workplace level. Over time the situation has become more complex as contracts have been subject to successive rounds of competitive tendering. Workers in the same workplace, undertaking the same work, can be employed under a plethora of different terms and conditions creating a multi-tier workforce. In one local dispute a UNISON branch reported staff being employed on nine different sets of terms and conditions in a single hospital trust (UNISON 2003b). The pressure on local resources is exacerbated by patchy local level organization and a shortage of workplace representatives (Bach and Givan 2004).

CCT also had significant implications for trade union organization and representation (Foster and Scott 1998). Colling (1999: 144) highlights the degree to which forms of contracting have disorientated unions. First, centralized union structures and officer resources designed to support national bargaining have needed to respond to the demand at workplace level for local bargaining expertise, legal advice and information about contractors' employment records as well as information about local labour market rates of pay. Whilst trade unions have been willing to follow their members into the private sector, this has been a more straightforward task – organizationally and ideologically – for those unions that already had a substantial private sector presence compared to those unions which serviced an almost exclusively public sector membership.

Second, trade unions have been fragmented according to subsector. As public sector organizations have been divided into separate business units and directorates, some services have been more exposed to forms of marketization than others. In a service like health, in which a highly diverse workforce exists, these market pressures have accentuated the potential for sectionalism, reflected in the existence of rival trade unions, with some groups transferred to the private sector and others remaining in-house, straining the scope for developing a common response to CCT. These potential cleavages could be expected to re-emerge under PFI because clinical staff are not transferred under PFI schemes. A further source of differentiation can arise between craft workers and manual workers with craft workers more likely to be beneficiaries of improved terms and conditions of employment. This may account for the findings of a survey of AMICUS-AEEU members which indicated that the majority of their members in PFI schemes were favourably disposed towards their new employers (cited in Maltby and Gosling 2003: 5).

The private finance initiative

Under the PFI system, a private consortium is contracted to finance, design, build and operate public service facilities, usually involving the transfer of ancillary staff. The NHS Trust makes an agreed annual payment for the duration of the contract (usually 25–35 years), which represents the first obligation on a trust's revenue. PFI is a system for the procurement of services, rather than only capital assets (like buildings). The attraction of PFI for the government and potentially for service users is that it enables the acquisition of new hospital services more rapidly than could be achieved via conventional financing because of the longer period over which assets are financed. This is in contrast with the upfront investment needed for conventional financing of hospitals, where the government must pay for the capital assets at the start of the project. PFI draws on specialist private sector expertise that can make efficiency savings and which share the risks of construction delays and other cost over-runs. In practice the degree of risk transfer has proved a highly contentious issue and UNISON (2002a) has argued that profits derived from PFI, including additional profits from refinancing deals, indicate unacceptable levels of profit accrue from PFI schemes. This view is contested by the private sector who argue that it is not straightforward attracting institutional investors to invest in PFI schemes and the recent financial difficulties of the contractor Jarvis indicate that PFI schemes are more risky than critics acknowledge.

Private finance initiatives are now the dominant method of procuring major new assets in the public sector. By the end of 2003, 617 projects had been signed under the PFI with a capital value of over £56 billion (Office of Government Commerce 2003). In the health sector, there are 64 major PFI schemes underway (17 of which are now fully operational), worth over £10 billion (Department of Health 2003). Due to the complex contractual arrangements, it is almost impossible to estimate the number of employees potentially transferred to the private sector under PFI. In 2002, the GMB estimated that 35,000 staff may be affected directly, and since then the number of health PFI schemes has risen by one-third (GMB 2002b).

As well as revitalizing the PFI the Labour government has gone much further than its Conservative government predecessors in boosting private sector involvement in health service delivery, as it shifts towards a mixed economy of welfare in which services are financed by central government but delivered by a range of providers. Overseas private sector health care providers have been invited to establish treatment centres to undertake £2 billion of routine surgery for NHS patients, to ensure that the government meets politically sensitive waiting time targets. There are some publicly owned treatment centres, others are owned jointly by the NHS and a private partner, and there are 11 wholly independent sector treatment centres planned, mostly provided by overseas health care corporations, with services purchased by the NHS.

In contrast to the voluminous data on the consequences of contracting-out, there is surprisingly little evidence available on the employment consequences of PFI/PPPs. The influential Institute for Public Policy Research's (IPPR) Commission on PPPs devoted just nine pages to workforce issues (IPPR 2001: 196–204) and the employment relations literature is largely confined to single case studies of hospital PFI schemes (Fischbacher and Beaumont 2003; Hebson *et al.* 2003). There are, however, important differences in the consequences of PPPs in comparison to the situation under CCT.

First, when services were contracted out there was a clear differentiation between the health authority and private sector employer. This enabled unions to undertake relatively straightforward comparisons between terms and conditions in the public and private sectors and to sustain an argument that contracting-out led to worse terms and conditions of employment. The position under PFI is more complex, because PFI schemes form part of an overall government approach that is blurring the boundaries between public and private sector provision. This stems from the government's support for the 'boundaryless', 'network' or 'extended' organization in which technological innovation enables organizations to work together in a cooperative manner to achieve their objectives, undermining the traditional antagonism between public and private sector organizations that has been the dominant narrative associated with contracting-out (see Colling 2000). This perspective is integral to the government's 'Third way' philosophy with its emphasis on 'what works' rather than who delivers public services. As John Kay argues:

> What is legitimate is what works: and this is true in both public and private sectors ... Our purpose should be to elide rather than emphasise the difference between public and private sector organizations.
>
> (John Kay 2003: 41–2)

In contrast to the transparency of CCT arrangements, the growth of public–private partnerships ensures a more embedded and diverse role for the private sector within the NHS. This makes it more difficult for trade unions to identify the boundaries between public and private sector provision, to establish the consequences for union members (e.g. the implications of staff working in private patient facilities within NHS hospitals), and to demarcate the 'red lines' of PPPs. In addition, public sector employees may be line-managed by private sector employers, further complicating the lines of accountability. The difficulty of articulating a clear union response is reflected in the terminology used. A 2003 RCN congress resolution referred to 'creeping privatization' whilst UNISON uses the term 'privatization by stealth'.

Second, the emphasis on 'what works' differentiates PFI from CCT. Under CCT, trade unions had some success in publicizing 'contract failures' and managed to shift debate from producer concerns about employment conditions towards service quality issues, reinforcing managerial and patient reservations about contracting out service provision. Indeed, some NHS trusts took services back in-house when the private contractor proved to be deficient. By contrast the benefits of PFI, especially the allure of a new hospital, are much more visible to staff and patients than under CCT and opposition to PFI can be portrayed as the dominance of sectional producer interests that are attempting to take precedence over the needs of users and staff. This procurement of new assets is the key distinction between PFI and CCT.

Finally PFI schemes represent a significantly more complex managerial process than CCT with a lengthy procurement process. This requires trade union representatives to develop a sound understanding of a highly technical process that involves a range of advisors to trust managers in order to influence the process. Gosling (2003) suggests that commercial confidentiality is often used as a cloak to discourage staff and patient involvement, although this was less evident in the NHS than other areas of the public sector. The consequences of PFI schemes have longer term repercussions than CCT because contracts are signed for 25–35 years, and in some cases up to 60, compared to three year contracts for CCT. This does have the potential benefit of providing more certainty and long-term employment security for staff than under CCT, but places a premium on ensuring effective protection for staff when the PFI schemes are completed.

To summarize, unions face two main challenges in confronting PPPs. First, there is a challenge of representation – how to provide representation for members employed in a variety of workplaces where recognition may not be automatic and in which terms and conditions are decided at local level. Second, unions face challenges as national organizations, in trying to influence government policy and develop credible responses in a rapidly shifting public service context.

Union responses to PFI

The response of trade unions to PFI and PPPs has taken a variety of forms that have included campaigning against PFI, lobbying the Labour government for enhanced staff protection as well as engaging with PFI implementation at workplace level. There are significant differences between trade unions in their response to PFI that stem from the occupational make up and professional identities of their membership, which affects the degree to which PFI has a direct impact on the terms and conditions of employment of union members. These different union strategies can be broadly divided into two main categories. The general unions have established well-resourced campaigns to discredit the private finance initiative and lobbied to end the two-tier workforce, whilst trade unions that represent predominantly professional staff have adopted a more cautious and low-key approach towards PFI.

Amongst the general unions UNISON has been most directly affected by the transfer of employment to private companies and the GMB also has a sizeable membership affected by PFI. UNISON and the GMB have adopted similar public stances towards PFI, but these similarities mask important differences in approach that stem from the composition of their membership and their differing historical evolution. UNISON defines itself as the union for the public services and organizes almost exclusively in the public services and privatized utilities in which national agreements are the preferred form of bargaining. The experience of membership losses arising from CCT, which in part precipitated the formation of UNISON, ensured unswerving opposition to PFI.

For the GMB, however, outright opposition to the PFI was less straight-forward. The GMB has a much more diverse membership then UNISON with the public services section comprising approximately 30 per cent of its total membership and it is more familiar with negotiating company specific agreements in the private sector. Organization and membership benefits could have accrued to the GMB by pursuing recognition deals with private contractors and becoming a preferred partner with these companies; downplaying their opposition to PFI. Although the GMB has a number of agreements with private contractors, forceful internal opposition to PFI led it to adopt a policy position that is not dissimilar to UNISON's. Members' ideological opposition to PFI proved a more potent influence on GMB policy than the uncertain longer-term organizational benefits of closer engagement with PFI contractors.

UNISON has taken the dominant role in mounting campaigns against PFI with lower-key campaigns adopted by the GMB to influence policy makers and the media. At the local level, however, the response has usually been pragmatic as these organizations have been forced to respond to the implementation of PFI schemes that impact on their membership. The professional unions such as those representing nurses and doctors have taken a much less proactive approach to PFI. Although the new facilities alter their work environment, for their members the terms and conditions of employment remain unchanged. Therefore the impact of PFI is less direct and these unions have been slower and more cautious in formulating responses to PFI, not least because there has been limited membership pressure to develop a coherent response to PFI/PPP.

PFI in the political arena: national level responses

In UNISON, the trigger for a more intensive engagement with the PFI agenda stemmed from hostility towards the government's plans for an expanded role for the private sector, unveiled prior to the 2001 general election, alongside an implicit acceptance that PFI was here to stay. This prompted UNISON to focus more attention on the consequences of PFI for their membership and in 2000 it became an explicit UNISON objective to campaign to end the two-tier workforce. A senior UNISON officer attributed this shift of emphasis to:

> the perceived need for a more pragmatic, twin-track approach in the face of a growth in private sector involvement and relatively low union membership density, and significant recruitment potential in parts of the private sector.
>
> (Wing 2003: 3)

UNISON and the GMB have therefore pursued a twin-track approach. The first strand has been to oppose PFI in principle and to discredit PFI, highlighting the lack of evidence that informed government policy. At the same time, the second strand has been to ensure that members are protected from the consequences of PFI. They have mounted high profile national campaigns against PFI specifically, and the private provision of public services more generally. UNISON's 'Positively Public' campaign and the GMB's 'Keep Public Services Public' campaign both sought to ensure that public services remained publicly financed and publicly provided. The GMB has emphasized the poor employment practices and high levels of executive compensation of the major PFI contractors (GMB 2002a). A GMB official highlighted the union's disappointment that Labour had embraced PFI so enthusiastically because 'we had been given assurances by government when in opposition that things would change, it hasn't, it's got worse' (Interviews). The GMB campaign also reflects competition for members; the GMB aims to appear as the most high-profile and effective anti-PFI union.

For UNISON the 'Positively Public' campaign 'has become the focus of our campaigning work. It is at the heart of the union's policy and campaigning agenda' (UNISON 2003a: 25). In 2001, £65,000 was spent on the campaign which included high-profile newspaper and cinema advertisements and a further £50,000 was committed to academic research (UNISON 2002b). UNISON has tried to respond to the government's emphasis on 'what matters is what works' by developing its own evidence base. The difficulty has been persuading key policy makers that its research is non-partisan, reflected in the unusually forthright criticism of UNISON-sponsored research by the Commons Select Committee on Health (2002: paras 65–9).

Trade unions have argued that PFI is unacceptable in principle because it allows private companies to profit from public services with shareholders rather than service users being the beneficiaries. They have also suggested that PFI has led to design faults and buildings of poor quality alongside sub-standard facilities management services ensuring that reports of hospitals with cleanliness problems or falling bed numbers following a PFI transfer gain a high media profile (Carvel 2003; Dunnigan and Pollock 2003). It is very uncertain, however, whether such difficulties can be attributed exclusively to the PFI process. Some hospitals have consistently performed well, achieving high star ratings and providing high quality services. Others have had performance problems, resulting in zero star ratings and the replacement of senior managers. There is no unambiguous relationship between the existence of a PFI scheme and hospital performance.

Although the general trade unions have not been able to persuade government to abandon PFI, their attempts to discredit PFI have influenced the government's willingness to address union concerns about the two-tier workforce (see next section). Senior union officials suggested that they have been effective in portraying PFI as 'a scam' in which benefits accrue to shareholders rather than patients and staff. This has been a source of frustration for the Labour government because its attempts to focus media coverage on the provision of new hospital facilities has been undermined by reports that emphasize the privatization and commercialization of the NHS.

Private sector companies involved in PFI schemes, frustrated with their inability to get their case over to the media, have established the Public Private Partnerships (PPP) Forum to present the private sector's case for PPPs and to respond to media criticism (see www.pppforum.co.uk). In addition, the Confederation of British Industry (CBI) has established a Public Services Strategy Board and Directorate to campaign on the benefits of private sector involvement in the delivery of public services. The CBI is publishing reports that highlight these benefits, most recently in relation to the contribution of privately managed prisons in transforming the prison service (CBI 2004).

In contrast to the open general public service unions, the more closed professional unions have generally not campaigned against PFI. The Royal College of Nursing (RCN) has adopted a pragmatic and cautious approach, neither condoning nor condemning the initiative, and supporting members affected by PFI schemes. The RCN's first publication on PFI outlines its advantages and disadvantages stating: 'to say that PFI offers no benefits to patients is an exaggeration' and the RCN claims that it 'assesses the merits of individual schemes with a view to its impact on the quality of services, patient access and the role of nursing' (Royal College of Nursing 2000: 3).

The response of the RCN is in keeping with its professional ethos and its orientation to service standards and quality issues that affect patients and members. The bulk of the RCN membership views the organization as a professional association rather than a trade union, and this translates into a reluctance to be overtly political with a preference for private lobbying rather than direct criticism of government. There is also a reluctance to engage with the consequences of PPPs because of a concern that criticism of PFI will be interpreted by RCN members as a criticism of the independent sector. The RCN has a sizeable membership in the independent sector and is sensitive to the views of this constituency who in the past have been concerned about their low-profile within the RCN.

The low-key approach of the RCN both reflects and reinforces limited membership concern or understanding of PFI/PPPs. In comparison to many other issues the RCN has published very little guidance on PFI/PPPs for members or stewards. The reluctance of the RCN leadership to engage with PFI is reinforced by other pressing membership concerns, such as the outcome of NHS pay modernization. Nonetheless, the poor experience of some RCN members at PFI hospitals has prompted activists and officers to encourage a more critical stance towards PFI. This pressure was reflected in resolutions that were passed at successive RCN Congresses in 2002 and 2003 (Royal College of Nursing 2003a : resolution 10; Royal College of Nursing 2003b: 32).[2]

Labour government policy and the two-tier workforce

Public campaigns against the principle of PFI by UNISON and the GMB have increasingly been supplemented by the second strand of national union policy that has focused on engagement with government and contractors to improve the terms and conditions of members transferred under PFI schemes. The GMB, for example, has national level agreements with 28 private sector companies, covering most of the major PFI service providers.

UNISON has been effective in raising the profile of its central concern about the existence of a two-tier workforce and has exerted continuous pressure on the Labour government to deal with its consequences. In its 2001 election manifesto, the Labour party conceded that support staff should not necessarily be employed by private contractors, stating: 'we will seek ways in which, within the framework of PFI management, support staff could remain part of the NHS team' (Labour Party 2001: 21). In autumn 2001 the health service unions achieved a notable victory when the government conceded that ancillary workers in three new hospitals could be seconded to the private sector, enabling them to remain on NHS terms and conditions, with a view to extending this model to all future PFI schemes. The Retention of Employment Model (ROE), as it has been termed, applies to five trades: catering, cleaning, laundry, portering and security services which are core areas of UNISON membership. Supervisors and managers were excluded from the agreement ensuring that the private sector retained some scope to alter job roles, although much less than they had sought. Staff covered by the ROE model not only secured the symbolic importance of retaining NHS employment[3] but it also ensured that they retained their membership of the NHS final salary pension scheme and can only be dismissed with the authorization of the NHS Trust (see Davies 2004).

Union misgivings remained, however, because enhanced protection of transferred employees in PFI schemes fell short of the unions' objective of full protection for all outsourced staff and the ultimate goal of retaining direct public sector service provision. Consequently, the Labour Party leadership suffered defeats on PFI and foundation hospitals at the 2002 and

2003 party conferences respectively, but the Prime Minister and the Chancellor have insisted that these votes will not alter government policy in which PFI is viewed as the way forward for public service procurement. The business community, conversely, has argued that PFI investments will not be desirable unless the investors have the ability to choose the most efficient employment strategy.

In February 2003, the Labour government announced measures to strengthen protection governing the terms and conditions of employees of contractors providing services to local authorities. Where new employees join an outsourced service their employment conditions must be 'no less favourable' than those of transferred employees, forcing private sector providers to compete more on the basis of quality than price (Office of the Deputy Prime Minister 2003). The Department of Health has been very reluctant to extend the Code of Practice to the health sector which has been interpreted as confirmation that the Department of Health anticipates the rapid development of a mixed economy of health provision and does not wish to jeopardize these developments by tighter regulation of private sector providers (Timmins and Turner 2003: 6). This stance has led to fierce condemnation from UNISON (2004) and a high-profile campaign to end the two-tier workforce which has worn down government resistance (Timmins 2004: 2).

The public service unions have demonstrated the capacity to highlight the problems of PFI schemes forcing some concessions from government. The Labour leadership has been inclined to make short-term concessions to make PFI more palatable to trade unions whilst increasing the role of the private sector in the NHS and refusing to concede ground on the fundamental direction of government policy. The campaign against PFI illustrates in microcosm the difficulties that confront the public service trade unions in respect of the Labour government. As Lewis Minkin argues regarding the evolution of New Labour, 'there was an emphatic repudiation of the idea of Labour as the Party which was more concerned with the producer than the consumer' (Minkin 1991: 467). This was particularly the case with regard to the public services.

New Labour perceived the historical strength of the public service unions as a threat to its electoral appeal and its attempts to court the business community. For Minkin, 'efficiency, quality and service began to be emphasized as incompatible with rigid employee protectiveness' (Minkin 1991: 476). This approach has ensured that the public service unions have been viewed as a special interest group that has to be placated rather than as 'partners' that share an agreed vision for the future of the public services. This divergent agenda, in which there is no clearly articulated role for unions, ensures that the relationship between the public service trade unions and the government will continue to be adversarial and union influence will be highly circumscribed (see Unions21 2004). These difficulties are reinforced by the reluctance of public service trade unions to develop an alternative vision for the future of public service provision that moves beyond the 1945 models of welfare state provision and which could engender wider public support for a *positive* change agenda rather than relying on the limited results that have accrued from opposition to PFI noted here and elsewhere (Ruane 2000).

Union responses to PFI in the workplace

At the local level, unions have tended only to respond to PFI where it has had a direct effect on their members. Responses have varied depending on the union and the nature of the PFI. Although professional unions have not taken a stance on the larger issue of PFI, they have tried to ensure involvement, particularly on design issues, for their members. In the well-functioning PFI hospitals (and wards), there was general agreement among clinical staff that they had been consulted from the early planning stages. Where doctors and nurses were not consulted, there was a greater tendency to identify problems with inappropriate room sizes, inadequate security systems and other basic building attributes.

Unions have found it difficult to actively engage members, as many staff are unsure of the implications of PFI prior to their transfer to a new facility. This process is made more difficult because of the technical complexity of the process and the degree to which trade union activists need to commit large amounts of time to analysing complex business cases and to attending numerous project team meetings, if they are to be able to influence the procurement process. In many cases a PFI scheme forms part of a larger re-configuration of service provision and the term PFI is rarely prominent in the public documentation associated with these schemes. As a result, few local branches have opposed PFI from the outset, and local and regional representatives have focused on negotiating the best possible terms and conditions for transferred staff. With variable degrees of local organization, unions have confronted difficulties in mobilizing members locally around the broader implications of PFI.

Although the underlying project financing changes under PFI, most PFI schemes are on sites that have been using private contractors for many years. Consequently employees, even those transferred under the schemes, may not see the employment changes as significant. It is difficult for unions to make a strong argument about potential service quality issues in a forthcoming PFI hospital because the experience to date has been highly variable.

With employees in a single workplace employed by several different employers, representation (even where there is recognition) becomes more complex. When an employer grants a public service union representative facilities time (paid time off for an employee to perform union work) it is generally not possible to use this facilities time to represent individuals that are employed by private sector contractors, because this would effectively result in the public service employer subsidizing the private sector. However, if the private contractor does not provide any facilities time for its own union representative, then a representation gap can arise, with the union unable to provide full services to subcontracted staff.

After staff transfers, due to PFI or standard contracting-out, there has been some industrial action in response to low pay from subcontractors. There has been industrial action in East London (at the Whipps Cross and Homerton hospitals) and strike action in North Lincolnshire (at Scunthorpe, Grimsby and Goole General Hospitals). In the case of the London hospitals, the build-up to the strike engendered significant advances in recruitment of contract staff, with union density rising to 80 per cent among contract cleaners at the time of the strike (see www.telcocitizens.org.uk). Low pay has been the primary issue around which unions have been able to recruit and mobilize members, especially in the open, more general, hospital unions. This is an important area of union activity but does not address concerns that arise from PFI as a form of service provision both for employees and service users, for example access to training and development opportunities and problems with hospital hygiene.

Those unions which do have a national strategy on PFI tend to provide much more support for local representatives. Indeed, a local representative of one professional union spoke of relying on the resources of another union with a more comprehensive approach to PFI in order to understand and engage with the substantive issues of PFI. In general, the unions had good cooperation at the workplace level, with a widespread recognition that UNISON and the GMB have national union material to draw on that outlines the issues which are likely to arise during the PFI process. The role of the staff-side chair (or coordinator) was crucial in determining the degree of staff-involvement in new PFIs and the possibilities for ongoing open communication. The individual staff-side chair (elected by staff unions) plays a crucial and high-profile role that requires support from the unions' full-time regional officer. In spite of clear differences in strategy at the national level, unions were generally willing to cooperate and share information locally. One staff-side chair stated: 'I had a very good relationship with [another union's] full-time officer who would feed me bits of information so that I knew I was going in the right way' (Interviews).

The professional unions, whose members are not transferred in PFI hospitals, tended to focus on design problems when criticizing PFI. As one representative of a clinical union put it, 'to be honest [about our] members within the trust, it didn't affect them. They were going to get a nice new building at the end of it' (Interviews). The contrast between a 'good' and 'bad' new hospital for these unions was dependent on whether the physical environment was functional and an improvement on the previous building. A crucial determinant of successful design was the degree of staff involvement, something that the professional unions are beginning to learn after some unsatisfactory experiences (see case studies for examples of differing degrees of staff involvement). For the professional unions, a PFI hospital is a success if it is well-designed and the contractor is providing high quality services; the terms and conditions of service for support staff are not relevant, as long as the service is adequate.

Nurses in PFI hospitals frequently complained of problems with cleanliness on the wards, although these problems seem to have originated when domestic services were initially contracted out rather than stemming directly from the PFI process. Nurses and their representatives consistently stated that wards were much cleaner when cleaners were part of the 'ward team', were direct hospital employees, and the same cleaner cleaned a ward every day. Ward managers expressed concern that they were not in charge of this particular aspect of ward operation, and in some hospitals there was very poor communication with the cleaning contractors (see case studies for more on the diversity of experiences with private contractors across PFI schemes).

At workplace level unions have tried to use concerns about PFI hospitals as a form of healthcare financing and delivery as further evidence of problems with PFI hospitals as workplaces. However, in one of the cases examined, the degree to which PFI can deliver high quality care for patients but not a positive employment relationship for staff was revealed. The interests of service users and employees are not always aligned. East Hospital's staff and managers cited design problems in the non-clinical areas of the new hospital, while the wards and other areas used for patient care were widely perceived as excellent. The cost of improving staff experience (by adding additional office space) would be high and, without heavy union pressure, the incentives are fairly low.

Case studies: North Hospital

North Hospital is an acute NHS trust, with over 700 beds, which was part of the first phase of PFI hospitals. It has been the subject of much criticism as the new building has been highly flawed in terms of both design and operation. Over time, and in the context of the PFI facility, this trust has fallen from a two star rating to zero stars.

This hospital had very limited staff involvement at the planning stages of the PFI. On the few wards where clinical staff were consulted on the design, the outcome has been significantly better than in the rest of the hospital. Staff complaints included inappropriate building design, poor quality support services and very limited communication and accountability structures between the trust and the private contractor. Staff involvement was minimal throughout the bidding and design process. When staff were consulted on planning decisions, they frequently felt that their input was ignored by the private consortium.

Clinical staff were particularly dissatisfied with the quality of cleaning and catering services provided by the private contractor. One nurse stated in an interview that 'cleaning and catering are awful'. Several interviewees complained of the large numbers of agency staff amongst the ancillary staff, many of whom were neither appropriately trained nor screened before commencing work.

This hospital has consistently received poor star ratings and CHI (the Commission for Health Improvement) clinical governance reviews. One Chief Executive has resigned because of the poor Trust performance. The 2003 CHI report stated that 'significant staffing issues exist and require immediate attention', confirming the opinions of union members who were interviewed for this research. The problems with the new hospital had precipitated higher levels of union membership and activism, particularly within the nursing unions. However, addressing such constant problems was a drain on union resources, particularly on the time and attention of regional union officers.

While North Hospital was one of the earliest PFI sites, it did not perform as well as other Trusts which were built at the same time.

East Hospital

East Hospital is of a similar size to North Hospital, and was also part of the first phase of PFI hospitals. The only major difference between East and North is that East has a small university research facility affiliated to it. This hospital delivers very well for patients. Front-line staff universally spoke of an appropriate physical environment and the Trust has consistently been rated very highly by CHI, as well as receiving plaudits in the media for its high quality services. Clinical staff stated that the design of the new hospital was very good. Staff had been involved in the planning of the new hospital from the very early stages, and the trust 'historically had a reasonably good working relationship with its staff-side organizations' according to a full-time union officer. Indeed communication was an obvious priority for the Trust managers as the PFI developed: 'they certainly went the extra mile in ensuring that the communication [was] as good as it possibly could [be]' according to a union representative. This is in stark contrast with staff at North Hospital who felt that there had been little involvement or communication between Trust management and staff from the earliest planning stages to the present.

The main criticism from staff at East Hospital has been from non-clinical staff. In particular, administrative and clerical staff have had insufficient office space and facilities. As new wards and additional beds have been added to the original design, no provision has been made for additional office space.

continued…

> One key element in the smooth functioning of this hospital has been the performance of the private services contractor and the frequent and open communication between Trust and contractor. The Trust Chief Executive described this relationship as 'superb' and interviews with trust management, union representatives and representatives of the contractor all demonstrated a high degree of trust and satisfaction in this relationship. This Trust has received two and three star ratings in the years since moving into the new PFI building.

Discussion

Since the election of the Labour government in 1997 the pace and degree of marketization of the health sector has increased substantially. PFI schemes have been the most visible and contentious part of this agenda, but the expansion of Treatment Centres, the increased use of overseas health care providers, the reinvigoration of the internal market reforms and the emphasis on patient choice indicate that an increasing proportion of health care staff may be employed outside of traditional NHS acute hospital environments. As the provision of health care becomes more diverse, and in a context in which the Labour government is advocating pay devolution and local flexibility, the regulatory influence of national agreements can be expected to decline further. The award of contracts for elective surgery to overseas providers has already forced the UK private health care sector to lower its prices with knock-on effects for medical staff fee levels. The experience of PFI therefore provides important pointers as to how trade unions are responding to the restructuring and marketization of public services.

Trade unions are by definition secondary organizations that operate within constraints and parameters laid down by other actors; in the public sector the key actor remains the government. This has always required a political response from trade unions to influence public policy and this remains the case in response to PFI. The difficulties for the public service trade unions are twofold. First, the increasing pace of reform in the public services and the ambiguities associated with public service 'modernization' has made the traditional opposition to private sector provision less effective as a guide to union action. It is not simply the blurring of the boundaries between public and private sector provision that complicates union responses, it is also that the outcomes for union members in PFI schemes are highly variable. Moreover, many trade union members remain unaffected by PFI schemes and other forms of PPPs and it has proved difficult for trade unions to animate their membership in response to a distant and highly technical series of reforms in comparison to more immediate membership concerns about pay and working conditions. The general trade unions have campaigned against PFI and gained concessions from the government; however, the fundamental direction of government policy is unaltered and this has necessitated trade unions examining the core values associated with public service employment and beginning to articulate the principles and values that should underpin public service modernization.

A second challenge confronting trade unions has been to influence government policy in relation to PFI. This has been difficult not only because of the *content* of the modernization agenda but also because of the *process* utilized by the Labour government. As noted earlier there is a high level of ambiguity about the role that trade unions are expected to play in the modernization of public services and the concessions granted to trade unions to protect terms and conditions of employment have required lengthy campaigning and been granted grudgingly. The Labour government's style of governing favours informal understandings and deals with union leaders which provide little transparency for union members. At the same time, the Labour government has emphasized its unwillingness to be guided by decisions of the Labour Party congress, which has passed critical resolutions on PFI. This style of governance potentially isolates senior union leaders from union members and carries the risk for trade unions that the government will subsequently modify or repudiate earlier 'agreements'.

In this uncertain terrain the unions have responded to PFI by building on their experience of CCT. The differing responses of professional and general unions to PFI therefore stem from strategies that evolved in the 1980s. UNISON and the GMB have combined the twin priorities of campaigning against PFI and seeking to extend protection for members linked to the theme of the 'two-tier' workforce. The RCN and other professional unions have adopted a much more cautious stance towards PFI at national level. At the workplace, however, responses to PFI across general and professional unions have had a great deal more in common.

At workplace level the PFI experience has varied widely. The level of staff involvement from the early planning stages of the project and the management approach of the private sector contractor are important influences on staff experiences of PFI schemes. In our case studies, where all staff (not only clinical staff) were consulted and provided with the opportunity for sub-stantive input over design and operational issues, staff and patients commented favourably on the functioning of new buildings and services. By contrast, the absence of meaningful consultation led to much less positive perceptions amongst employees.

There was also a strong sense amongst trade union officers and activists that some private sector contractors were much more open to staff and trade union involvement than others. When trade unions were involved in interviewing short-listed bidders they were able to question contractors about union recognition, the type of staff-side structures that would be established and related issues including the form of work reorganization planned. Formal structures for communication and accountability between the contractor, Trust management and staff representatives were viewed as integral to effective service provision.

The selection of the contractor therefore had a major impact on the employment relationship. The dominant public services unions already have general recognition agreements (that tend to exclude bargaining over pay) with some contract companies and trade unions are continuing to build relationships with those contractors who have shown a willingness to negotiate with unions and invest in employees. By assisting Trust managers in the selection of 'good' contractors in PFI schemes, unions and private services providers are able to build more mutually beneficial arrangements and crowd-out less scrupulous private contractors. This process may be facilitated by the gradual extension of protection for staff in PFI schemes which by providing more regulation of employment conditions may enable more fruitful relations to develop between public service unions and private contractors.

The experience of PFI has highlighted the degree to which public service trade unions operate in a context of continuous restructuring, in which they have to contend with numerous public and private sector employers, and invest in workplace organization and representation to ensure a visible union presence that can deal with multiple terms and conditions of employment. At national level there is still much work to be done to persuade the Labour government that the union movement has a convincing vision for the future of public services as the government continues to embrace a more mixed economy of welfare provision. At the workplace, challenges remain in terms of union organization and representation, but continuous pressure on the Labour government has led to increased protection for employees within PFI schemes, providing opportunities to move away from adversarial patterns of employment relations that characterized much of the past experience of CCT.

Notes

1   The authors acknowledge the Department of Trade and Industry, The Economic and Social Research Council, the Advisory, Conciliation and Arbitration Service and the Policy Studies Institute as the originators of the 1998 Workplace Employee Relations Survey data and the Data Archive at the University of Essex as the distributor of the data. None of these organizations bears any responsibility for the authors' analysis and interpretations of the data.

2   The position of the professional unions in health has largely been echoed by the professional unions in education, who are also dealing with widespread PFI building projects. In general the major teaching unions have been pragmatic and have not mounted anti-PFI campaigns, while responding locally to the workplace issues that arise.

3   There are echoes here of the reaction of NHS staff to Conservative government attempts to introduce local pay determination in the mid-1990s. NHS staff proved extremely reluctant to transfer to trust contracts, even on more favourable terms and conditions of employment, because of the familiarity and security associated with NHS (Whitley Council) terms and conditions of employment.

Chapter 7

Unions and performance related pay

What chance of a procedural role?

David Marsden and Richard Belfield

Key points

- Performance related pay (PRP) and performance management (PM) are now a part of the organizational landscape that unions face in the UK's public services.
- While PRP and PM threaten the scope of traditional union bargaining activities, they simultaneously offer a new role to unions as providers of 'procedural justice services' to both union members and employers.
- Our survey evidence shows that classroom teachers experiencing the introduction of PRP have expressed a strong demand for such services from the teachers' unions.
- Analysis of the implementation of PRP for classroom teachers indicates that the teachers' unions have progressively assumed a 'procedural justice role' since its introduction.
- Union action in this regard has led to substantial modification over time of classroom teachers' PRP and PM. These changes have addressed many of the concerns of teachers, have created a new institutional role for the unions, and may permit the systems to avoid the operational difficulties they have experienced elsewhere in the UK's public services.

Introduction

The recent spread of individual performance related pay (PRP), particularly in the public sector, has been seen as a challenge to union effectiveness in two senses. First, by enlarging the zone of management discretion over individual pay, it increases the power of managers to reward certain kinds of behaviour and punish others. Second, it potentially reduces the influence of collective action on employee welfare, and hence the perceived usefulness of unions to their members, further tipping unions towards their 'demise' rather than their 'resurgence'.

However, a countervailing trend emerges from research by the Centre for Economic Performance (CEP) on performance pay for public service employees in Britain. This work has highlighted the difficulty such schemes face in motivating staff, and the widespread employee view that they are a source of divisiveness (Marsden and Richardson 1994; Marsden and French 1998). A key source of demotivation appears to lie in the way the schemes have been operated rather than in their basic principles. This point was stressed in the government's Makinson Report on civil service PRP (Makinson 2000), which contrasted general approval of the principle of linking pay to performance with widespread 'disenchantment' with its operation. A major factor explaining why employees have seen the schemes as divisive is connected in particular with weaknesses in the goal setting and appraisal systems used, so that when employees see these as poorly operated, they find PRP demotivating and harmful to work relations (Marsden 2004).

These twin developments – of growing use of PRP alongside employee disenchantment with its operation – potentially offer new opportunities to unions, and it is these which we explore in this chapter. Can unions develop a new role in establishing what we term a 'procedural justice' role within new employee management systems, and thereby create a new demand for their services from both their members and from employers? A growing body of literature suggests that modern performance management systems, such as those combining performance pay and appraisal, fail to motivate staff if they are judged to be unfairly operated (Milkovich and Wigdor 1991). Further, working in a divisive environment can be an active source of employee discontent, as is the suspicion that managers are allocating rewards unfairly, and one recent study has shown that such employee perceptions of workplace injustice are associated with increased union participation (Brown Johnson and Jarley 2004). Given that incentive schemes that fail to motivate staff are of little use to management, and those that cause conflict are unlikely to be welcome to employees, both parties would have a strong interest in unions' being able to provide a solution to these problems by their provision of procedural justice services.

In this chapter, we explore the scope for such a union role by analysing the introduction of a new PRP system for classroom teachers in England and Wales. This instance is ideal for the testing of our ideas, as it concerns a segment of the labour market that has a strong union presence, and as such represents a kind of 'best-case scenario' for unions seeking to assume the role we propose. We begin by sketching out the potential for union adoption of the 'procedural justice' role, and contextualizing this within the new teachers' pay system. Subsequently, we use data drawn from a survey of teachers' opinions to assess the extent of demand for procedural justice, and whether this demand is directed towards the unions. The last stage of our study considers union activities in the procedural justice arena, and the modifications to the new teachers' pay system thereby achieved.

It emerges that, although the teachers' unions were not invited to ensure that the new pay system was fairly operated – and to a large extent, that is not how they saw their role at the outset – they have progressively taken on a procedural justice role through their representational activities. In the concluding section, we argue that this role represents a significant departure from more traditional bargaining methods over pay levels. In addition, we present evidence that union representation has helped to adapt the new system from its initial design to one that is much more closely aligned with classroom and head teachers' understanding of the reality of performance in schools. An important consequence of this shift is that the PRP scheme for teachers has the potential to bypass some of the operational weaknesses of schemes previously implemented in the civil service.

The 'procedural justice' role: an opportunity for unions?

Where PRP is introduced, the key issue for management is to induce employees to use their work discretion to the benefit of the organization. Employee perceptions of the risk of bad faith by management greatly complicate the operation of such incentive schemes. If employees don't believe the rewards for extra effort will be forthcoming, they are less likely to respond to the incentive scheme. Indeed, a relevant prediction is provided by the psychological theory of expectancy, which asserts that performance pay systems will not work unless employees regard them as fair in their design and operation, and corresponding to their own preferences for incentives and pay variability (Lawler 1971; Furnham 1997).

This argument is extended by Cropanzano and Greenberg (1997), who affirm that 'procedural justice' can be as important for motivating employees as 'distributive justice'. Whereas the latter relates to the structure of rewards provided, the former is concerned with the fairness of procedures which determine whether an employee gains a particular reward – in our context, a performance increment. Cropanzano and Greenberg propose that employees' motivation is more likely to withstand adverse performance ratings if they believe management's procedures are fair and conducted in good faith, and hence one can argue that 'procedural justice' is a key element in the motivational aspects of incentive pay systems.

According to these arguments, then, we can point to three critical areas in which intervention in PRP systems could ameliorate their procedural justice outcomes, and thereby augment their positive incentive impact. First, the choice of incentives must align with both the employer's goals and employees' feelings about what is appropriate for their work. Next, employees must be assured that management's assessment of their performance is both valid and reliable, in the sense that it reflects accurately the main components of performance and that it does so without bias. Lastly, employees must feel that management is committed to observing the spirit as well as the letter of the rules in the administration of the system.

Previous CEP research on the subject of PRP indicates that unions have a potentially important part to play in all of these areas (Marsden 2001; Marsden 2004). Compliance with the first two of the above procedural justice criteria requires the honest communication of feedback about the pay system from employees to management. Individuals may well be unwilling to express their opinions fully for fear of some manner of reprisal. Unions, however, can by their collective nature represent their members' opinions clearly with virtual impunity, at least as far as it will affect the individual member. Furthermore, they can use their organizational strength to ensure that management plays fairly, both by monitoring management behaviour and by leaning on it where necessary.

Where unions are able to enforce the criteria in these ways, they can be said to be playing the procedural justice role effectively. Consequently, employers can benefit by ensuring that PRP systems create the intended incentive effects; and employees can benefit because they gain insurance against unfair assessment by their managers, and they are less likely to work in a demotivating and conflictual environment. Unions, therefore, might exploit this potential dual demand for their services in this area.

Performance related pay for classroom teachers: a new pay system

For classroom teachers, the new PRP policy took effect from September 2000, having first been presented in the Labour government's 1998 Green Paper, 'Teachers: Meeting the Challenge of Change' (DfEE 1998). This document had proposed a broad, articulated set of policies for the upgrading of the state schooling system, largely inspired by the three themes of leadership, teaching quality, and expanded resources. The PRP programme fell under the rubric of teaching quality, and it was foreseen as playing the dual role of motivating existing teachers to higher performance, and, by providing a more attractive pay and career structure, of attracting high quality recruits to the profession and retaining them in the classroom.

The new scheme comprised three key elements. First, there was a system of annual goal setting and appraisal, or 'performance reviews'. Second, it offered eligible teachers the opportunity to apply to cross the 'Threshold' test of teaching competence and performance. The eligible group consisted of those with eight or nine years' experience in the job, that is, those who had likely already reached the top of the old 'main professional grade' pay scale for classroom teachers. Success in this test would bring with it an immediate pay uplift of around £2,000. The third element, a new 'upper pay scale' (UPS), flowed from the second, as passing the Threshold (i.e. moving to UPS point 1) gave access to further opportunities to increase one's pay.

Initially, the UPS was composed of a five-step ladder, progression along which would be performance-related and progressively more challenging.

The term 'performance management' was used to describe the combination of stick and carrot incentives, that is, of performance reviews and PRP. However, while intended to be mutually reinforcing, these two components differed slightly in their scope. All teachers, whether or not they have passed the Threshold, have to go through an annual performance review with their head teacher or their line manager. The purpose of this is to agree a set of work priorities for the coming year, and to appraise performance for the previous year. In the process, individual teachers' objectives are to be determined in relation to those of their school, as set out, for example, in the School Development Plan.

Whereas the performance criteria in the annual performance reviews are integrated into the school's objectives, those for passing the Threshold and for UPS progression are more specific and more standardized. Those proposed in the Green Paper, and largely implemented in 2001, included measures of the following (DfEE 1999, Annex 1: Draft Standards for Threshold Assessment: 38–9):

1   Pupil performance;
2   Use of subject/specialist knowledge;
3   Planning, teaching and assessment; and
4   Professional effectiveness.

Similar performance criteria were to apply to movements along the upper pay scale. Under the new system, the Threshold assessment would be carried out by head teachers, and was initially validated by an 'external assessor'.

In terms of its impact on pay, the new system avoided awarding a general pay increase to all teachers, and concentrated the extra money on extending the teachers' pay scale upwards, from its then ceiling of about £24,000 to about £30,000. On passing the Threshold, teachers would gain an uplift of £2,000 to £26,000, followed by scope for further increases by progressing along the upper pay scale. This had obvious appeal, given that about 70 per cent of classroom teachers at the time were at the top of the main professional grade scale, able to increase their pay further only by taking on managerial duties, and moving away from classroom duties (STRB 2000a: Table 10). It was also thought that the longer scale might be more attractive to new entrants.

A further key outcome relating to pay concerned how many teachers could aspire to move up the full length of the UPS, and at what speed. Whereas all teachers might reasonably have expected to reach the top of the old main scale, the government's thinking was that the new upper pay scale should be 'tapered', that is, that fewer teachers should be able to reach the performance standards demanded for access to the top points, and that progression should be awarded at intervals of several years instead of annually (STRB 2000a: para 88).[1] This no doubt had a budgetary justification, but the key reason stressed by Estelle Morris, the then Secretary of State, in a letter to head teachers was that tapering would provide more of an incentive (DfES 2002).

The initial reaction of the teaching unions[2] was mixed, although two distinct types of response could be discerned: the NUT was the most outspoken in rejecting any connection between pay and appraisal, whereas others (including the ATL and the NASUWT) cautiously accepted this principle, but strongly questioned certain aspects of the proposal, in particular the link to pupil performance in examinations. This difference of approach has continued up until the present.

The government delayed implementation of the system from September 1999 to September 2000 in order to engage in 'constructive dialogue' with the unions, but indicated that significant alterations to the proposed scheme would not be considered. The conflict between this position and that of PRP's stronger critics was manifested in the NUT's attempt to block implementation of the system by means of a High Court challenge in July 2000, which charged that the Education Secretary had no right to order change to teachers' conditions of service without due consultation. The resulting deadlock caused a delay in the introduction of the system, which was ended by the court's finding in favour of the union. However, this finding was only a partial victory for the union, as it essentially enabled the scheme to be implemented with minor modifications, chief among them the diluting of the pupil progress performance criterion for passing the Threshold (STRB 2000a: para. 13).

In England, the first round of assessment at the Threshold, for which a near-majority of teachers was eligible, took place during the winter of 2000–1. The system was also rolled out in Wales, but according to a different timetable, as it was agreed that the Welsh National Assembly would become involved in its funding there. According to the Department for Education and Skills (DfES), about 250,000 teachers were eligible for the Threshold. About 201,000 (80 per cent) teachers applied. About 97 per cent of those who applied met the Threshold standards and passed onto UPS point 1, a rate that was sustained in the years immediately following (DfES 2001: Annex A, Appendix B; DfES 2004: para. 3).

Since this first fraught year, the scheme has bedded down and become a more established part of the school environment. The second round of assessment, which took place in autumn 2002 and saw movement up to pay point 2 on the UPS, was a more regular affair, although it too was remarkable for its high application and pass rates (only slightly lower than for the first step). Many of those in the initial cohort who successfully applied for the Threshold in autumn 2000, would be eligible to apply for UPS 3 in the autumn of 2004.

Teachers' perceptions of the new pay system: does procedural justice matter?

Our main source of information about the effects of the introduction of PRP on classroom teachers is a nationally representative survey conducted by the CEP over two waves, the first in February–March of 2000 in anticipation of the implementation of the new pay system, and the second a little more than a year later (May–June 2001), shortly after teachers were expected to know the results of their Threshold assessments. The survey probes teachers' attitudes to PRP in the light of their existing attitudes towards teaching, and its time-series nature enables us to investigate the effects of experiencing the appraisal process for the first time. We restrict the sample to England, given the different nature of implementation in Wales, and to those teachers who respond in both waves, which delivers a sample of 1,876 individuals. The restricted sample does not differ significantly from the broader first wave cross-section sample on any observable dimension of individual or school characteristics.

We begin by exploring summary results from the two waves of the survey of teachers for some of the key perceptions regarding the operation of performance management that could signal a lack of procedural justice. Further, we also compare these results to earlier CEP studies of attitudes to PRP in the civil service, which themselves suggested the potential for a procedural justice role for unions (see Table 7.1). In absolute terms, teachers do not seem very keen on the idea of PRP, nor do they feel that its incentive impact would be very great. Conversely, though, they do not appear to think that PRP would have a strong negative impact on cooperation in the workplace, either among classroom teachers or with management. This result is particularly marked in the second wave of the data, by which time teachers had already lived one year with the new pay system. A notable point in this respect is that whereas before implementation teachers mostly believed that there would be a quota at the Threshold – that is, that there might be insufficient funding available to reward everyone in the event that the majority did well in the assessment – the experience of very high pass rates (see previous section) appears to have substantially allayed this fear.

There emerge a number of differences in attitude between teachers and civil servants. First, it appears that teachers are less supportive of the principle of PRP. At the same time, they are less likely to feel that PRP gives them genuine incentives to increase their performance. However, while the overall incentive effect of PRP seems to be weaker for teachers than for their counterparts in the civil service, its impact on cooperation among employees appears less marked. Similarly, PRP seems to have less harmful consequences for employee-management relations in the case of teachers, who appear less suspicious of management's oversight of the system than civil servants. These divergences can substantially be ascribed to differences in the respective approaches to PRP of bureaucratic and professional employees, the former

Table 7.1 Comparison of attitudes to PRP in schools and in the civil service

% in each cell replying 'agree' or 'agree strongly'	Civil service			Schools	
	Inland Revenue 1991	Inland Revenue 1996	Employment Service	Class teachers 2000	Class teachers 2001
Pay and work orientations					
PRP a good principle	57	58	72	26	32
Motivation: perceived incentive					
PRP gives incentive to work beyond job requirements	21	18	12	13	8
PRP gives incentive to show more initiative in my job	27	20	20	N/A	12
PRP means good work is rewarded at last	41	19	24	25	37
Motivation: perceived divisiveness					
PRP causes jealousies	62	86	78	88	64
PRP makes staff less willing to assist colleagues	28	63	52	N/A	23*
PRP has made me less willing to cooperate with mgmt	10	30	26	N/A	10
Relations with mgmt: non-manager replies					
Mmgt uses PRP to reward their favourites	35	57	41	54	39
There is a quota on good assessments	74	78	74	81	22
Relations with mgmt: line manager replies					
PRP reduced staff willingness to cooperate with managementt	20	45	39	N/A	18
PRP has increased the quantity of work done	22	42	28	N/A	34

Sources: Marsden 2003: Table 1 (Civil service); CEP survey of class teachers (schools).

Note

Based on five-point Likert scales: 'strongly disagree', 'disagree', 'no view', 'agree' and 'agree strongly' (except *, answered 'yes' to yes/no question). Teachers' results based on panel respondents from England sample only.

being more comfortable with following performance directives from management, and the latter being accustomed to exercise relative autonomy over work targets and patterns (Marsden *et al.* 2001). Furthermore, the shared professional identity of classroom teachers and those in managerial roles may well contribute to a more amicable relationship between these two groups. In the big picture, however, these results indicate that, as in the case of the civil service, teachers harbour concerns about a number of the procedural justice aspects of the new pay system.

We can examine this possibility in more detail by studying the relationship between teachers' perceptions of the effects of PRP and their reports of a number of aspects concerning its operation which are likely to reflect inadequacies in procedural justice. Our chosen outcome variables are those of 'perceived incentive' and 'perceived divisiveness', which we derive from a factor analysis of relevant variables (see Table 7.5 in the appendix to this chapter). We regress these factors on variables that capture teachers' potential concerns with the issues of the choice of incentives, measurement difficulty, and management good faith, according to models derived from previous work in this area (Marsden 2003: 9; Marsden 2004). We further control for individual and school characteristics, and for a measure of affective commitment to the job, which we expect to mediate perceptions of working conditions.

The results of this analysis are largely consistent with our expectations (see Table 7.2). Clear setting of targets and the existence of scope for performance improvement are both positively and significantly related to the perception that PRP provides genuine work incentives. These relationships are robust to the inclusion of controls. The financial incentive variable predicated by the model is only weakly relevant, but in any case we feel that it is the least well measured of those included in the regression. Surprisingly, the effectiveness of the appraisal appears to have no effect on this perceptual outcome. This is not the case with the other outcome: perceived divisiveness is significantly reduced in concert with the effectiveness of appraisal, as it is with the clarity of target setting. Here, neither the scope for performance improvement nor the financial incentive variables have any impact. However, it seems that a teacher's sense of affective commitment to their work considerably reduces the divisiveness engendered by the PRP system. As above, these results are robust to controls.

Perhaps most importantly, this set of results is consonant with those derived from similar analyses conducted for other public servants studied by the CEP (Marsden 2003). This is to say that the dimensions considered contribute to teachers' perception of a lack of incentive, and the presence of a sense of divisiveness, associated with the PRP system. The key aspects of this finding appear to be weaknesses in the processes of goal setting and appraisal, and a lack of confidence that the employers will deliver on promises made concerning the rewards for performance. Thus, the early stages of the teachers'

Table 7.2 Correlates of perceived incentive and divisiveness

Regression (robust standard errors)	incentive		divisiveness	
Operation of PRP				
Effective appraisal	−0.006	0.064	−0.342**	−0.240**
	(0.068)	(0.075)	(0.072)	(0.081)
Clear targets set by managers	0.355**	0.350**	−0.112**	−0.110**
	(0.032)	(0.035)	(0.034)	(0.037)
Scope to raise performance	0.321**	0.325**	−0.037	−0.040
	(0.048)	(0.055)	(0.046)	(0.049)
Financial incentive	−0.217*	−0.154	−0.185	−0.037
	(0.131)	(0.164)	(0.122)	(0.145)
Commitment				
Affective commitment	0.019	0.020	−0.243**	−0.229**
	(0.031)	(0.034)	(0.030)	(0.033)
Control variables				
Personal characteristics	No	Yes	No	Yes
School characteristics	No	Yes	No	Yes
Constant	−1.332**	0.177	0.794**	0.635
	(0.168)	(1.122)	(0.182)	(1.091)

Source: CEP survey of class teachers (2001 data only).

Notes
Significance: ** 1%; * 10%. Personal characteristics comprise age, tenure in school, highest qualification, FT/PT, member of leadership group, trade union member, partner in employment, and any dependants; and school characteristics comprise primary/secondary, region, any pupil selection, and school size by pupil numbers.

scheme are marked by procedural weaknesses similar to those which have marked those implemented elsewhere in the public service. Procedural justice issues, it seems, are of importance to teachers working under the new pay system.

Do teachers see the need for a union role?

From the perspective of the unions, it is important to know whether teachers believe unions to be capable of protecting them from unfair treatment related to the pay system. One way we can get at this information is to refer to the survey questions that relate to the perceptions of shared or conflicting interests with other groups that teachers hold (see Table 7.3).

Teachers' responses to these questions suggest that they feel a strong sense of shared interests with their colleagues, with the unions, and, to a lesser extent, with the leaders of their schools. However, this contrasts starkly with their perceived absence of shared interest with the system's designers (government) and those responsible for overall control of the system (government, governors), which, although slightly reduced by the experience of the Threshold, is relatively stable across waves. It would seem therefore that

Table 7.3 Which groups do teachers identify as sharing the same interests in connection with performance management?

	Wave	Broadly the same (%)	Mostly different (%)	It's hard to say (%)
Your school's governors*	2000	22	17	61
	2001	30	21	49
The leadership group/management team in your school*	2000	49	20	32
	2001	60	21	19
Other teachers in your school*	2000	79	5	16
	2001	84	5	11
Other teachers in your union or professional association**	2000	65	5	30
	2001	67	5	28
Your union or professional association**	2000	63	7	29
	2001	62	9	30
The DfEE (sic) or your LEA*	2000	9	39	52
	2001	13	32	55

Source: CEP survey of class teachers.

Notes
* differences between waves significant at 1% level; ** differences between waves insignificant at 10% level.

teachers would be strongly supportive of union efforts to use their institutional resources to represent employee interests in the assessment procedure. This interpretation is buttressed by the results of logistic regressions which find that teachers who actively identify their interests with those of the unions are also significantly more likely than others to fear quotas and favouritism, and to believe that an appeals procedure is necessary to ensure fairness, in the operation of PRP (see Table 7.6 in the appendix to this chapter). Although these results are weaker in the second wave of the survey that follows the initial Threshold assessment, they indicate that teachers who identify with the unions (nearly two-thirds of the population) represent a constituency to which the unions could plausibly offer services relating to procedural justice.

We also asked who might provide a legitimate voice for teachers' views about the goal of performance standards: who should determine standards of excellence in teaching? The teaching profession emerged as the leading candidate (Marsden 2000). As the unions play an important part in maintaining the overall coherence of the teaching profession, this suggests that they can have a clear role.

Procedural justice and the unions

In the case of classroom teachers, therefore, we observe both employee demand for procedural justice in the operation of the new pay system, and evidence that employees believe unions to be the most plausible providers of services to meet this demand. In the wake of our discussion (see the second section) of the critical areas of intervention in such a system to the end of procedural justice, we now look for evidence of the following types of union activity as they relate to our case:

- Informing employers about the kinds of incentives that employees feel are appropriate for their work;
- Conveying employees' views about the practicalities of applying performance measurement to their jobs; and
- Working to ensure the fair operation of PRP schemes by management.

Choice of incentives: information about teachers' work motivators

A consistent feature of public sector performance pay schemes has been the emphasis on the role of individual performance pay as an incentive for better performance. One of the presuppositions of individual PRP is that employees will increase their individual effort, physical or mental, in order to achieve the extra performance required for the additional reward. This assumes that the employees concerned value that kind of extra reward at the margin, as distinct from having a good basic salary. It also assumes that changes in performance can be clearly attributed to the efforts of particular individuals. Imposition of inappropriate incentives can undermine employee perceptions of procedural justice in two ways. At one level, the mismatch of incentives with employee motivations will increase the unpredictability of rewards, and teachers may see what they regard as the wrong kind of performance attracting rewards, and the most valuable performance going unrewarded. At another level, it displays a disregard, or a lack of respect, for employees' own judgement, sometimes referred to as the 'interactional' component of procedural justice (Folger and Cropanzano 1998).

The teachers' unions have been collating and communicating such information on several occasions during the period of discussions about performance pay and appraisal. Among the classroom teachers' unions, the ATL joined forces with the head teachers' unions to commission research on 'what makes teachers tick', exploring the factors which they judge important for morale and motivation for themselves personally, and for teachers in general (Vaarlem et al. 1992). This research, which was fed into the national deliberations about teachers' performance management, showed that 'good pay' came a long way down their list of factors boosting their morale and motivation, ranked 27 out of 38 items. At the top of the list were job satisfaction, good relations with pupils and a manageable workload. Even among the items judged 'unsatisfactory and very unsatisfactory', pay came one-third of the way down the list of priorities.

No doubt there is a degree of self-selection – teachers who wanted more money may have already left the occupation, or never entered it – but central to the issue of PRP is whether employees find extra pay for increments in performance attractive. The same union-commissioned survey showed that teachers ranked extra pay for individual or for school performance as the least important items for teachers' morale and motivation (respectively 13th and 14th out of 14 items). At the top were better media portrayal, fewer out-of-school hours, and improved pay for all teachers. Pay emerges as a major source of dissatisfaction, but it not a major source of good morale or motivation. Thus we can see that the union message that management must consider the broader motivational environment if it is to elicit maximum 'performance' within schools – and not just rely on monetary rewards for a narrow set of behaviours – is substantially supported by empirical evidence.

Measuring performance: 'pupil progress' and its construction

One of the biggest problems in designing a workable model of performance pay for schools has been the operationalization and measurement of suitable performance criteria. If teachers deem these criteria inappropriate because they do not accurately reflect their work, it is most unlikely they will find them motivating. The psychological research around goal-setting theory has often stressed the importance of agreed goals that are jointly set by management and employee, on the grounds that this approach will lead employees to adopt and apply them as their own (Locke and Latham 2002). Thus, if the criteria are judged inapplicable, employees will not adopt them voluntarily, and are only likely to apply them if their work is closely monitored.

In this respect, the criterion of 'pupil performance' – central to the government's efforts to raise standards in the educational system – makes an interesting example. The DfES under Labour (DfEE 1998), like other government actors, has tended to see this outcome as a function of the input of individual teachers, rather than of a broader context or system, e.g. a school or a community. However, it is apparent that teachers, and the unions, prefer to conceive it as transcending the efforts of any individual teacher (Marsden 2000). As a result, they argue that if pupil performance is to be included as a criterion in the calculation of teachers' pay, then it must be articulated in a manner much different to the simple tabulation of exam outcomes. This concern is expressed in the joint union submission of evidence to the STRB in September 2001, which sketches out Threshold criteria the unions feel to be more appropriate. These standards largely consist of 'input factors' such as 'skill, knowledge, classroom management, planning, and preparation', and the unions assert that where teachers satisfy them, it can be concluded that their pupils are 'making appropriate progress' (ATL et al. 2001).

Case study: setting targets for pupil progress for a primary school teacher

Commentary by chapter authors

This official guidance was given to teachers in 2000 as PM was introduced. It illustrates aspects of the most novel and controversial of the criteria for teacher assessment: that of pupil progress. In this case study, for primary schools, one can see the scope for variation in the approaches to measurement between schools. Some could emphasize quantitative outcomes, while others could take a much broader approach. One can also see the amount of data collection and paper work that could become involved.

What Does The Annual Performance Management Cycle Look Like For A Class Teacher?
An Example for a Year 4 Class
QUESTIONS

(Examples of available information underlined)
1. What information does the teacher have on which to base pupil progress objectives (end of year targets) at the start of the year?
Information directly related to the class:
– Information from the School Development Plan relevant to the class
– provisional end of key stage targets set for cohort at the beginning of the key stage (see page 3)
English: 65 per cent to reach level 4, 15 per cent level 5 (80 per cent L4+); mathematics: 60 per cent level 4, 15 per cent level 5 (75 per cent L4+).
– interim end of Y4 targets set at the beginning of the key stage (set so that staff would know what pupils needed to achieve by the end of Y4 in order to be on track for end of key stage targets – see page 3)
English: 10 per cent to have emergent skills within level 3; 55 per cent to be working securely within level 3; 15 per cent to have emergent skills within level 4.
Mathematics: 10 per cent to have emergent skills within level 3; 50 per cent to be working securely within level 3; 15 per cent to have emergent skills within level 4.
– progress made by class over the previous year (end of year review of progress within Performance Management Cycle)
End of Y3: 50 per cent of pupils achieving learning objectives indicating emerging skills within L3 for reading/writing with 5 per cent working securely within level 3.

continued...

(Note – this is unlikely to be sufficient progress for pupils to be on track for Y4 interim targets.) Mathematics: 55 per cent are working securely within level 3 and 10 per cent have emergent skills within level 4 (i.e. on course for the end of Y4 interim targets).

Other information of relevance:

- issues/trends identified from the analysis of whole school performance data (see page 2)

Value added analysis has indicated that lower performing pupils at the end of KS1 are making less than expected progress in both English and mathematics by the end of KS2. Boys make less than expected progress in English.

Higher performing girls (at the end of KS1) make less progress in mathematics by end of KS2.

- issues identified from the evaluation of previous teaching and learning in the teachers' classes (End of year review of progress within Performance Management Cycle)

End of year performance management reviews indicated that Y4 pupils in the previous year had achieved a less than expected number of learning objectives from medium term planning for writing.

PUPIL PROGRESS OBJECTIVES/DEVELOPMENT PLANS

2. What pupil progress objectives (end of year targets) might be set with this information in mind?

(Agreeing objectives within the Performance Management Cycle)

Considering all of above information, it was decided that interim Y4 targets already set for the cohort at start of the key stage (see above) should remain in place as pupil progress objectives for the coming year, with priority being given to achieving the English targets.

3. How is teaching and learning to be planned so that pupils meet pupil progress objectives (end of year targets)?

(Work and development planning within Performance Management Cycle)

- Review of key learning objectives within medium term plans for English and review of implementation of literacy strategy (with emphasis on writing).
- Review of how learning objectives in medium term planning are translated into short term learning objectives and activities in short term planning, how these learning objectives are shared with pupils and how they are used as basis for giving them effective feedback.

> – <u>Training to look at approaches to writing (focus on boys and lower performing pupils)</u>.
> **4. How is pupil progress towards these objectives to be monitored through the year?**
> (Monitoring progress within Performance Management Cycle)
> <u>See page C of this document for what this process might look like</u>.
> **5. How is progress of the Year 4 class reviewed in relation to the set objectives?**
> <u>(End of year review of progress within Performance Management Cycle)</u>
> <u>Consideration of all of the information available about this class at the end of Year 4, e.g. summary teacher assessments, optional test results including standardised scores. Were pupil progress objectives met, what was successful in terms of teaching and learning and what was not? What factors if any prevented achievement of objectives? Ensure all findings feed back into next year's planning/ review cycle.</u>
>
> Source: Recognising Progress – Getting the most from your data, Primary School. Dept for Education and Employment, London. Date of issue: Oct 2000; Ref: DfEE 0253/2000

Working for fairness: provision of information to members

An important factor in promoting procedural justice is the provision of trusted information on what teachers need to do in order to apply for the rewards attached to good performance. All the teachers' unions, whatever their official position on PRP, have provided advice to their members on how to apply to pass the Threshold. Usually this has been supported by material and advice made available to members from their union's website. ATL provided a set of booklets of its own offering advice and information to members; the NASUWT teamed up with SHA to offer a joint model policy for performance management; and the NUT, in addition to such materials, set up its 'Threshold watch' to monitor problems posed by the scheme.[3] These documents gave teachers step-by-step accounts of how to apply with hints and tips gleaned from many sources.

How extensively these were used by teachers is shown by the MORI poll commissioned by the DfES in spring 2001 (see Figure 7.1). Two-thirds of teachers obtained information and advice about applying from their unions, and over half from their head teacher. This compared with only a quarter who used the DfES publications and website. It is clear, therefore, that this support by the unions proved very effective in diffusing information about the scheme that teachers felt was fair and reliable.

Q: Where did you obtain information and advice about applying?

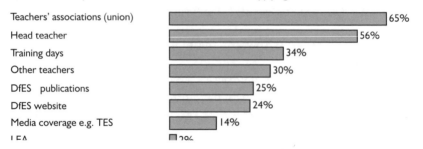

Teachers' associations (union) — 65%
Head teacher — 56%
Training days — 34%
Other teachers — 30%
DfES   publications — 25%
DfES website — 24%
Media coverage e.g. TES — 14%
LEA — 2%

Figure 7.1   Sources of information used by teachers for Threshold applications (Source: DfES 2001)

Note
Base: 92 teachers who applied and met standards (Source: MORI).

In each of the above critical areas of intervention, then, we detect union involvement to the end of procedural justice. Certainly, this means that the unions have at least partially adopted a procedural justice role in relation to the new pay system. This observation, however, raises the question of the effectiveness of their activities in the role, and it is to this subject that we turn in the next section.

Changes to the pay system achieved by the unions

As a measure of the success of the teachers' unions in gaining procedural justice-related adaptations to the pay system, one can point to three significant areas of change: the pupil progress element in assessment; the criteria for moving up the UPS; and the *de facto* resumption of collective bargaining as a means of establishing new procedures.

Softening of the 'pupil progress' criterion

In the Green Paper, the first – and perhaps most controversial – performance criterion was 'pupil performance' (DfEE 1998: para. 86). The subsequent Technical Consultation Document defined this standard as comprising measures of classroom management ability, pupil results, and teacher development (DfEE 1999: para. 24). By the autumn of 2000, after the NUT challenge of the new pay system in the High Court, the criterion's label had changed to 'pupil progress', but it appeared that the underlying concept remained unaffected, as the statutory amendment of teachers' pay and conditions dated November 2000 defined pupil progress predominantly in terms of examination results (DFEE 2000: Annex 1, para. 5).

Though seemingly constant across time at the level of policy, this emphasis on pupil test results in the assessment of teacher performance was less salient at the level of practice. Indeed, there had been total union opposition to the rigid interpretation of the pupil performance Threshold standard in the run-up to implementation of the pay system in 2000, although there was some variation among the unions in the intensity and precise focus of their opposition. This opposition was registered by the STRB in the course of the consultation process underlying its special review of the Threshold (STRB 2000b, October), which was itself triggered by the High Court's finding against the government. In its pronouncement on the issue, the STRB took particular care to acknowledge the concern of a number of unions that the criterion might be applied in a 'formulaic' way, asserting that pupil progress should be 'fairly assessed in the context of the school and the pupils' backgrounds' in order to head off this possibility (STRB 2000b: 3). As a result of union pressure and action, including from the two head teacher associations, the pupil progress standard was substantially loosened in practice relative to the government's original proposal.

Reduced 'tapering' of the UPS

The nature of movement along the upper pay spine was also subject to conflicting views. The government's initial view was that the access to the top of the UPS should not be automatic, but 'tapered': it should require increasingly high standards of performance. This view was expressed by the DfES in its evidence to the STRB in 2000 (STRB 2000a: para 88), and confirmed by Estelle Morris, Secretary of State for Education and Employment, in her letter to head teachers of March 2002 (DfES 2002). She stressed that whereas passing the Threshold should be 'demand led', moving up the UPS should not be so. Otherwise, there would be no incentive for teachers to improve. The same view was expressed by the Secretary of State to the STRB in 2003 (STRB 2003: para. 7.3).

However, by March 2004, the 2004 STRB report confined its agenda to progression to UPS3, and reported that progression on the UPS had not been working as originally intended (STRB 2004: ch. 2, para. 2.18ff). 'Tapering' was not much in evidence as a large proportion of those applying were successful. It also recommended that progression to the top two points be replaced with a new 'Excellent Teacher Scheme' (ETS). Promotion to the latter would be strongly 'tapered' (STRB 2004: paras 2.29–2.31). In any case, the issue of 'tapering' had been deferred to a future – and as yet not fully defined – scheme by negotiation between the unions and the government.

In April 2004, the Rewards and Incentives Group (RIG), established following the 2003 STRB report, started work on a revision of the UPS and clarification of the procedures for progression to UPS2 and UPS3. This group comprised the DfES and all the teachers' unions except the NUT. It agreed that progression should be based on two consecutive successful performance reviews. To ensure that the teachers' contributions had been 'substantial and sustained', the review would need to assess whether teachers had 'continued to meet Threshold standards' and had 'grown professionally by developing their teaching expertise in their field' (RIG 2004).

Such criteria clearly imply progression on individual merit, rather than according to any form of quota, and there is an emphasis on increased skill rather than increased performance. Thus, one can argue that the UPS has undergone considerable change away from the former concept of tapered progression towards a much more inclusive system, in similar manner to passing of the Threshold. This change is clearly consistent with the arguments put forward by the teachers' unions.

Resumption of collective bargaining

Finally, the RIG agreement represents an important procedural step, as it is an agreement between the DfES and all the teachers' unions (except the NUT) over matters relating to the allocation of pay and its underlying procedures. It comes after a similar agreement on measures to rationalize teachers' workloads reached in the autumn of 2003, again with all the unions except the NUT, and is the first such agreement since the previous Conservative government withdrew from collective bargaining for teachers in 1991. Significantly, the government's decision to bring the unions onboard with the pay system may be interpreted as emerging evidence of employer demand for unions' procedural justice services.

To whom do teachers attribute these changes?

A final piece of evidence for the effectiveness of this new role for unions concerns whether employees themselves believe the changes have occurred, and if so, to whose actions do they attribute them. Provisional results from the third wave of the survey in 2004 indicate that among the teachers who believe there have been significant changes in performance management, ending the 'tapering' of the upper pay scale, and broadening the criterion of pupil progress, significant numbers attributed these changes to the actions of their unions. Over half credited the unions with the end of 'tapering' and nearly two-thirds with the change on pupil progress. The next most important agents, by a wide margin, were individual head teachers who voiced their concerns about the operability of the scheme. Thus, the teachers' unions were seen not just as potential guarantors of procedural justice, but were also seen by teachers as having been effective in changing key aspects of the new scheme.

Conclusions

One possible objection to the argument in this chapter is that the history we have traced does not demonstrate the scope for unions to develop their procedural justice role because the conflict is a standard one over distributive justice. From this point of view, the Threshold and UPS progression were simply devices by the employer to phase teachers' access to what is effectively a substantial pay increase, and to restrict its coverage in order to reduce the impact on the overall salary bill. For their part, then, the teachers' unions were simply fighting to get the pay increase for as many teachers as they could. This view is not implausible. Successive CEP surveys of PRP show that many employees believe the employer's purpose is primarily to save money. Why else, one might ask, would ministers and top public management under successive governments persist with PRP schemes which the government's own report (Makinson 2000) suggested did not motivate staff?

Further, there is a possible theoretical objection, which arises from the research literature on organizational justice. This literature encompasses a debate as to the importance of the distinction between distributive and procedural justice in the minds of those working in organizations, and whether for them procedural justice is more than just an instrument for achieving distributive justice (Greenberg 1990; Cropanzano and Ambrose 2001). Clearly, if this is so, it makes little sense for unions to develop new representational strategies based around procedural justice.

However, we reject these interpretations for three reasons. First of all, our interest has been in what might be called an emergent strategy. This is not necessarily one that the parties recognized at the outset, but as the experience with PRP has progressed, unions have developed new capabilities to serve their members. This has been the first full-blooded experience of the classroom teachers' unions and classroom teachers' managers with the type of performance management and performance pay systems which have spread rapidly across the public sectors of advanced industrial countries (OECD 2004b). Such pay systems pose a new set of problems for unions and for management because of the increased management discretion in their administration, and out of these new challenges, one can observe new responses. In fact, in this chapter, we present examples of both traditional and new responses to PRP. The traditional union response to attempts by management to increase its discretion over pay is to seek to rein it in by means of fixed and objective rules, such as happened with older payment-by-results schemes like piece rates. Elements of this approach can be seen, for example, in the NUT's counterproposal to the government's original plan for PRP. This recommended an alternative logic for rewarding 'senior' teachers, stressing that pay should be tied to the demands of the job, rather than to individual-level variables such as skill and performance (NUT 1999: para. 343). In contrast, the NASUWT and the PAT have stressed the need to reward qualities and expertise of the teachers themselves, albeit by a process of evaluation similar to that for promotion (NASUWT 1999; PAT 1999). This is taking a step towards giving management greater scope to reward variations in teacher quality, albeit in a way that seeks to make it fair. Thus, both approaches have been present in the way the unions have responded to the new pay system.

The second reason is that there is a degree of consistency in government policy on performance across a range of public policy areas, and this extends far beyond PRP. Management is trying to do something different. The development of performance targets as a means for democratically elected governments to steer the performance of public servants has been applied and developed progressively across all levels of organizations. For instance, in the civil service, during the period surveyed by Makinson, it has been shown that PRP did in all probability contribute to higher productivity because it was articulated with middle-management and organization-level targets (Marsden 2004). By virtue of this, the government was able to use PRP to negotiate a change in performance norms across the organization. Although important, the control of salary bill costs is only one of the employer's objectives in schools in relation to pay. Just as important an objective of this pay system is to help management steer the performance objectives and attainment of teachers and their schools.

The third reason is that many public employers are aware of the problems posed by lack of procedural justice. This was precisely the meaning of the Makinson report when it contrasted the evidence on civil servants' support for the principle of pay for performance with their disenchantment with its practice. The relevance of this finding for classroom teachers is reinforced by the near-identical results obtained when we apply for teachers the same regression models of perceived incentive and perceived divisiveness as were applied for civil servants. The importance of effectively operated appraisals and clear goal setting is apparent for both sets of employees. This outcome responds to the question raised in the research literature regarding the true status of 'procedural justice', and underlines the salience for employees of the procedural fairness of reward systems.

Thus, we infer that the negotiation and representational activity by the teachers' unions, after the government's initial proposals, have focused effectively on operational issues of performance management and performance pay. Moreover, their actions seem to have led to substantial changes in the way the new pay system is operated. This amounts very much to a focus on the procedural justice of the new pay performance management system in schools, and it appears to be a major concern of the majority of the teachers' unions. Nevertheless, one should remember that the NUT's statements and policies display much greater scepticism as to reform of the new pay system.

To conclude, performance pay systems which are designed to give management more scope to reward individual employee performance depend for their effective operation on a reasonable degree of procedural justice. If they lack this, the schemes are unlikely to motivate staff, and unlikely to help management mobilize the discretion that employees have in their jobs. For unions, this provides a new challenge and a new opportunity. The challenge is that the more individualized reward systems are often seen as a threat to collective solidarity and to union effectiveness. The opportunity is that such schemes need an element of independent employee voice if they are to be seen to operate fairly. If unions can develop suitable representational strategies, then they have the opportunity to boost the services they provide to their members, and also a means to reduce management opposition to union presence. It would seem from our analysis of the case of classroom teachers' PRP that this role can be, and has been, effectively played by unions.

Acknowledgements

We wish to thank all of the teachers' unions and professional associations, and the DfES, for their help, and especially the many classroom and head teachers who gave up their valuable time to respond to our questionnaires. We also wish to thank our colleagues on the Future of Unions project and the editors for their helpful comments on earlier drafts of this chapter.

Notes

1   The idea of 'tapering' was expressed thus by the STRB:

> The Secretary of State believes that these points should normally be awarded at intervals of several years, rather than annually, against levels of performance which would become progressively more challenging towards the top of the range. However, it was suggested that it might be appropriate for schools to have the flexibility to award performance points to teachers demonstrating exceptional performance over a single year.
>
> (STRB 2000a: para. 88, p. xxvii)

This approach did not endure, however. Note the contrast with the STRB's 2001 report, which now advised against making the performance criteria increasingly demanding:

> The criteria for progression above the starting point of the scale should be as already defined in the School Teachers' Pay and Conditions Document and explained in the related DfEE guidance – in essence that progression is at the discretion of the relevant body to recognize substantial and sustained performance and contribution to the school as a teacher. This should take account not only of particular performance objectives but also the totality of the teacher's work looking at all of the elements covered by the Threshold standards. We do not think it appropriate to lay down that the levels of performance required should become progressively more challenging towards the top of the scale.
>
> (STRB 2001: para. 88, p. 20)

2 The classroom teacher unions and professional associations referred to in this chapter comprise:

- The Association of Teachers and Lecturers (ATL)
- The National Association of Schoolmasters and Union of Women Teachers (NASUWT)
- The National Union of Teachers (NUT)
- The Professional Association of Teachers (PAT)
- Undeb Cenedlaethol Athrawon Cymru (UCAC).

We also refer to the following head teacher professional associations:

- The National Association of Head Teachers (NAHT)
- The Secondary Heads Association (SHA).

3 Four examples include:

- ATL (2000) *Performance Management and You: Advice and Information for Members. London, Association of Teachers and Lecturers.*
- ATL (2001) *Setting Objectives: Advice and Information for Members. London, Association of Teachers and Lecturers.*
- NASUWT and SHA (2000) *NASUWT Performance Management: Teachers, Team Leaders: A Practical Guide*, National Association of Schoolmasters/ Union of Women Teachers and Secondary Heads Association, August 2000.
- NUT Media Centre (2000) 'NUT Launches Threshold Watch as Confusion and Inconsistency Hit Government Scheme', National Union of Teachers, 15 June 2000.

Appendix – the samples

Table 7.4 Summary statistics for panel sample of individuals

Variable		%	Mean	Standard deviation
Sex	Female	59.7		
	Male	40.3		
Contract type	Full-time	91.3		
	Part-time	8.7		
School type	Primary	18.2		
	Secondary	81.8		
Member of leadership group		34.3		
Member of ethnic minority		2.9		
Member of a teachers' union		95.2		
Eligible for Threshold in 2000		75.4		
Age (yrs)			42.6	9.0
Tenure in current school (yrs)			10.5	8.0

Source: CEP survey of class teachers (2000 data).

Table 7.5 Derivation of measures of perceived divisiveness and incentive by factor analysis

Rotated factor loadings	Factor 1: Perceived divisiveness	Factor 2: Perceived incentive
The higher levels of pay above the Threshold mean that good teaching is rewarded at last	0.414	0.583
Linking pay with performance will give me more incentive to work beyond the requirements of my job	0.028	0.854
Performance management has made me want to show more initiative in my job	0.041	0.806
The Threshold has caused resentment among teachers who feel they already meet the standards but are not eligible to apply	−0.642	−0.212
The Threshold is the cause of divisions between management and staff in my school	−0.745	0.013
Performance management has reduced my wish to co-operate with management	−0.732	−0.071

Source: CEP survey of class teachers (2001 data only).

Note
Principal component factors after Varimax rotation.

Table 7.6 Association between identification with unions and procedural preferences

Coefficients (logit) expressed as odds ratios (robust standard errors)	Identifies shared interests with unions	
	2000	2001
Threshold quota certain	1.126*** (0.041)	1.070* (0.043)
Hard to relate work in schools to performance	1.300*** (0.073)	1.046 (0.053)
Mgrs will reward favourites	1.088** (0.045)	1.059 (0.046)
Appeals procedure needed	1.133** (0.059)	1.215*** (0.066)

Source: CEP survey of class teachers.

Note
Significance: *** 1%; ** 5%; * 10%.

Chapter 8

From the Webbs to the Web

The contribution of the Internet to reviving union fortunes

Richard Freeman

Key points

- In the 2000s unions in the UK and US made innovative use of the Internet to deliver union services and move toward open source unions better suited for the modern world than traditional unions structures.
- In contrast to analysts who see unions as being on an inexorable path of decline, it is argued that these innovations are changing unions from institutions of the Webbs to institutions of the Web, which will improve their effectiveness and revive their role as the key worker organization in capitalism.

Can the Internet produce more effective and successful unions and help resuscitate the labour movement in the UK and US?

Some labour experts in the UK and US claim that the Internet will fundamentally alter employee representation and the way unions operate (Shostak 1999; Diamond and Freeman 2002; Darlington 2000; Lee 1996). Freeman and Rogers (2002a, 2002b), in particular, have outlined the elements of a new 'open source' union form designed to deliver union services and connect activists over the Internet at low cost, regardless of management recognition. Some readers will undoubtedly be sceptical about these claims or forecasts, and not only because they originate with pointy headed intellectuals. A substantial minority of persons in both countries do not use the Internet. In 2004 37 per cent of US citizens and 44 per cent of UK citizens were non-users and many had no intention of going on-line.[1] Internet hype fuelled the dot.com bubble of the late 1990s and led some to foresee rapid development of a referendum-style democracy. The collapse of the bubble and gradual growth of e-democracy and e-government[2] are reminders that economic and social patterns change more gradually than innovations in computer speed and the growth of Internet hosts.

Still, it would be foolhardy to reject visionary claims out of hand. The e-economy has grown steadily post the dot.com bust.[3] The Internet propelled an obscure ex-governor of Vermont to be Democratic party front runner in early 2004. Activists have created powerful political sites independent of the standard political parties. And an increasing proportion of citizens in the UK and US use the Web to obtain government services.[4] Whether the Internet will have similar transforming effects on union activities is an empirical question.

To see how far unions have come in using Internet technologies to improve their services to members and to reach unorganized workers, this chapter examines the content of union websites in the UK and US and reviews eight significant union innovations in applying the new technologies. The evidence shows that while visionary ideas of open source unions have yet to be fulfilled, union progress using the Internet and related technologies has been sufficiently rapid to suggest that unions are indeed in the process of morphing from institutions of the Webbs to institutions of the Web. While by itself this may not resuscitate the labour movement in the UK and US, it will greatly increase the chances of such a change in fortunes.

Union presence in cyberspace

From the mid-1990s to the mid-2000s, unions in the UK, and in the rest of the advanced world, developed a Web presence. In 1995 the only UK union with a website was UNISON. In 2001 there were 373 union websites in the UK (Diamond and Freeman 2002, based largely on data in www. cyberpicketline.org.uk). In the US, all international federations and thousands of local unions developed websites. Worldwide, the number of union websites has risen rapidly, as many developing country unions have gone on-line, and as the global union federations and International Confederation of Free Trade Unions have made the Internet integral to their operations. In 2004 the global union federation, Union International Network (UNI), launched a Web-based helpdesk to assist union Web workers in running or improving their websites (http://www.e_tradeunions.org).

Many union leaders in the UK and US had come to view the Internet as part of their strategy for the future. The TUC's Internet strategy has produced a website that provides information largely to non-union workers (www. worksmart.org.uk); another site that links union representatives around the country (www.unionreps.org.uk); as well as a site reporting its activities (www.tuc.org.uk). The general secretary for NAPO, the UK's probation officers' union, uses a blog to communicate with her members (www.napo. org.uk/napolog), and so too does the general secretary of the Communication Workers Union (www.billyhayes.co.uk). In the US, the AFL-CIO has created an e-mail list of approximately 2 million members and activists to use in union campaigns (www.unionvoice.org/wfean/home.html). The president of the highly successful Service Employees International Union uses a weekly blog on the union website to converse with members (www.fightforthefuture. org/blog).

For the visionary claims to come true, unions need high quality websites that give them a significant place in cyberspace. Analysing the content of UK union websites in 2001–2, Ward and Lusoli concluded that the bulk of the sites were mediocre, at best. The vast majority of UK unions had 'signpost websites' that gave the name of the union and some minimal information, together perhaps with a picture of the union president. This finding is consistent with what union workers said about their unions' websites on the 2001 British Workplace Representation and Participation Survey. Only 20 per cent of Internet active union members reported having ever visited their unions' website; 22 per cent didn't know if their union had a website; and 6 per cent claimed their union did not have a website. Of those who used their union website just 14 per cent reported that the site was excellent, while 14 per cent reported it as poor (Diamond and Freeman 2002: table 7).

But UK unions improved their websites in the early 2000s. The development of standardized commercial programs made it easier to produce user friendly and informative sites. Technologically sophisticated Web workers created professional expertise in many unions. Innovative use of Internet technology by the Trades Union Congress and improved websites broadly set a standard to which many individual unions responded. Most important, as noted above, many union leaders came to recognize the need for an effective Web-based strategy to carry out union functions.

Because central federation websites are the face of unionism to much of the world, I begin my assessment of the UK union presence in cyberspace by comparing the content of the TUC's main website to the content of websites of the central union federations in the US, Canada, and Australia. I use the methodology developed by Ward and Lusoli (2003) to analyse individual British union websites, supplemented by some additional information. This methodology scores the content of union websites along three dimensions: provision of information, such as information about union history, policies, media releases, an FAQ, and so on; options for participation, for instance an e-mail sign-up, member forum, on-line joining; and provision of services, such as purchase of insurance, training, professional development. The protocol codes 13 items relating to information as 1 for provision or 0 for absence of information. It codes 4 items from 0 to 3 on participation, depending on strength of the form of participation. It codes 12 services as 1 for provision and 0 no provision. For ease of analysis, I scale the sum of the scores in each area from 1 to 100 and average them to obtain a summary measure of content quality.[5]

Figure 8.1 gives the content quality scores for the websites of the TUC and the other major English-speaking union federations as of 2004. All of the websites score relatively highly on the measures for information and services. In part, this reflects the importance that central federations give to their web presence, since websites are one of the few ways for a central federation to reach union members and other workers. But most of the

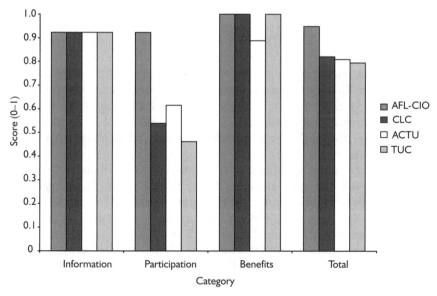

Figure 8.1 Content analysis of the websites of major English-speaking union federations
(100 is maximum score)

websites score less on participation. One reason for this is that unions have
shied away from developing interactive websites that might encourage
members or others to be critical of union leadership and policies. Another
reason is that central federations are cautious about interacting with the
members of their affiliates. Overall, the AFL-CIO obtains the highest score
for its website, achieving 95 per cent of the maximum possible score, while
the TUC scores lowest of the federations, at 79 per cent. One reason for this,
however, is that the TUC has three websites – the main TUC site and the
workSMART site and the unionreps site – which divide some of its
information, services, and participative features. A content analysis of all
three treated as a single site gives a score of 90 per cent.

To see whether individual UK unions had improved their sites since the
Ward-Lusoli study, I computed the content of the websites of the same unions
they had studied in 2004. Because of union mergers and other changes, not
all of the sites in their study were still operating, but the majority were. Table
8.1 summarizes my results in terms of the average content score across the
three domains of participation, services, and information. The figures in the
first column give my rescaling of the scores for 30 unions in 2001–2 reported
by Ward and Lusoli overall and divided between larger and smaller unions.
The average for all UK unions in 2001–2 is just 38 per cent of the maximum
possible score, with, however, considerable difference between the larger
and smaller unions. The second column shows that in 2004 the UK unions

averaged 54 per cent of the maximum score in the categories – a substantial improvement in a short period of time. The table differentiates between larger and smaller unions. In both years larger unions had better websites than smaller unions. In addition, since 2001–2, the larger unions improved their websites more rapidly than the smaller unions. As an example of the change in the quality of websites for large unions, consider the Transport and General Workers' Union (TGWU). In 2001–2 this was largely a signboard, with limited information and interactive features. It scored 29 on the 0–100 scale. In 2004, the TGWU scored 58, which put it slightly above the average for UK unions.

Because US unions went on the Web earlier than UK unions, US union sites are likely to be more advanced than UK union sites. To compare the websites of UK unions to those of US unions, I paired unions in the two countries by sector or type of worker (for instance, comparing the websites of teaching unions, of communication workers and so on), and analysed the content of the US union websites. I obtained 22 matches. Columns three and four of Table 8.1 give the results of these calculations. In 2004, the content scores of US unions averaged 69 per cent – 11 points above the scores for their UK counterparts. But there was virtually no difference in the quality of UK and US union websites among large unions. Indeed, the UK's UNISON was tied with one other union at the highest score of 90, above the 82 for its US peer, the Association of Federal, State, County and Municipal employees. The reason for the lower average rating of UK websites is that smaller UK unions have fewer features on their sites than smaller US unions – possibly because they have fewer members and thus fewer resources than their US pairs.

In sum, UK union websites have improved to the extent that the sites of large UK unions have attained rough equivalency with the sites of large US unions. While smaller unions have a way to go to improve their websites, and almost all unions could add more participative features, UK union websites are no longer the dredges of cyberspace that they were just a short while ago.

Table 8.1 Content analysis of websites of individual unions in UK and US, scaled from 0 to 100

	The same UK union sites in two periods		UK union sites vs paired US sites	
	UK 2001/2	*UK 2004*	*UK 2004*	*US 2004*
All unions	38	54	58	69
Larger unions	52	73	76	74
Smaller unions	35	49	49	66

Source: 2001/2 calculated from Ward and Lusoli (2003: Table 7), tabulated by Centre for Economic Performance, London School of Economics.

Innovative uses of the Internet

Union development of a modern Web presence is necessary but not sufficient to fulfil the visionaries' picture of the Internet strengthening trade unions. To fulfil the vision, unions must use Internet technology to deliver services to workers and connect activists and develop some of the attributes of the open source form. To determine how far unions moved in these directions, I examine eight innovative uses of the Web by unions and labour activists. I focus primarily on innovations by British unions, with some attention however to US and Dutch union innovations.

Providing information to workers: the TUC's workSMART

Before the Internet, it was difficult and expensive for unions to provide information to workers outside the organized sector and to aid organized workers in small work places. The Internet gives unions a low cost tool for informing workers in any locality about workplace conditions and rights and for advising them how to deal with workplace problems. In a world that obtains its information on-line, moreover, it is critical for unions to take advantage of this new way of reaching workers. As Bibby has stressed, a union's 'website acts as the most prominent public shop-window of the organization, providing an opportunity to explain the services and benefits which union membership can bring' (Bibby 2004: 4).

To see how important a strong Web presence is for unions, consider a world where non-union websites, such as commercial job boards, NGO sites, government sites or employment law office sites, offered easier access, better information, and superior advice about workplace problems than union websites. Non-union workers would see unions as irrelevant to their needs. Union workers might wonder about the value of their subscriptions. By contrast, if union websites provide workers with the best information and advice about workplace problems, workers will naturally see unions as a helpful institution. They will be more likely to join unions and support union campaigns. The information-laden union website advertises union expertise to workers and shows how unions can help workers with specific problems, as well as directly aiding those workers.

In 2002 the Trades Union Congress developed www.worksmart.org.uk, 'to be a one-stop shop for everything to do with your working life', particularly for non-union workers. The workSMART site contains basic information about workplace problems and worker rights and links to other sources of information and advice. Its union parentage is presented discreetly, with no reference to union campaigns or TUC events. Box 1 describes the site and gives some sense of how it is organized. In its first year the site reported 20,000 monthly visitors; in its second year, it reached 40,000 visitors in peak months.

Box 1 Welcome to workSMART

workSMART, brought to you by the TUC, is here to help today's working people get the best out of the world of work

your rights at work: employment law explained
your health at work: keeping well in the workplace
your money: simple advice on your pay, taxes, and pension options
union finder: help in choosing a union
email newsletter: key and quirky stories from the world of work

We aim to be a one-stop shop for everything to do with your working life.

Free help
TUC rights leaflets. The TUC's know your rights line provides a range of helpful leaflets which cover a wide range of employment rights information (available on line at www.tuc.org.uk/rights), and can advise you on which union you should join by calling 0870 600 4882.
ACAS help lines. ACAS (The Advisory, Conciliation and Arbitration Service) is a government-funded agency that promotes good relations in the workplace. It operates a national help line on 08457 474747 that can give free information on employment issues to both employees and employers.
Advice agencies. Law Centres provide a free and professional legal service to people who live or work in their catchment areas. The Law Centres Federation can tell you if there is a Law Centre near you. Its number is 020 7387 8570, or visit their website at www.lawcentres.org.uk.
The National Association of Citizens' Advice Bureaux can give you information about your local CAB at www.nacab.org.uk.
On the web. We've tried to give helpful links where appropriate. One good general advice site is provided by the National Association of Citizens Advice Bureaux at www.adviceguide.org.uk. ACAS www.acas.org.uk also provides some general employment law advice. Click here for other useful links to employment rights sites.
Benefits for union members. If you are in a union you can also ask them for advice. Unions are experts at solving problems at work. Use the workSMART unionfinder to contact a union in your work sector.

Pensions
The Financial Services Authority offers general information about financial services and products. Phone 0845 606 1234. Lines are open Monday to Friday, 8am to 8pm. Calls are charged at local rates.

OPAS is an independent, non-profit organization that provides information and guidance on the whole spectrum of pensions covering State, company, personal and stakeholder schemes. They can help you if you have a problem, complaint or dispute with your occupational or private pension arrangement. OPAS operates a national telephone helpline on: 0845 601 2923. Calls are charged at local rates.

If you are a union member and have a problem with your occupational pension you should approach your union. Many unions employ pensions specialists. You can get contact details for your union from the workSMART union finder.

The workSMART site is a work in progress. The site lacks a sophisticated artificial intelligence program along the lines of www.askjeeves.org or medical advice sites that would allow an AI 'workplace expert' to answer detailed questions about problems. It does not provide labour market news, career or salary information, a discussion forum, or information on particular employers that many workers report that they would find useful on a website (see Table 8.2). The site specializes in rights at work; a Google search for 'workplace

Table 8.2 Percentage of workers who would find 'personally useful' services on the Web

	Very useful	Quite useful	Not useful/ don't know
Advice about your rights at work			
Union members	37	48	15
Non-members	39	40	21
Information and reviews about employers			
Union members	34	46	10
Non-members	37	49	14
Advice about pensions and personal finance			
Union members	36	39	25
Non-members	30	44	26
Information about salaries for people in your line of work			
Union members	36	34	40
Non-members	36	40	34
Discussion forums for people at your workplace or doing your type of work			
Union members	26	42	32
Non-members	22	40	38

Source: Derived from Diamond and Freeman, 2002: Table 6.

rights, UK' places the site tenth on the list of relevant sites. But at this writing workSMART is not well-linked to other sites: in June 2004 it had just 157 other website links compared to 2,440 links to the TUC website.[6] The TUC plans to increase the site's visibility and reach by syndicating it to commercial sites and search engines as the marquee site with workplace information. The Tiscali Internet Service Provider (the fourth largest in the UK) made workSMART its site for workplace information. In 2004, the TUC estimated that about 15 per cent of users come from that source.[7] In 2004, moreover, workSMART developed special projects on working proper hours and increasing the number of bank holidays that drew national media coverage.

The TUC effort to reach non-union workers contrasts with that of the AFL-CIO, which has shied away from developing a site targeted at largely non-union workers. If you want to learn about your pension rights in the US, the AFL-CIO's own website is useful, but if you are a non-union worker who does not readily think of the AFL-CIO as the place to go, you may be unable to find the information readily. The AFL-CIO alternative has been the organization Working America (see 'Open source union designs'), which provides considerable information to non-union workers on-line but under a strong union label.

Obtaining and publicizing wage information: the Dutch wage indicators survey

The wage indicators website (www.wageindicator.org/index.php?pag=home) developed by the University of Amsterdam Institute of Advanced Labour Studies, working with FNV (Dutch Confederation of Trade Unions), and Monsterboard (the Dutch Monster.com Internet recruitment firm), gathers and delivers wage data through an Internet survey.[8] Originally started in 2001 to allow Dutch women to compare pay across jobs, the survey has expanded to cover Dutch men, and to cover workers in several other countries. The survey asks users to fill out a questionnaire about their salary, which it uses to obtain wage, salary or earnings data for occupations, with which they can check their relative pay. Apart from questions about earnings, the survey asks about working hours, work history, company, contract, attitudes toward work, including preferences on working hours.

Why did the Dutch Confederation of Trade Unions support this survey? In the Dutch industrial relations system, unions bargain over wages for broad sectors, and thus establish what amounts to minimum levels of pay in those areas. Union involvement in the wage indicators survey was motivated by a desire to find the actual wages paid workers in different settings. This would illuminate the impacts of collective bargaining and the extent of pay dispersion independent of collective agreements. The wage indicators survey was sufficiently successful that in July 2004, comparable surveys were launched in eight other EU countries, including the UK, and in China.

International union news: www.labourstart.org

Eric Lee has argued that the Internet will create a more global trade union movement by providing information on labour issues around the world and a mode for initiating and conducting campaigns on those issues at low cost (Lee 1996, 1999). The major website connecting unionists around the world is Lee's www.labourstart.org, which has become the primary source of international labour news. The site lives on the volunteer activity of correspondents, who upload labour stories from their local newspapers to the site. As of 2004 over 500 unions made the site their channel for helping members keep abreast of international labour developments. In addition to providing news, the site uses its 15,000 or so e-mail list to engage readers in on-line campaigning on particular problems, and offers free Web forums to any union which wants one and links to other forums around the world. In 1999 the site sponsored a 'Labour Website of the Year' competition, in which users of the site voted by e-mail for the best site. Lee reports that dozens of votes were cast for some 25 sites. By 2003, the competition had attracted nearly 6500 votes among 27 sites (Lee 2004). Box 2 describes www.labourstart.org.

Box 2 About LabourStart: 'Where trade unionists start their day on the net'

LabourStart is an on-line news service maintained by a **global network of volunteers** which aims to serve the international trade union movement by collecting and disseminating information – and by assisting unions in campaigning and other ways.

Its features include daily labour news links in 11 languages and a news syndication service used by more than 500 trade union websites. News is collected from mainstream, trade union, and alternative news sources by a network of over 230 volunteer correspondents based on every continent.

LabourStart has been involved in on-line campaigning for several years but moved up a gear with the launch in July 2002 of the **ActNOW campaigning system**. Tens of thousands of trade unionists have participated in its various on-line campaigns and more than 15,000 are currently subscribed to its **mailing list**. They receive weekly mailings, usually on Thursdays.

Creating union campaigns: the AFL-CIO's Working Families Network

In 2002–3 the AFL-CIO organized the development of what amounts to a massive e-mail list of union members and activists – the Working Families Network (see Box 3). Since member unions feared that they would lose power

---

Box 3 The AFL-CIO Working Families Network: Campaign for Overtime Pay, 2003

The Working Families Network is an AFL-CIO created e-mail list of 2 million union activists and supporters that the union movement uses to generate community support in important labor disputes. In winter 2003, the Federation was campaigning to prevent Congress from weakening overtime legislation and removing overtime pay, particularly for white collar workers. The Families Network sent an email to their eActivist list asking people to carry out a complicated series of steps: click on a link in an email; which goes to a web page; where they would download a pdf petition form related to overtime; which they then printed on their home printer; then carried the petition to their workplace; where they were asked to sign up co-workers; and finally to fax the completed petition form to the AFL-CIO office in DC (a long distance fax).

The administrator of the program wrote that 'We figured that no one would really do this because it was so many steps and required many things (printer, Adobe acrobat reader, fax machine, etc). Somewhat incredibly, we received petition forms in our office with over 180,000 names and addresses, including more than 50,000 new email addresses. We probably had more come in, but our fax machines ran continuously for an entire week and were often blocked. My phone rings one day and there's this guy with a heavy Southern accent on the line calling to ask if I was part of the Working Families Network. He was a union member who worked in a nuclear power plant in Tennessee, and he had signed up 250 of his co-workers onto the petitions, but couldn't get through on the fax machine. Amazing!'

---

by giving the central federation access to their e-mail directories, the AFL-CIO did not ask for such direct access. Instead, the affiliates kept control of their own e-mail lists and thus can accept or reject AFL-CIO sponsored e-mail campaigns or those of other organizations as it sees fit. If a union was e-mailing its list as part of a campaign and feared that members would suffer from on-line campaign fatigue from AFL-CIO messages or if it had a different view of a particular issue than the AFL-CIO, the union could veto the AFL-CIO appeal. Organized in this way, the central federation was able to gain huge buy-in from affiliate organizations and to encourage the affiliates to build their own activist lists. In summer 2004 the AFL-CIO had over 28 participating national unions, 84 geographically defined State Federations and City Labor Councils, and over 400 local unions and other union organizations involved with its Family Network. There were more than 600 local administrators responsible for particular lists. The overall network included over 2 million union 'eActivists'. This large number allowed the AFL-CIO to e-mail small proportions of the list and still engage large numbers of persons, and to send localized appeals to particular areas. During the 2003 Safeway strike in California, the AFL-CIO directly raised nearly $350,000 for the Safeway grocery workers via two e-mails to 400,000 people on their main activist list.

The large numbers also allows the AFL-CIO to link on-line appeal to off-line activity in a locality. To pressure management in the California Safeway strike, the AFL-CIO e-mailed persons in the District of Columbia and asked them to join local teams to confront their local Safeway stores, even though those stores were not on strike. Each person on the team was given the e-mail address and phone number of all the other people on their team, plus the local store information. The success of this activity led the AFL-CIO to recruit volunteers from the eActivist list to go door-to-door in targeted areas to talk to union members about the issues related to the 2004 national election – tapping a big network of activists who otherwise would not be involved in local mobilization efforts.

The AFL-CIO regards its e-mail Working Families Network as a success. The former director of Working Families wrote in July 2004:

> The scope of this is overwhelming at times—I checked this morning and there were 306 live on-line campaign sites in the system today, each producing campaign messages by union activists, and also generating new list members through tell-a-friend and related pages.
>
> (Fox 2004)

Industrial disputes: the UK firefighters dispute websites

In November 2002, the UK Firefighters Brigade Union (FBU) struck over wages and working conditions. The firefighters wanted a 40 per cent pay increase to bring pay to £30,000 per year. The government offered much less and wanted productivity improvements through changes in work conditions. The dispute continued until 2004, when the firefighters signed an agreement for a smaller pay increase and disaffiliated from the Labour Party. Three union websites played a role in the dispute: the FBU site, a TUC support site, and a rank and file site set up by a Manchester firefighter to allow members to discuss freely issues relating to the strike and union policy.

The FBU site (www.fbu.org.uk) chronicled the dispute and efforts to negotiate its resolution. It presented union policies and tactics to members but did not engage union members in an interactive way. The TUC sites (http://www.tuc.org.uk/fp4f and http://www.fire.org.uk) were set up to publicize a December demonstration in support of the firefighters. TUC officials reported that the latter site received 40,000 visitors in the two weeks it operated and gave information to activists around the country that helped make the demonstration a success. The site did not report any of the misgivings that TUC leaders felt about the FBU's strategy.

The rank and file site, www.30KFirePay.org.uk (now defunct) provided space for members to discuss the dispute without censoring views that might conflict with those of the leadership. The site was put up rapidly at low cost and was of sufficiently high quality for labourStart users to vote it the third best website in 2002 in the annual labourStart poll of best labour websites.[9] The militancy expressed on the rank and file site provided a more accurate view of the feelings of firefighters about the dispute and the decisions made by their leadership and the government than that given on the other union sites.[10]

These websites did not produce victory for the firefighters in the dispute. Arguably, the websites had the opposite effect, feeding unrealistic expectations by members and reducing the possibility of compromise at critical times. Still, the use of the Web to provide information to union members and the general public during a strike and the rapid creation of the TUC and rank-and-file temporary sites are likely to be imitated in future disputes.

E-mail bulletins and on-line learning: TUC risk e-mail bulletins

Beginning in 2002, the TUC sent a weekly e-bulletin, *Risks: weekly health and safety update*, to union health and safety reps and others seeking information about occupational health and safety issues. By 2004 some 8,000 people had signed up for the e-bulletin. Given the success of the Risk e-bulletin, the TUC developed five other e-mail bulletins for interested representatives and workers.[11] Taking Web use a step further, the TUC's education and training division developed on-line training in health and safety to union representatives unable to otherwise access classroom training, which it will launch in 2005 and follow with on-line courses in other areas. In the pilot project that preceded the national launch, reps from smaller firms and shift workers made up a disproportionate share of on-line course enrollees. Several individual unions also offer on-line safety rep training for their members. Finally, the TUC also uses the Internet to deliver training to union members (http://www.learningservices.org.uk).

Toward open source unions

So I am asking you to authorize SEIU to create Purple Ocean, the world's first 'open source', virtual union – with a goal of uniting one million more people who want to join our campaigns for justice.

(Andy Stern, President, Service Employees International Union,
San Francisco, California, 21 June 2004
http://www.seiu2004.org/press/keynote.cfm)

The open source union form uses the Internet to provide information and services to workers at low cost; makes the union website a virtual union hall for supporters and activists to exchange information and views; includes workers/supporters outside of collective bargaining as union members; uses the interactive features of the Internet to increase union democracy; and combines on-line Internet communities with off-line activities in local areas to create a social movement.

The principal UK innovation in the open source direction has been the third of the TUC's sites mentioned earlier (www.unionreps.org.uk) – a website linking union representatives. The principal US innovation has been a set of competing open source union forms for workers outside of collective bargaining, of which the SEIU 'purpleocean' site is the most recent.

Strengthening union representatives: www.unionreps.org.uk

In July 2003 the TUC established www.unionreps.org.uk to help union representatives carry out their jobs around the country. The site contains bulletin boards, e-mail news for reps, a directory of on-line resources, a calendar of key events and training courses for reps, and other features. The site is limited to union representatives from UK unions and the TUC. While representatives are the face of unions in most workplaces, they are not union officials but rather workers usually elected by their peers to help resolve workplace problems and make collective agreements and unionism succeed. Some reps are health and safety specialists, some are learning specialists, some specialize in defending workers against ill treatment by management, and so on. Many representatives conduct union business on company time but many work outside normal working hours. In 2004 there were approximately 230,000 union representatives in the UK.[12] The site reached 5,000 unique visitors in August 2004, so that it was being used by approximately 5 per cent of all reps and 10 per cent of those likely to use the Internet.

To see how union reps use the new site and the Internet more broadly in their work, Freeman and Rehavi surveyed some 900 union representatives who underwent TUC training in 2003–4 (regular reps) and some 400 users of the unionreps.org site. The sample of reps who underwent classroom training are essentially a random group of local reps with respect to Internet use. The majority of these reps reported that they used the Internet frequently, making it clear that access and familiarity with the Web is no barrier to an open source form.[13] By construction, the users of the unionreps site are all Internet users and can be viewed as the union reps of the potential open source future.

Table 8.3 summarizes the survey responses regarding use of the Internet for representative duties. The largest proportion of regular reps report that they used materials from their representative training courses for their training,

Table 8.3 Union representatives' use of the Internet to perform their job (%)

	Often		Rarely or never	
	Reps under training	Union reps.org users	Reps under training	Union reps.org users
1 *Percentage of union reps who 'use the following sources to obtain information' for their representative duties often and rarely/never*				
Union reps training material	42	43	11	11
Full-time union staff	34	29	26	25
TUC	5	5	71	75
Older/experienced workers	31	22	22	28
Internet	31	66	35	4
2 *Percentage of union reps Internet users who use the Internet for*				
Union rep duties	32	63	26	6
Current job	30	43	43	32
Other union activities	24	50	41	11
3 *Frequency of visits to websites*				
Your union's web site	9	19	57	31
TUC web site	6	11	70	46
unionreps.org website	3	15	83	29

Source: Tabulated from union representatives survey, 2003–4, Freeman and Rehavi 2004.
Note
Often is more than three times a week; rarely or never is once a month or less.

Table 8.4 Use of websites by union representatives under training and users of unionreps.org.uk (%)

	Reps under training	unionreps.org.uk users
1 *Percentage of respondents who agree strongly that specified website is very useful*		
My union website	22	31
TUC website	28	35
unionreps.org website	20	39
2 *Percentage of union reps that use Internet to support specified duties*		
To find out about training possibilities	61	78
To inform workers in your workplace about your union activities	60	76
To find out about worker rights and employment legislation	82	96
To find out about pay levels and working conditions elsewhere	43	60
To keep in touch/exchange information with your union officials	56	72
To keep in touch/exchange information with other union reps	59	80
To keep in touch/exchange information with contacts with other unions/worker organizations	38	60
To communicate with the workers you represent	N/A	69

Source: Tabulated from union representatives survey, 2003–4, Freeman and Rehavi 2004.

but a substantial proportion report using the Internet as well. Representatives from the unionreps.org sample differ in one important way from other union representatives: *they make more extensive use of the Internet for their work.* Sixty-six per cent of the unionreps.org users reported using the Internet 'often' compared to 31 per cent of the other representatives. Modestly fewer unionreps.org representatives said that they relied 'often' on union officials and senior workers for information than the other representatives, which implies that the Internet adds a source of information to a greater extent than it substitutes for existing sources.

Item 2 in Table 8.3 compares representatives' use of the Internet for their representative work with their use of the Internet on their regular jobs and on other union activity. The regular reps use the Internet approximately as much for representative work as for their other work or union related activities. The users of the unionreps.org.uk site use the Internet more widely for all activities, but the difference is largest for their representative duties, which suggests that the site again increases use of the Internet for that specific function.

Which websites did union reps visit often and how useful did they find those websites?

Item 3 in Table 8.3 shows the responses to a question about how often per week users went to their own union's site, the TUC site, and the unionreps.org.uk site. It shows that regular reps went most frequently to their own union website, fewer went to the TUC website, and the fewest went to the newly launched www.unionreps.org site. By contrast, 19 per cent of the unionreps.org users visited their own union site more than three times a week, but almost as many said they went to the unionreps.org site. In terms of usefulness of the websites, item 1 of Table 8.4 shows that the regular reps scored the TUC as the most useful site and scored the new unionreps.org.uk site, with which most were barely acquainted, the lowest.[14] By contrast, the unionreps.org sample rated that site as the most useful to them, with the TUC site rated second and their own union's site rated third. Still, these unionrep.org.uk users viewed all of the Internet sites as more valuable than did the regular reps.

For which issues do union reps use the Internet in their work?

The survey question here allowed for multiple answers and item 2 in Table 8.4 shows that most representatives use the Internet for more than one purpose. Among regular reps, the average number of items cited was four. Among unionreps.org users, the average number of items cited (exclusive of the last item, which we asked only of those respondents) was 5.2. Among both groups the most cited use was finding out about worker rights and employment legislation, while the least cited uses of the Web were for keeping in touch with other unions and finding out about pay and conditions elsewhere. The biggest gap in usage between the regular representatives and the unionreps.org users was in the items about keeping in touch/exchanging information with other union reps and with other unions/worker organizations. To the extent that advice from a group of knowledgeable persons improves decisions (Surowiecki 2004), the site has the potential for harnessing the collective wisdom inherent in union organizations and thus improving the ability of reps to provide union services at their workplace. Eighty per cent of the unionreps.org users said that the bulletin board, where they could interact with other reps or follow discussions, was the most appealing feature.

Finally, the last line in Table 8.4 gives what was the most surprising finding for us: that 69 per cent of unionreps.org users used the Internet to communicate with the workers they represent. On the (possibly mistaken belief) that very few regular reps were using the Internet to communicate with the workers they represented, we did not ask that question in that sample. However, the 1998 WERS survey did ask it: among the reps in the WERS in 1998, 14 per cent reported using the Internet to communicate with the workers they represent.

Open source union designs

In 2001 three US unions had open source forms: www.alliance@ibm.org, an affiliate of the communication workers union organized as a minority union at IBM; www.washtech.org/wt, another communications workers affiliate based on IT workers in Northern California and Washington; and the National Writers Union, an affiliate of the United Automobile Workers that organizes freelance writers around the country (Diamond and Freeman 2002). Since then the open source notion has expanded in the US (see Box 4) and in other countries,[15] though not yet in the UK. I review US initiatives in two categories: jurisdictional-based organizations, in which particular unions have sought to use open source designs to enrol workers outside of collective bargaining; and national organizations, which seek to enrol members from almost any group, just as the Knights of Labor did in the 1880s.

Box 4 Newest open source union experiments

Jurisdictional-based experiments
Communications Workers Union Techs Unite (www.techsunite.org)
Following on its experience with washtech (www.washtech.org), the CWA developed techsunite as a national site for IT workers around the country, with organizing groups in seven different geographic areas. Oregon IT workers set up their own organization, www.ortech.org, with $24/year dues payable through

the CWA Local 7901 Associate Member program. Each organizing committee is geographically centred, rather than company centred.

International Association of Machinists CyberLodge: An Open Source Union Project (www.cyberlodge.org)

Organized over web: 'a guild-like structure where workers retain their traditional employee–employer relationship while enjoying benefits normally reserved for employees with collective bargaining agreements'. One-year charter membership of $120 gives access to portable health insurance free web hosting, and other benefits 'But the most important benefit is power – the ability to influence the movers and shakers who affect our working lives'.

United Steel Workers: (www.uswa.org/am) – New Form of Associate Membership

'A new form of individual membership in our union – open to anyone regardless of where they work or even if they have a job! We hope this program will revolutionize the American union movement and fundamentally alter how the American people think about unions and belonging to them'. Membership at $40 per year; on-line recruitment 'get access to union-only benefits like confidential workplace assistance, health care savings, job training and educational opportunities'.

National-based experiments

AFL-CIO WorkingAmerica (www.workingamerica.org)

Organized through communities, with Internet structure. Based on local organization in ten cities in five states, with 400 staff signing up members. Will use lessons from Working Families Network to recruit on-line and develop strong e-mail linkages. Members to vote on-line to determine priorities of organization. Asks for $5 in voluntary dues. 400,000 members as of summer 2004. Goal to enroll 1 million members by end of 2004.

SEIU – Purple Ocean open source union (www.purpleocean.org)

Formed 2004. Goal is to enrol 1 million members into non-collective bargaining organization. 'PurpleOcean.org is the latest wave of the American labor movement. Through actions, both on-line and offline, we seek to ensure fundamental human rights in the workplace and ensure that workers here and abroad are treated with dignity. By building a powerful grassroots network dedicated to social justice, PurpleOcean.org members will 'spotlight' employers and politicians who respect workers and 'hotlight' those who don't. In addition to direct action, PurpleOcean.org will be a place for fun discussions and education, where workers and their allies can debate and discuss today's paramount issues – from outsourcing and offshoring to health care and pensions'.

Box 4 highlights three jurisdiction-specific developments. First is the CWA's establishing www.techsunite.org as a national site for connecting IT workers. This extends the CWA's Washtech experience[16] from the Washington state area to Oregon, and five other geographic centres of IT work. That the union has chosen a geographic form rather than the company-based open source structure of www.alliance@ibm.org suggests that specific precipitating events may be needed to create company-based open source unions (the event at IBM was the company's change in its pension fund, which greatly reduced benefits for some workers). Second, in November 2003, the Machinists established Cyberlodge (www.cyberlodge.org), an Internet-based union for IT workers. The International Association of Machinists (IAM) describes the organization as having a guild-like structure where workers retain their traditional employee–employer relationship while enjoying benefits normally reserved for employees with collective bargaining agreements. Box 4 shows that the union offers personal benefits for a $120 per year membership fee, but makes its main selling point the potential clout the workers will have by associating with a relatively powerful union of skilled workers. Third, in 2004, the Steelworkers also initiated a 'new form of individual membership – open to anyone regardless of employment' that gave services at modest dues and encouraged on-line enrolment, but the Steelworkers have not yet developed a separate website for this group of workers.

The two national open source designs are a greater break with the tradition of organizing by occupation or industry. In 2003 the AFL-CIO developed a 'community affiliate' Working America (www.workingamerica.org). Working America began by organizing members in local neighbourhoods, with a focus on community and national issues as opposed to problems at workplaces (which affiliate unions might view as encroaching on their territory). Most of the initial organizing was done via door-to-door canvassing. In summer 2004, Working America had offices in ten cities in five states, and 400 staff knocking on doors daily.[17] It signed up some 500,000 members and anticipates having 1 million members by 2005. In contrast to the associate membership scheme that the AFL-CIO encouraged affiliates to try with minimal success *prior to the Internet*, Working America stresses participation in a social movement rather than savings by purchasing with a large group.

But while the organization started through community organizing, it has put considerable effort into e-mail collection and on-line campaigns, centred around its website. Working America has been adopting many of the techniques that proved effective with the Working Families Network and has used http://www.workingamerica.org/ on-line initiatives to build membership. Its intent is to combine Internet communication with the door-to-door effort: indeed it promises members that they will help determine policy through on-line ballots. In summer 2004, when the Bush administration changed the administrative rules governing overtime, Working America added the 'Is Your Overtime Pay at Risk?' page to its website (see Box 5), in which

Box 5

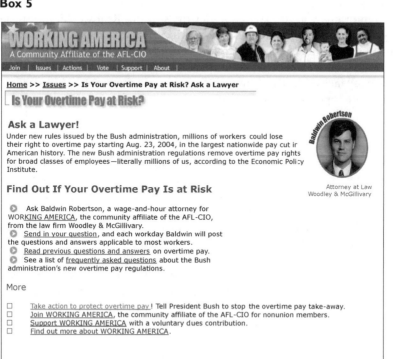

a lawyer responded to questions about the new regulations, and where the site posted questions and responses from various workers and an FAQ.

Finally, indicative of the future development of national unions, who have focused almost exclusively on collective bargaining since the demise of the Knights of Labor in the early 1900s, the Service Employees International Union announced in summer 2004 an explicitly open source design, www.purpleocean.org, with the goal of enlisting 1 million members in the near future.[18] Since SEIU is the most successful and innovative union in the US, increasing membership in the 1980s–1990s through smart organizing campaigns, its decision to develop an open source form could have immense spillover effects on the entire US labour movement.

There are unresolved design issues in open source unionism. The AFL-CIO started its organization with off-line organizing. SEIU has started on-line. Which will work better? Alliance at IBM is firm based. Washtech is occupation based. Which will work better? But arguably the most important design issue is how to link on-line and off-line activities. As a collective group, unions need members' trust and commitment, which presumably requires that members get together at least sometimes in the real world. The website www.meetup.com organizes local gatherings of people brought together by a common interest on the Web under the slogan, 'Real world, face-to-face, maybe over coffee or a beer'. At this writing, none of the open source unions uses the meet-up structure for taking on-line linkages to the real world.[19] Given the cost of meetings, it is critical for open source unions to determine how many face-to-face meetings suffice to create the personal links necessary for a viable open source organization.

Conclusion

When I began this chapter, I expected to conclude by explaining why unions were slow adaptors to the Internet. It was because they were democratic organizations that operated according to median member principles; were risk averse with members' money; operated in a market with low entry and exit; and were run by conservative bureaucracies, per Robert Michels' 1915 analysis of oligarchic tendencies in organizations.

The preceding review of union responses to the Internet as of the mid-2000s has forced me to scrap this conclusion. Unions may have adapted less rapidly than firms to the Internet, but even so unions are innovating and experimenting with the Internet at unparalleled rates. The TUC and major UK unions are experimenting with diverse ways to strengthen unionism through the Internet. Having discovered that organizing through normal channels has not delivered the renascence of unionism that they had hoped, the AFL-CIO and major US unions are probing the open source design to see if it can produce greater support and membership. These efforts will expand in breadth and depth. In the UK the formation of works councils will induce the TUC and member unions to provide on-line services to councils, many of whom may be majority non-union. In both countries unions will continue to improve the content of their websites; construct e-mail lists of members; find ways to link on-line and off-line activity; create more options for workers to join on-line; and personalize services to members. Activists will connect on the Web independently of union officials and develop websites to press for more democratic and transparent procedures.

These changes will profoundly affect union membership and density. Historically, unionism has never developed smoothly. In virtually all advanced economies, growth in membership has occurred in great spurts, with new union forms and new groups of workers leading the way (Freeman 1996). The opportunity to deliver union services to workers through the Internet and other new technologies combined with the necessity of finding new forms and modes of operation has spurred the kind of creativity and experimentation necessary to produce a new spurt. From this experimentation, some open source form may find the 'killer application' service to workers and mix of on-line and off-line activities for the next union spurt.

Notes

1   Surveys show that during the first part of 2004, 56 per cent of adults in the UK used the Internet (www.statistics.gov.uk/cci/nugget.asp?id=8) while in the US, 63 per cent of adults were regular Internet users in 2004 (www.mediamark.com/mri/TheSource/sorc2004_06.htm).

2   Accenture, E-Government Leadership: High Performance Maximum Value (May 2004) found the growth of the Internet in providing government services was tailing off in 22 countries, including the UK (www.accenture.com/xdoc/en/industries/government/gove_egov_value.pdf).

3   See http://www.esa.doc.gov/DigitalEconomy2003.cfm.

4   The most notable political site in the US is www.moveon.org. UK government services on the Internet are given at http://www.direct.gov.uk/Homepage/fs/en. For US use of the Internet for government services see http://207.21.232.103/pdfs/PIP_E_Gov_Report_0504.pdf.

5   In addition, the Ward-Lusoli content analysis examines numbers of links with other sites, which I ignore in this chapter.

6   This count is for 28 June 2004.

7   As of 31 March 2004, Tiscali had 8 million active users of whom 1.2 million were broadband customers.

8   As with other Web-based surveys, the sample is non-representative of the population (Tijdens et al. 2004). This cannot be remedied simply by weighting responses by population demographics, since the workers who fill out the survey may differ from others with the same demographics. Still, the survey can provide correlations among variables that are likely to generalize to the broader population (Freeman 2004).

9   Labourstart.org runs an annual 'beauty contest' in which users of the site vote on the best labour websites of the year. The number of participants voting in the contest has risen substantially over time.

10 Swedish unions have used the Internet to poll members during negotiations, while both the CWU and Connect have polled members regarding agreements with employers, see Bibby (2004: 7–8).

11 These are: Changing Times News: Fortnightly work/life balance update; Education update: three times yearly newsletter; Equality news: monthly update; In ToUCh: the monthly TUC round-up; International Development Matters; Organise!: bi-monthly update for union organizers.

12 Data from the 1998 WERS survey suggests that there were about 250,000 union reps in that year. The TUC estimates 230,000 in 2004.

13 Forty per cent of the union reps said that they used the Web daily, 20 per cent reported using it 2–3 times a week, whereas just 20 per cent said that they either never used it or used it at most once a month.

14 In fact, this sample was selected as a 'before' sample for assessing the impact of the new site; the regular reps were introduced to unionreps.org as part of their training. A follow-up survey will assess their usage after training.

15 Bibby (2004) reports on French and Italian unions that have set up Internet-based organizations to attract freelance and professional workers and on the creation of a Norwegian form for self-employed workers, www.rom.no. Australian unions have formed www.itworkers-alliance.org for IT workers.

16 While initially developed without collective contracts, Washtech established collective bargaining arrangements with a handful of very small IT firms during 2004.

17 Steven Greenhouse, 'Labor Federation Looks Beyond Unions', NY Times, 11 July 2004 discusses the AFL-CIO effort.

18   See Leigh Strope, 'Labor's fight for its future takes to the Internet', Associated Press, 6 July 2004. *Albany Times Union* discusses the SEIU endeavor.
19   Union activists use the meetup site to organize some meetings, such as an international union organizers meeting on 21 July 2004 (http://unionorganizers.meetup.com).

Chapter 9

The public policy face of trade unionism

Robert Taylor

Key points

- The peculiarities of British industrial relations history will make it difficult – if not impossible – for the country's trade unions in the future to develop an effective and important role as public policy makers.
- Traditionally most took a sceptical, even hostile, view of the state in its interference in their own affairs and collective bargaining and they rejected any desire to become responsible social partners in the running of the modern economy.
- Today trade union strength stems increasingly from legal rights obtained from the country's membership of the European Union. But there are few signs that most trade unions want to shoulder responsibilities in return for a role in public policy making.
- The forces of our own industrial traditions and culture as well as the new forms of work in the post-industrial world are both likely to restrict the trade union role in the wider economy.

Trade unions in Britain – as everywhere else – have always been in practice far more than collective bargaining institutions, intent both on the defence and improvement of the wages, benefits and material conditions of their members at work through negotiation. They are also social and political organizations who historically were concerned with the broader emancipation of labour in an unequal world divided by class, status and power. This is why they played such an important role in progressive reform movements, designed to extend the franchise to all citizens as well as advance and protect the civil liberties and status of the working classes they claimed to represent. But of course trade unions were also voluntary professional associations, who sought to raise the labour value of their members through the provision of education and apprenticeship training as well as use of forms of job control such as the closed shop. Some of those who represented skilled craft workers also even acted as employment exchanges in accommodating supply and demand in local labour markets. Most were understandably friendly societies and mutual aid bodies, dedicated to the propagation of virtues of thrift and self-reliance among their members and keen to protect those who could become vulnerable and insecure through the poverty of old age and arbitrary experience of unemployment. They established savings schemes and personal insurance systems and in return provided a range of personal benefits to cover funeral expenses, health treatment and support during bouts of no work. In other words, trade unions – from their very origins – always regarded themselves as necessary voluntary and autonomous institutions in the social and political as well as industrial advance of their members in the wider society.

Visionary statements

In the nineteenth century trade unions in Britain staunchly supported a range of single-issue pressure groups – from the cause of temperance to that of unadulterated food, from the extension of free non-denominational education to the provision of public libraries and parks for all citizens. They saw themselves as important, respectable and proud bodies in the development and widening of the concept of the public interest and civil society. Above all, they believed they were increasingly the representative voice of labour in a rapidly industrializing nation.

Trade unions were concerned in their wide range of activities to uphold the integrity and self-respect of working people and their families. Their idealism was reflected in the often visionary statements that prefaced their detailed rule books and intricate procedures. Increasingly they came to embrace collectivist notions such as the creation of a Commonwealth of Labour or forms of Socialism where capital and labour worked in harmony or were to unify together in the promotion of the general good of humanity. Trade union leaders usually brought an ethical and religious code of beliefs to their activities. They were often non-conformists and they drew no distinction between their work as collective bargainers on behalf of their members and their deep commitment to the creation of a better, more socially just and humane world. Indeed, most made no clear or rigid distinction between their industrial and political purposes. Trade unions may have sought to become vested interests and struggled to establish a monopoly bargaining power for their members as producers but they were always to be far more than narrow-minded practitioners of a selfish pursuit of material gains at the expense of the rest of society.

The complex multiplicity of the often competing and contradictory roles that trade unions played as public actors in the past is of crucial importance when we come to examine their future prospects for survival and growth in today's wholly different world of paid work. In fact, historically Britain's trade unions found they could only pursue an effective industrial role in the workplace if they established and maintained recognition for their legitimacy in the political economy as representative and voluntary autonomous institutions who were outside the direct control of both the state and employers. They needed to maintain and extend their influence and authority in society and politics in order to safeguard their primary industrial role as collective bargainers. But the legal security of trade unions in Britain was often thrown into serious question by the action of the legal system. They found themselves vulnerable to the arbitrary interpretations of the common law with its primary concern for individuals and the sanctity of property and not in accepting any general notion of a public interest. In their lobbying of Parliament trade unions were concerned to apply pressure on governments, troubled by what they saw as the real threat posed by what was termed the 'labour question'. This meant the passing of legislation that gave trade unions not positive rights and responsibilities but legal immunity from adverse court judgements.

This was why most trade unions in Britain believed it was necessary for them to seek specific political objectives beyond the immediate concerns of the workplace. Unless they were able to influence the legal framework within which they operated their very existence as free, autonomous and independent institutions would be put at risk. They needed to secure legal immunities by statute from Parliament so they could act on behalf of their members and avoid the restrictive conditions of the common law that regarded combinations such as trade unions as restraints of trade and therefore as unlawful bodies. The need to defend and advance the cause of organized labour through political action was therefore an understandably important function for trade unions in Britain that dated back to before the industrial revolution.

However, with few exceptions, trade unions in Britain – at least until the end of the nineteenth century – saw no need to develop a coherent ideology of collectivism that would have involved the creation of a separate political party to represent their cautious and limited aims. Nor – unlike their counterparts in Western Europe at that time – did they see the need to become organizations dedicated to the creation of a Socialist society to replace capitalism. Most trade unions believed on principle in free trade and open markets. Indeed, most of them shared a deep and instinctive scepticism, if not genuine dislike for the emergence of any intrusive and centralizing state that governed in the interests of labouring people.

This does not mean that trade unions were satisfied with the existing social and political distribution of power. They believed not only in the cause of individual freedom, but in the need to promote the self-respect, integrity and independence of their members and this, they used to argue, stemmed in most part from the practice of manual work. They argued that those who laboured through the sweat of their brow were as much entitled to democratic and constitutional freedoms as anybody else. This is why trade unions placed themselves at the forefront of so many of the great progressive issues of the Victorian age. They sought the creation of a rational and civilized society that upheld the liberties and obligations of all free-born Englishmen. They were also genuinely internationalist in their commitments such as the cause of Polish and Italian independence and the abolition of Negro slavery in the United States. Karl Marx found staunch allies among British trade union leaders in the First International. Moreover, trade unions were often hostile to imperialism, believing that free trade and the free movement of labour promised the most civilized way to organize society. Nonetheless, our trade unions remained ambivalent or sceptical about the positive use of state power that was exercised on their behalf.

As Reid has argued, the economic beliefs of many trade unions

> were still frequently associated with broader commitments to the demo-
> cratic traditions of religious nonconformity and the libertarian traditions
> of popular radicalism. This combination therefore began to produce a
> dynamic vision of full employment, higher standards of living and the
> redistribution of wealth, achieved without the direct intervention of
> central government through the spread of powerful new forms of
> collective self-organization.
>
> (Reid 2004: 169)

Robert Applegarth, secretary of the Amalgamated Society of Carpenters and Joiners, explained this distinctive public role for trade unions when he wrote in the 1860s:

> We do not wish to turn our trade societies into political organizations,
> to divert them from their social objects; but we must not forget that we
> are citizens and as such have citizen's rights. Recollect also, that by
> obtaining these rights we shall be able more effectively to secure our
> legitimate demands as unionists.
>
> (Pelling 1968: 86)

But as Frederick Rogers, general secretary of the Bookbinders' union explained, in the 1890s the objectives of trade unionism were quite different and separate from those of the state:

> We shall enlarge the frontiers of the state and control, so far as govern-
> ment, can control, the power of the capitalist over the labourer more
> and more. But there must be an independent life within the state to
> prevent government becoming tyranny and the trade unions will be chief
> among those who shall bring that independent life into being.
>
> (Murray 1980: 85)

Political role

But in 1900 this attitude appeared to change dramatically. The trade unions agreed to form the Labour Representation Committee that sought the election of trade union sponsored working class candidates to the House of Commons. That body became the Labour Party six years later after victories in the 1906 general election. The trade unions thereafter were to provide Labour with its peculiarly distinctive ethos and ideology for much of the twentieth century and they always retained a formidable if under-used power to determine its programmes and policies. After the introduction of its constitution in 1918 the Labour party was committed to a Socialist objective but this reflected very much the direct concerns of the trade unions. Labour's defined interests championed very much those of the worker as a producer rather than consumer or citizen. But at the same time an unwritten and informal general understanding was to determine the complex relationship between the party and the trade unions who were to dominate its internal structures – the annual conference and the national executive committee – outside Parliament. The collective bargaining and economic functions of trade unions were to be upheld and strengthened but through the maintenance of legal immunities from the common law and not as a result of the introduction of positive legal rights for workers or their own organizations. Elsewhere in Western Europe, and especially after 1945, trade unions benefited from the existence of national social settlements that they negotiated with the centre-left political parties and governments they supported. These arrangements helped to establish welfare states based on redistributive forms of personal taxation and the state ownership of key industries and services. But they also provided workers and their trade unions with recognized rights and obligations under positive frameworks of legally enforceable regulation. This development was not to happen in Britain, despite the existence of majority Labour governments between 1945 and 1951, until the end of the century and even then only in a piecemeal and often incoherent, *ad hoc* way. For the most part, our trade unions remained determined to uphold their role as collective bargainers but in a system that upheld the informal and the voluntary that was based on hallowed custom and practice. They may have exercised substantial influence on Labour governments in the strategic direction and detailed content of social, economic and industrial policies, but they expressed no enthusiasm to transform themselves into corporatist partners in the administration of the modern state. As the TUC general secretary George Woodcock argued as late as 1968:

> For the most part the attitude of the trade unions towards the government is that we would just as well that you left us alone. If you do not think it is possible for you to help the trade unions then the least you can do is not to impede us.
>
> (Woodcock 1968: 6)

Of course, such a position grew increasingly untenable in the post-war years as governments wrestled with the seemingly intractable problems of wage-push inflation, high unit labour costs and low productivity in a fragile political economy that was increasingly exposed to uncertain external pressures and financial speculation. Successive Labour and Conservative governments, especially between 1948 and 1979, tried to secure permanent trade union support for voluntary wage restraint through the means of an agreed prices and incomes strategy. They failed and the state was compelled to resort to restraints on collective bargaining backed up by the threat of legal sanctions against those who defied Treasury-determined wage norms. Government endeavours were to founder inevitably in a free society in self-destructive bouts of workplace militancy and inflationary pay settlements that were the consequence of full employment and a decentralized and ossified structure of trade unionism that was too often focused on the defence of hallowed wage relativities and differentials.

In practice trade unions acted rationally as sectionalist and self-interested organizations who were able to take advantage of favourable economic conditions for their members. But the resulting inherent instability under-mined the capacity of trade unions to play any positive role in the advance of their wider objectives outside the workplace. In principle, most of their leaders argued that they remained committed Socialists who wanted to bring about the creation of a planned economy through the use of a powerful centralizing state. They tried to use the Labour Party that they had created to bring about their collectivist political and industrial objectives but at the same time they insisted on preserving their freedom to bargain with employers in isolation from any wider obligations. Moreover, they displayed little consistent interest in the development of social partnerships or forms of tripartism that required trade unions as well as employers to shoulder responsibilities in the governance of the political economy. As a result, Britain failed to build the kind of voluntary national representative institutions of capital and labour that under-pinned many of the successful economies of post-war western Europe. It is true that an impressive range of intermediate or non-governmental organiza-tions were established during the trade union–Labour Party social contract era of the 1970s. These were often designed to further the aspirations and rights of workers through trade union representation. Bodies such as the Health and Safety at Work Commission, the Equal Opportunities Commission and the Advisory, Conciliation and Arbitration Service provided trade unions with important roles. They continue to exist and their future may not be in doubt but they were usually seen as second-best supplements to the existing system of voluntary collective bargaining and not as genuine alternatives. Even the limited employment protection legislation of the period was regarded by the trade unions as more a sign of the failure of their own collective efforts to achieve their aims rather than evidence of their power and influence. They did not really want to see an advance in the interests of workers as a whole through the establishment of a political regime of positive employment regulation but sought to limit the extension of state support only to those workers who were trade union members. It is not surprising that the trade union campaigns for an extension of industrial democracy during the 1970s usually opposed the creation of consultative works councils or forms of worker participation that were applicable to all employees and not just to those workers who belonged to trade unions. Trade unions in Britain may have partially abandoned their older ambivalent attitudes to the positive use of the state to improve the position of their members at work but they were far from accepting that all workers should be treated as industrial citizens with universal and legally enforceable entitlements.

Limitations of voluntarism

It was not really until the last decade of the twentieth century that the trade unions began to acknowledge that their traditionalist views of voluntarism and limited state involvement in their affairs were no longer credible. Increasingly they came to recognize that they lacked the collective strength to remedy their own structural weaknesses and vulnerability. Their attitudes were reshaped by their experience at the hands of Margaret Thatcher's Conservative government as it pursued a so-called 'step by step' strategy between 1980 and 1990 which was designed to limit trade union powers by restricting their legal immunities in industrial disputes, putting an end to so-called secondary picketing and abolishing the closed shop. In doing so the Prime Minister worked very much with and not against the grain of the voluntary system of industrial relations. She was helped in her undoubted success by her willingness to tolerate high levels of open unemployment in defiance of the post-war consensus that governments could not survive the existence of lengthy dole queues. This helped to weaken trade union bargaining strength. She also displayed an unyielding determination to confront damaging industrial disputes in the public sector. The gradual transfer in the ownership of state-run industries to the private sector also challenged the public role of trade unions. In fact, the resulting demise of the nationalized industries dealt a fatal blow to the intricate network of power and influence that helped to shape the political economy and in which trade unions had always played an important if not determining part. The ensuing liberalization and deregulation may not have been initially a part of any grand design but it did much to marginalize the trade unions in the making of public policy. Perhaps even more crucially, it helped to strengthen the forces of employee individualism that were already undermining older notions of social cohesion and class solidarity. In fact, Mrs Thatcher's achievement in settling the post-war trade union 'problem' that had troubled all previous governments since 1945, was to reveal what was always the fragile and contested nature of trade union power in a market economy. In their traditional unwillingness to press for legally enforceable rights in employment contracts and the establishment of statutory positive regulation to protect and strengthen the position of workers, the trade unions had relied too much on their complacent assumption that they would always continue to enjoy the kind of industrial leverage that they had so often achieved as collective bargainers through their own negotiating efforts.

Belatedly the trade unions now began to reassess their attitude to their relations with the state and they began to change the nature of their demands. Now they called for the introduction of the kind of social rights and legally-enforceable regulations that were in existence across most of the rest of the European Union, designed to improve the position of employees and trade unions through the use of statute law. The incoming Labour government's decision in June 1997 to end the UK's opt-out from the provisions of the Social Chapter of the European Union's Maastricht treaty was crucial to the advance of what was a new public policy agenda for the modernization of employment relations. As a result an impressive range of legally transposed measures were introduced into Britain to universalize the rights of employees in areas such as holiday entitlement and paid maternity and paternity leave. In addition, the Labour government agreed to introduce a statutory national minimum wage for the first time in Britain to deal with poverty pay and they created an independent Low Pay Commission to supervise its implementation and advise on what its level should be. Laws were also passed to provide trade unions with the legal right to recognition for bargaining purposes from an employer if a majority of workers in a designated workplace voted for such an agreement. It is true that the government took an increasingly sceptical view of the widespread use of such regulation to manage workplaces. Ministers opposed the proposal to establish consultative and information mechanisms for employees in companies under a proposed European Union directive until they found they were completely isolated in their resistance to its introduction. The government also supported Britain's employers in their opposition to protective regulation that would establish pro-rata employment rights for agency workers as well as an end to the opt-out for many workers from the European Union's working time directive, designed to restrict the number of hours they worked in the week by law. The British state's response to the social Europe agenda has often turned out to be half-hearted if not hostile, sceptical at best and always less than fulsome. Increasingly employment regulation in the workplace achieved by the law and not collective bargaining has been seen as a genuine obstacle to business efficiency and a threat to industrial competitiveness although the empirical evidence available has not proved to be conclusive.

In fact, contemporary attitudes reflect the legacy that has come from Britain's complex tradition of voluntarism in collective bargaining and ambivalent trade union attitudes to the positive use of government power in order to shape workplace relations. This approach looks likely to remain a dominant constraint on the public role of trade unions in the foreseeable future. In fact, the British state seems likely to take increasingly less responsibility for the defence and promotion of the public interest. The continuing introduction of private market incentives and short-term employment contracts into every aspect of health and education provision, as well as the creation of an increasing number of public/private partnerships and the extension of the sub-contract culture of work into the administration of the civil service and local government by private firms, points towards the emergence of an increasingly limited role for the state in the direct provision of public services and above all in the employment of public sector workers. The political economy is likely to be dominated by the interests and attitudes of private entrepreneurs and the consumer citizen, by the cash nexus and the dominant ideology of personal choice in the provision of public services. This development, however, threatens to impose a severe constraint on any advance in the concept of social citizenship as practised by many countries in mainland Europe. Perhaps this may stem, in part, from the logic of remaining a relatively low tax country which is prepared to accept and tolerate a widening inequality in income and wealth distribution. In such a future it is hard to envisage any obvious public role for trade unions that would involve an extension in their collectivist functions or a commitment to wider social responsibilities and obligations, partnerships and ethical forms of corporate governance. Outcomes will be determined overwhelmingly by a resort to what a person can afford to pay and commercial criteria will remain paramount in the assessment of business success. The resulting commodification in the provision of a wider range of goods and services is likely, therefore, to endanger any remaining notion of what constitutes the public interest.

But if the modern, enabling state in Britain is unprepared to seek out or offer any open and explicitly negotiated social partnership with employers, trade unions and employees in the management of the political economy, it is also unlikely to seek any further advance in the regulation needed to defend worker and trade union rights if they come into conflict with the needs and demands of capital in an increasingly competitive globalizing economy. A campaign of radical economic reform which is designed to enhance labour market flexibilities across Europe, as envisaged by British governments of all the mainstream parties, suggests we can expect to see a resulting diminution in the role of trade unions as active participants in the making of future public policy. In this scenario trade unions would become little more than learning organizations, tolerated by governments and employers but only as long as they adjusted themselves rapidly to meet the changing demands of employers in the modernization of work organization and job restructuring. Trade unions under such a neo-liberal economic agenda would be expected to demonstrate their continuing relevance by raising the labour value of their own members through the provision of better training and learning. The decision by the government to create a modestly financed union modernization fund in 2004 suggests that some ministers are keen to try and help unions make themselves more presentable, professional and adaptable to the new world of paid work.

The future

It is true that the August 2004 accord reached at a meeting at Warwick University between the Labour Party and trade union leaders appeared to point to the emergence of a more positive public policy role for the trade unions. Warm words were written of the continuing importance of the party–union relationship and a number of specific policy proposals were made that appeared to satisfy the new generation of union leaders, not known for their agreement with the nature of the New Labour project. However, even the most optimistic reading of the agreement's contents cannot disguise the fact that we are unlikely to see any return to the kind of formal relationships that used to exist in the era of the social contract in the 1970s or even the close alliance of previous decades. The possibility of new forms of social dialogue between the state, the trade unions and employers looks improbable in the current political climate even if these remain commonplace in the rest of Western Europe. The British government may have been compelled to accommodate the social market agenda from Brussels but it has done far more in the letter than in the spirit and usually in a more begrudging than enthusiastic manner.

However, even if the British state now seems increasingly unwilling to strengthen and work with trade unions as legitimate social partners in the wider political economy, it may not be possible to avoid having to come to terms with those broader principles and detailed regulations that are still promising to emanate from the European Union's social market model. The ideological assumptions of that model stem from distinctive and powerful influences that were always less apparent in the British tradition of industrial relations outside wartime conditions. The more progressive form of liberalism that influenced the British voluntarist trade union tradition was mainly absent from the continent. Now Britain has to come to terms with and absorb a substantial flow of Brussels-based social regulation into its own world of paid work that tends to conflict with the more individualistic and voluntarist system of collective bargaining.

This is why it is likely that over the coming years a number of important reforms look set to change or at least modify the existing public face of trade unionism in this country. The government may have opposed, for example, European Union derived information and consultation rights to the bitter end, but the introduction of the new laws, in phased stages from March 2005 to March 2008 into all firms employing more than 50 workers, is going to provide the opportunities for a revival of trade unionism at company and sector level. This important if underplayed reform could also help to stimulate a belated reassessment of trade unions as representative institutions that are essential to the creation of a more competitive market economy. The creation of high performance workplaces may require a more systematic approach to how companies should organize and involve their employees and provide them with necessary opportunities to influence decision-making. The state's role in this strategy may become vital. By the end of the decade trade unions could find their position has improved as a result of that public policy initiative.

However, trade unions in Britain have lost much of their influence on Labour policy making. It is true that the four largest of them now constitute as much as 40 per cent of the total number of votes that are cast at the Labour Party conference and this provides them with a substantial voice. They still remain important sources of finance for the Labour Party. From time to time, they can be expected as a result to exercise some power over the direction of party policy but this is far less than it was 30 years ago. It is hard to see any circumstances when the trade unions can hope to re-establish the position of authority and influence they used to enjoy in the Labour Movement 30 years ago. On the contrary, underlying trends point in a quite different direction which looks likely to make it harder and not easier for the trade unions to re-establish any undisputed position in public policy making.

First and foremost, the world of organized labour that dominated the decades after the Second World War has gone and it seems very unlikely to return. As Dr James Cronin (2004) has argued recently, this has meant the passing away of the distinctive Old Labour ethos and traditions that were shaped by the defensive aspirations and restrictive attitudes of the manual industrial working class. It has resulted not only in the abandonment of any recognizable form of democratic Socialism but the disappearance of many of the values and attitudes that avowedly underpinned the social structure of post-war British society. It seems highly improbable that we are going to see any revival in forms of work organization that will involve the creation of large plants and offices and labour-intensive manual occupations. The forces that helped to establish forms of social cohesion and solidarity also appear to grow weaker all the time. The emphasis is not only on the advance of worker individualism, on the primacy of personal lifestyles and aspirations rooted in hedonism and affluence, but on the advance of individual and not collectively negotiated rights at work and in the wider civil society.

This does not, however, mean that trade unions in principle can no longer enjoy an effective future as public policy advocates with influence and authority on the way that governments behave. On the contrary, we can find countless examples in mainland Europe where trade unions continue to play active roles as partners in the existence of social dialogues with national governments and employer associations in the making of micro-economic policies. The Netherlands, Ireland, Sweden, Austria and even Germany despite that country's current difficulties illustrate this. Such arrangements of national coordination are often designed to ensure monetary stability with a negotiated trade-off between the protection and creation of jobs and restraints on wage bargaining. Moreover, the pursuit of active labour market policies by the state to boost training and employment creation remains central to the public activities of many national trade union confederations. It is true that such arrangements are no longer as comprehensive or as centrally directed as they used to be. Competitive pressures in global markets on the activities of many companies have brought a greater decentralization in bargaining and decision-making, with a resulting weakening in the collective strength of national accords and understandings. But this has so far not led to any radical abandonment of traditional forms of social consensus that have involved the provision of an important public policy role for trade unions, especially in northern Europe. It is true that many Social Democratic parties are no longer as strongly linked to national trade union federations as they used to be. There is a greater degree of diversity of practice and a clearer division in trade union functions and responsibilities between political and industrial life. In Denmark, for example, the main LO trade union federation ended its historic organic ties with the country's Social Democratic party in 2003. This move has not occurred elsewhere although public debates elsewhere in the region continue on what kind of future relationship there should be between political parties and trade unions.

The example of Scandinavia can also point to the relative success of a different kind of progressive public policy agenda for modern trade unionism that is rooted in the new world of paid work. This is focused in particular on the quality of working life throughout its length – from school to old age. Sweden, in particular, has pioneered public policy strategies that focus on the occupational health of workers in a preventive and not a litigious way. The belated interest in the cause of widely available and affordable child care in Britain as part of a better work/life balance looks set to dominate public policy debates in the future and this is particularly well developed among the Nordic countries with active trade union involvement. The growing role of the trade unions in the provision of pension schemes and the administration of an active labour market may also become more credible as governments grapple with the difficulties of ageing workforces and rising pressure on the demands for greater public expenditure with increasing resistance to high levels of taxation.

But such public policy reforms are only a beginning if trade unions hope to respond effectively to the changing world of work. Women now make up nearly half the labour force in Britain and they constitute almost a majority of trade union members. Increasingly their specific interests and needs will have to achieve a much higher priority on both government and collective bargaining agendas. This looks likely to take the form of rising demands for the introduction of more comprehensive forms of universally applied social regulation that would seek to establish a minimum legally enforceable framework in workplaces within which trade unions will have the opportunity to strengthen entitlements through collective or even individual bargaining.

Trade unions can also be expected to try and strengthen their position as social movements in the wider community. Under John Monks' leadership, between 1993 and 2003 the TUC made some efforts to maximize its influence as the country's leading voluntary pressure group in forming strategic alliances with a diverse range of non-governmental organizations from greater assistance to the disabled to the cause of debt relief and cultural and environmental causes. This approach can be expected to grow under Brendan Barber, Monks' successor as TUC general secretary. It also seems probable that Britain's trade unions will want to establish stronger ties with the European Trade Union Confederation and use the well-established public policy processes that exist in Brussels where the ETUC plays an important part in order to advance a wider trade union agenda applicable across Europe. On the other hand, trade unions may find it much harder to establish much collective influence over so-called globalization. Well-meaning rhetoric can so often outpace practical realities. But trade union efforts can be expected to grow for a more effective public policy response at the international level to combat the abuse of labour rights in developing countries.

However, trade unions cannot expect to re-establish their former dominance in the making of public policy. Although a complete rupture between the industrial and political wings of the Labour Movement may still look doubtful, a number of trade unions (the RMT transport union and the Fire Brigades Union) have disaffiliated from the party in protest at what they regard as its anti-union policies. Other unions have reduced their financial affiliation to the Labour Party. But most remain loyal despite the strains on their historic alliance. The introduction of the state funding of political parties would bring the relationship into serious question but this is not yet on the public policy agenda.

And yet there can be nothing inevitable about the continuing public policy role of trade unions unless they can reverse the decline in their memberships and establish greater relevance. But they will find it harder to gain and hold on to members in the new workplaces in the private services sector and in small firms. The authority and influence of trade unions in the public arena stems from the degree of power which they can exercise in the political economy. Increasingly they are unable to assert themselves with a public policy agenda that can establish a strong hold on the Labour Party.

But there is a more serious and fundamental problem than the apparent lack of any credible programme for the advance to a more modern kind of trade unionism. Historically the trade unions were able to build their wider political aspirations because they believed they were an inexorable force in the evolution of society. It is true that there was nothing inevitable about the rise of organized labour. But – as we have argued – from at least the 1860s the political system came to recognize and respond to the emergence of trade unions as potentially powerful organizations. Their leaders saw themselves as important partners in a loosely organized progressive movement that sought to become a countervailing influence to the power of capital. In the United States and Britain, but also across much of the industrialized world, trade unions turned themselves into advocates of the public interest. As a result they came to help shape and influence the world of work in the twentieth century. But the onward march of the Labour Movement came to an end at least 30 years ago and it fell into prolonged retreat. The underlying social trends that determined its advance are no longer apparent. Unless the public policy climate changes more favourably it seems highly improbable that trade unions will be able to reassert themselves in the way they were able to do 50 years ago. Moreover, they may find their existing structures and cultures remain too deeply entrenched to be either reformed or modernized in ways that would enable them to renew their basic political and industrial purposes.

The forces that influence public policy in the world of work are now much more shaped by the competitive needs of capital. Employers in Britain and elsewhere are increasingly more effective in public policy lobbying than they used to be. Official anxieties about lack of relative competitiveness, high labour costs and poor productivity are tending to lead to more deregulatory and liberalizing measures that are undermining the social cohesion and stability that used to be associated with trade unions. Increasingly trade unions are finding themselves being pushed onto the margins without any recognized role to play in existing modernization strategies. Of course, their crisis is not unique to Britain. Across most of the industrialized world trade unions are in retreat both as public policy makers and collective bargainers. But their troubles remain perhaps more acute in this country. To a very great extent this stems from the particular and often confused way in which they sought to reconcile their differing roles. The burdens of their own peculiar history make it hard to believe that the trade unions can once again turn themselves into effective and representative institutions capable of exercising a power and influence in what is a far more fragmented, individualistic and competitive world than the one they had to deal with over the past two centuries.

This chapter forms a part of a much wider study of trade union futures in a globalizing world that is being prepared for publication under the Leverhulme Future of Trade Union project.

Chapter 10

Follow the leader

Are British trade unions tracking the US decline?

Morris M. Kleiner

Key points

- During the past 50 years, the US has been the leader in the decline of union density among major Western industrial countries. In the early 1950s, about one-third of American workers belonged to a union in the US, but by 2003, about 12 per cent of the workforce was a union member. In the private sector, the density figures show a decline to about 8 per cent in the US by 2004. A central element of this analysis is to examine whether this decline in unionization in the US is foreshadowing a similar further decline in UK union membership and political influence. The results show a modest positive relationship between the US decline and declines in the UK given the close economic link between the two nations.
- As much as 30 per cent of the decline in American union density has been attributed to employer opposition policies and practices that focus on stopping unions. Compared to the US, the economic incentives to try to stop unionization efforts in the UK are small; therefore, employer opposition to unionization in the UK would be less intense. Further, the large US union wage gap relative to that in the UK is unlikely to be made up by productivity improvements driven by unionization and therefore provides additional incentives for employers to oppose unionization in the US.
- The average penalty for violating the National Labour Relations Act in the US is slightly more than $2,700 whereas the average penalty for a violation of the Employment Relations Act of 1999 in the UK is more than £75,000. This difference may have a deterrent effect on managerial violations of the Act, especially ones at the margin. Consequently, the level of unionization is likely to remain much higher in the UK relative to the US.
- Both the US and the UK have seen union member contributions to political organizations increase during the past 40 years. Given the decline in union membership, the impact of unions on the electorate

is bound to have declined. Consequently, their influence on policy is also likely to have been reduced relative to the levels that unions enjoyed in the 1950s in the US and the 1970s in the UK. Nevertheless, unions continue to have an important role in the political arena.

• Labour leaders in both nations have undertaken policies like associate membership, consultations with management, use of pension funds, and the Internet to stop the decline in rates of unionization. Nevertheless, in the US, without a change in public policy that makes organizing easier, there is little likelihood that the decline in US union density will be stopped.

Introduction

During the past 50 years, the US has been the leader in the decline of union density among major Western industrial countries (Freeman and Rogers 1993). In the early 1950s, about one-third of American workers belonged to a union in the US, but by 2003, about 12 per cent of the workforce was a union member. In the private sector, the density figures show a decline to about 8 per cent in the US by 2004. The causes of this decline have been attributed to both structural economic changes in the US and the increases in employer opposition to unionzation (Farber and Western 2001; Kleiner 2001). A central element of this chapter is to examine whether this decline in unionization in the US is foreshadowing a similar further decline in UK union membership and political influence.

The US has often been a leader among Western industrialized countries in setting trends for many labour market institutions. In many areas of the labour market, such as increasing labour force participation of women and expansion and enrolment in higher education, the US has been at the forefront in establishing trends followed by Western Europe (Blau and Kahn 2000). The movement toward a high technology workforce with an emphasis on the service sector has been a hallmark of the US industrial transformation (Lee and Wolpin 2004). Union membership had seen a decline not only in the US, but also in the EU.

The objective of this chapter is to examine under what conditions industrial relations institutions in the US and the UK will continue the downward trends in unionization. The focus of this chapter is on the American experience, since the UK experience with unions is discussed throughout this volume. This chapter also will provide statistical evidence on the extent to which unions will follow a similar path in both nations. Initially, I present the organizing trends in the US, followed by a brief review of those in the UK. Next, a comparison of the trends in both countries is developed. This is followed by an examination of the incentives for unionization in both countries. Since both nations have a higher percentage of the public sector organized than in the private sector, I examine the level of political contributions in both countries. The following section presents some policies that unions in both nations are implementing to stem the decline of unionization. The conclusions provide an assessment of the likelihood that unions in the UK will continue to follow American unions into a decline in the private sector.

One unique aspect of this chapter is a comparison of the penalties for violations of labour laws in both nations. This is one gauge of the incentives for managers to comply with labour laws in each nation. Another issue that is developed elsewhere in this volume is that technological innovations on organizing in both the US and UK, like the ability of union members to communicate more effectively through the Internet, may serve as a focus for another spurt of unionization (Freeman 2004).[1] Of all the nations in Europe, the UK has developed labour market institutions most similar to the US. This may have been a contributing factor to the UK being the largest beneficiary of American foreign direct investment and foreign trade (Kleiner and Ham 2002). These close economic ties may also result in complementarities in labour market institutions such as labour unions and the role of public policy in shaping the employment relationship.

American trade union organizing trends

US unions have experienced both an overall decline in membership, but a smaller decline in political influence over the past 50 years.[2] One reason for this is that the American labour movement has seen a major decline in private sector unionization, but an increase in the percentage of the workforce who belonged to public sector unions, over which politics has a greater influence.

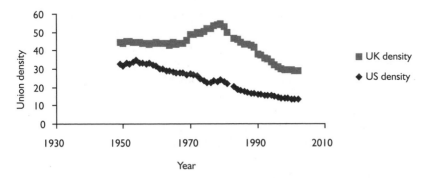

Figure 10.1 Trends in UK and US union density, 1949–2002 (Sources: UK data: a) Bain and Price (1980) (1949–77); b) Annual statistics of Britain (1978–2000); c). LFS (2001–2). US data: a) 'Handbook of Labor Statistics 1978', US Dept. of Labor Bureau of Labor Statistics, 1979 (1949–74); b) Hirsch and Macpherson (1975–76, 1981); c) 'Handbook of US Labor Statistics' 1988 (1977–80, 1983–97); d) 'Handbook of US Labor Statistics' 2004 (1998–2002))

The trends, as shown in Figure 10.1, give the decrease in unionization from 1949 to 2002 in the US and UK. This trend shows a declining rate of unionization over the past 50 years in the US but an increase in the 1970s in the UK and then a steady decline.

The often analysed reasons for the decline in private sector unions vary from industrial shifts away from traditional union strongholds such as manufacturing to industries like finance, insurance, and real estate, to the inability of unions to win elections and first contracts in large bargaining units, and the decline in union expenditures on organizing new workers (Farber and Western 2001). In the US, there has been a geographic population and employment shift from more union-friendly regions and states in the Northeast and Midwest to states in the South and Southwest, which have fewer 'pro-worker' labour market institutions. Finally, there has been an increase from the 1950s to the current period in overt employer hostility toward unions as measured in the increase in violation of US labour laws (Kleiner 2001). The wage gap between union and non-union workers is much higher in the US relative to most other industrialized nations (Blanchflower and Freeman 1992). One argument has been made that employers in the US view the economic cost of violating labour laws as small in comparison to lower wages and flexible work rules that avoiding unions brings to the enterprise. The union/non-union wage gap in the US is close to 25 per cent and productivity differences between union and non-union firms is small, but favours unionized establishments (Freeman and Medoff 1984). Estimates of the ability of employers to use anti-union tactics suggest that this tactic can explain up to 30 per cent of the decline in American unionization (Freeman 1985).

A further reason given for the decline in the membership rates of American unions is the decline in the amount of effort and resources put into organizing drives (Bennett and Kaufman 2001). Currently, some factions of the labour movement are challenging the leadership of the labour movement to be more creative in organizing more Americans (Bernstein 2004). Moreover, the business community has stated that it now has adopted more pro-worker policies such as employee involvement and other 'high performance workplace practices,' which include financial incentives to give voice to workers in a non-union environment. With the establishment of financial incentives such as profit-sharing, and productivity-focused gain-sharing policies, the interests of the employees have been aligned with those of the owners. There is less demand for unionization by workers as a consequence of these policies (Freeman and Rogers 1999).

Has this decline in membership also meant a decline in political influence? During the rise of unions in the 1930s and 1940s, national Democratic Party political candidates were virtually required to obtain permission from labour leaders for individuals to run for office. This is epitomized by a statement from President Franklin D. Roosevelt, who, when choosing Vice-Presidential nominee Harry Truman, told his advisors to 'Clear it with Sidney', the powerful labour leader of the largest textile union, Sidney Hillman. Does labour still have similar political clout in either the US or Great Britain?

Unions like the Service Employees have spent more than 65 million dollars on political campaigns during the 2004 presidential campaign almost exclusively for Democratic candidates (Bernstein 2004). In spite of the decline in density, American unions have maintained their contributions to the US political arena, thereby increasing their expenditures per member. When 'in-kind' assistance such as volunteer work to political campaigns is taken into account, overall contributions have grown in the US. This has resulted in the maintenance of a strong influence in American politics since the days of Sidney Hillman. In large part, this is a consequence of increased participation by unions in the public sector. Public sector unions have an incentive to lobby political leaders to shift the demand for government services outward, thereby making the resources available to unions for wages and benefits much greater. In spite of the increase in political contributions, the impact of unions has diminished, in part due to their decline in membership. Although financial contributions are growing, their influence over the electorate has diminished as their percentage of the workforce has dropped. Unions in the US have adapted to the change from private to public sectors by lobbying legislators and members of congress rather than focusing on collective bargaining, which in the past required less of an overt emphasis on politics (Freeman and Ichniowski 1988).

British organizing trends

To what extent are these institutional arrangements likely to be replicated in Great Britain and are they likely to have the same result leading to a similar decline in British Trade Unions? Since the mid-1970s British Trade Unions also have experienced a rapid decline in membership and influence in the political and economic arena. With the election of Margaret Thatcher in 1979 and her successor John Major in 1992, there began a rapid decline in British union membership. Of interest in Figure 10.1 is the growth of union density until 1979 and then the sudden slide following the election of Prime Minister Thatcher. One issue is whether the institutional setting they established and changing economic structure result in a decline in British trade unions similar to the US decline, and whether the long-term level of unionization will be higher than in the US (Metcalf 2004). In 1999, the UK passed the Employment Relations Act that regulated labour relations law in the UK. However, compared to the US, violating labour law is more expensive in the UK with potential penalties several times greater than those imposed through the US National Labour Relations Act. Moreover, the union/non-union wage gap in the UK is 5 to 10 per cent versus more than 20 per cent in the US (Hirsch and Macpherson 2003; Metcalf 2004). Consequently, even though British unions may decline as a result of shifts away from manufacturing, and as a consequence of better managerial practices, the expected decline would be lower than the one in the US, in part because managerial incentives to fight unionization efforts would be much lower.

In the political arena, British Trade Unions have also seen their influence slip. For example, as Figure 10.1 showed, membership has gone from 54 per cent in 1979 to under 30 per cent in 2003. Moreover, similar to the American case, political influence has declined somewhat as contributions to the Labour Party have decreased as a percentage of the total but per member contributions have increased (Ludlam and Taylor 2003). Some of the reasons for this decline may be similar to the rationale in the US. In the UK, public sector union membership is approximately 60 per cent as opposed to slightly more than 20 per cent in the private sector (Metcalf 2004). In spite of this dramatic decline, the level of union density in Great Britain is likely to remain well above the level in the US as a consequence of the narrower wage gap between union and non-union employees and a higher level of penalties for violations of labour relations law. The next section details these differences.

Comparisons of British and American union wage costs and public policy penalties

As much as 30 per cent of the decline in American union density has been attributed to employer opposition policies and practices that focus on stopping unions (Freeman 1985; Blanchflower and Freeman 1992; Kleiner 2001). Unlike the US, where there are substantial incentives to try to stop unionization efforts, in the UK the economic incentives are smaller and I would expect that employer opposition would be less intense. The large US union wage gap relative to those in the UK are unlikely to be made up by productivity improvements driven by unionization (Freeman and Medoff 1984; Metcalf 2004). Although employers in both countries would rather manage without consultation with a union and the threat of an occasional work stoppage, the economic incentives to remain union-free are substantially greater in the US. Moreover, workers in the US would rather obtain voice benefits by working with management rather than through an adversarial relationship that sometimes accompanies a union (Freeman and Rogers 1999). A calculus by management in both societies would gauge the costs of unions relative to the costs of stopping an organizing drive, including the penalties of being found guilty of violating employment laws.

Table 10.1 shows the costs of violating relevant labour laws in the US and Britain using estimates from academic studies and data from government sources. Several different labour laws are presented to show variation in the types of laws that may be the subject of disputes. Moreover, the union impact is much larger because they usually encourage the enforcement of these statutes by employees or the government relative to non-union establishments (Budd

Table 10.1 Employer costs of violating the National Labour Laws in the US and UK

US		UK	
Regulations and Laws	Penalty in dollars	Regulations and Laws	Penalty in pounds
Equal Employment Opportunity Commission (EEOC)	Average back pay is $8.5 million from 109 decisions and is $4.9 million from 169 settlements between 1964 and 1986 (Hersch 1991)	Sex Discrimination Act, Race Relations Act, and Disability Discrimination Act	In 2002/3, average award was £27,041 for race discrimination, £8,787 for sex discrimination cases, and £10,157 for disability discrimination cases (Employment Tribunals Service 2003)
Occupational Safety Health Administration (OSHA)	Average penalty was $275 per violation and $366 per serious violation in 1993 and average fine was $50 per violation in 1995 (Weil 1997)	Health and safety law	Average penalty per conviction was £4,167 and was £3,418 per deflated conviction from 1990 to 2002. The severest penalty can be a fine of £20,000 with six months imprisonment.
Fair Labor Standards Administration FLSA (Minimum wages and overtime)	Average back pay per employee is $169 in 1988 (Lott and Roberts 1995)	National Minimum Wage (NMW)	There are six criminal offences relating to the NMW with fine up to £5,000 for each offence
Employment-at-will/ Wrongful discharge	Average initial award in unjust dismissal cases was $180,000 (Addison and Hirsch 1997)	Unfair dismissal regulations in the Employment Protection (Consolidation) Act	Average compensation award was £6,776 in 2002/3 (Employment Tribunals Service 2003)
National Labor Relations Act (NLRA)	Average amount of back-pay reward was $2,733 in 1991 (Dunlop Commission 1994: 83)	EWC	The penalties can be up to £75,000 where management acts in breach of its main obligation

and McCall 2004). Table 10.1 gives the employer public policy costs of violating major labour laws in the US and the UK. These estimates do not include the costs of legal representation, which far outweigh the penalties for violation of the law. Except for discrimination by age, race, and gender and for plant closings legislation, the financial impact of public policy penalties for firms is greater in the UK than for the US. One of the reasons for the larger penalties in the US is that the American sample largely includes firms that are publicly traded, whereas the British sample includes a more diverse sample of firms. Given the focus of this volume, the average penalty for violating the National Labour Relations Act in the US is slightly more than $2,700 whereas the average penalty for a violation of the Employment Relations Act of 1999 in the UK is more than £75,000. This difference may have a deterrent effect on managerial violations of the Act, especially ones at the margin. Moreover, the Employment Relations Act in the UK requires arbitration of first contracts, an issue raised and recommended by The Dunlop Commission on the Future of Worker–Management Relations (1994) for changes in US labour policy in order to stop employers from curbing organizing at the negotiations stage. For most areas of public policy presented in Table 10.1, British laws have stronger financial penalties than those in the US, and this may contribute to greater compliance with the law. Coupled with the lower wage differential in the UK, the expectation is that the long-term level of unionization would be higher in the UK. Nevertheless, issues such as changes in the economic structure of the product and labour market may lead to continuing declines in union density along the lines estimated by Metcalf in this volume.

The declines in the private sector do not necessarily mean that public sector unions are moving in the same direction. In the public sectors of both the US and UK, there are low wage differentials between public union and non-union workers. Moreover, the funds that unions in the public sector provide to politicians help reduce the likelihood that managers will engage in anti-union tactics to the extent of their private sector counterparts. Similar to the private sector, the density differential in the public sector is likely to be maintained.

Re-examining Figure 10.1 suggests that there appears to be a correlation between union density trends in the US and UK. Moreover, the simple correlation over time between US and UK density or membership is greater than 0.82. However, Table 10.2 presents a time-series regression between unions in the US and UK, with time trends accounted for in the regression analysis. The estimates are of the Granger time-series model which shows that when lagged levels of unionization in the UK are controlled for, US union density rates are modestly significant, but always positive, suggesting that US lagged density is associated with UK trends in organization density (Studenmund 2002). However, using measures of union levels are not significant when the lagged variables are accounted for in the regression equation.

Table 10.2 Ordinary least squares (OLS) with UK union statistics on US union statistics from 1949–2003

Independent variable	Membership					Density				
1 year lag value of UK union statistics	1.16*** (11.26)	0.99*** (21.89)	1.01*** (22.74)	1.04*** (21.98)	1.04*** (22.42)	1.19*** (11.68)	0.94*** (24.63)	0.96*** (22.40)	0.98*** (21.15)	1.00*** (21.62)
3 year lag value of UK union statistics	−0.02 (−0.10)					−0.28* (−1.76)				
5 year lag value of UK union statistics	−0.16 (−1.00)					0.06 (0.39)				
7 year lag value of UK union statistics	−0.03 (−0.30)					−0.06 (−0.51)				
1 year lag value of US union statistics	0.01 (0.13)	0.04 (0.83)				0.15* (1.73)	0.19*** (2.78)			
3 year lag value of US union statistics			0.002 (0.04)					0.13 (1.65)		
5 year lag value of US union statistics				−0.04 (−0.66)					0.12 (1.23)	
7 year lag value of US union statistics					−0.03 (−0.60)					0.06 (0.56)

Notes
1 Sources for UK data: a) Bain and Price (1980) (1949–77); b) Annual statistics of Britain (1978–2000); c). LFS (2001–2).
2 Sources for US data: a) Handbook of Labor Statistics 1978, US Dept. of Labor Statistics, 1979 (1949–74); b) Hirsch and Macpherson (1975–76, 1981); c) Handbook of US Labor Statistics 1988 (1977–80, 1983–97); d) Handbook of US Labor Statistics 2004 (1998–2002).
3 One control variable of UK GDP was used in all regressions.
4 T-statistics are in the parentheses.
5 *** refers to significance at level of 0.01; ** refers to significance at level of 0.05; and * refers to significance at level of 0.1.

Perhaps changes in technology or other structural economic factors that often occur in the US prior to the UK may explain this relationship. Moreover, since US foreign direct investment goes disproportionately to the UK, this may also help explain why UK economic structure may reflect what has occurred in the US.

Union political contributions

Both the US and the UK have seen union member contributions to political organizations increase during the past 40 years. Figure 10.2 shows US political receipts from unions and contributions per member from 1979 to the present in constant 2000 dollars (Masters and Jones 1999). The figure shows both increasing contributions and contributions per member. As presented earlier, American unions are increasingly in the public and service sector, which means they think it is important to be a force in the political arena both to increase demand for public sector goods and to obtain state and national legislation that is favourable to unions; unlike the early days of the American Federation of Labour, when their first President Samuel Gompers warned against political involvement by stating, 'I contend that trade unions are the natural form of organization for wage earners under existing economic conditions, and I propose (so far as I may be able) to keep them undefiled and free from alliance with any political party' (*New York Herald* 1891). American unions, in contrast with Gompers' warning, now see the need to have an important role in the political arena and to financially support mainly the Democratic Party in order to maintain their status and protect union jobs.

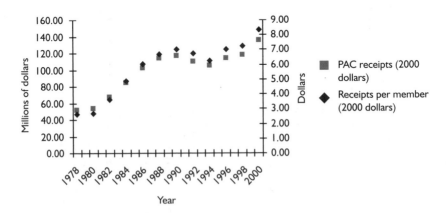

Figure 10.2 US union member political financial contributions and contributions per member, 1978–2000 (in constant 2000 dollars) (PAC = Political Action Committee)

Unfortunately, there is less publicly available data in the United Kingdom on political contributions over time. Data from the 1970s shows that contributions to the Labour Party varied a great deal from a low of approximately 54 per cent but with substantial variations during political campaigns when contributions were as much as 80 per cent of total contributions to the Labour Party (Ewing 1987). From more recent data, contributions relative to the total have fallen somewhat (Ludlam and Taylor 2003). However, contributions per member have increased given the decline of union membership by more than 5 million since the mid-1970s (Metcalf 2004). Unlike political contributions in the US, which go to both Democratic and Republican candidates, union political contributions in the UK go almost exclusively to the Labour Party.[3] Consequently, the expectation is that unions would have a greater influence with the political party but not within the political system.

Given the decline in union membership, the impact of unions on the electorate is bound to have declined. Consequently, their influence on policy is also likely to have been reduced relative to the levels that unions enjoyed in the 1950s in the US and the 1970s in the UK. Nevertheless, unions continue to have an important role in the political arena. For example, union-related contributions continue to be the largest single contributor to the Democratic Party and they have virtual 'clear it with Sidney' authority with most political candidates within the Democratic Party at the national level.

Prospects for an American or UK union resurgence?

Union leaders in both the US and UK are well aware of the decline in union density in both nations and have implemented programmes to reverse the trend. The major new approaches, have included unions providing productivity assistance for management, better use of technology like the Internet, the use of associate memberships to spur prospective membership growth, and the use of union pension funds to influence firms on their policies toward unions. These issues are the focus of much discussion among union leaders. All of these policies offer the potential for a union resurgence.

In the UK, the TUC has formed the TUC Partnership Institute in 2001, which focuses on providing employers with consultation on how to make the enterprise more productive through the use of 'high performance workplaces'. The stated objectives are twofold. First is to show how organized firms can compete with and be as profitable as unorganized ones. A second objective is to reduce employer animosity toward unions by showing unorganized firms that unions can grow the company and not only reallocate resources away from owners and toward employees. To the extent that the Partnership Institute can reduce employer opposition to unions, this may spur union growth. If successful, this may be especially useful in the US, where the incentives to stop unions are especially high. This approach focuses on the potential benefits that providing advice on how labour and management can increase productivity will lead to more trust and acceptance of unions by management.

As the chapter in this volume by Richard Freeman shows, there are many examples of technology making organizing easier by getting information to employees at less cost through the Internet in both the US and UK. It also has the potential to circumvent the employer's ability to stop information from reaching employees. Since the vast majority of American and UK employees use the Internet, the promise of the use of this technology has the potential to lead to another union spurt in density. However, to the extent that employers also can get their 'message' to employees through the Internet, this new technology may not provide the large boost in membership hoped for by unionists.

A focus of some efforts at union growth in the US is through associate membership. In the US, one of the leading unions to focus on this method to revitalize membership is the Steelworkers Union (USWA) (Grow 2004). This non-collective bargaining form of being a union member offers counselling services and help on issues of workplace safety or discrimination by race and gender. Associate members also have rights to union health care savings, job training, and educational opportunities typically reserved only for members. Associate members only need to pay a nominal $40 annual fee. The long-term goal of this programme is to acquaint a new generation of workers with the benefits of unions with the hope that they will help with organizing and later, collective bargaining. This method of introducing workers to unions may also be transferable to the UK environment as an introduction to the benefits of the TUC. This policy has been proposed for some time with little impact on the growth of union membership in the US.

An alternative method for unions in the US to gain influence is to use their financial influence through pensions. In the US, the AFL-CIO established a unit called the 'Center for Working Capital' in 1997. The goal is to harness the financial power of union-influenced pension funds to spur organizing efforts. Workers' savings have grown in the past two decades from $538 billion to $6 trillion, and now account for the largest pool of investment capital in the United States (Center for Working Capital 2004). Given this financial clout, the goal is to use union affiliated pension funds in a way to promote investments that are friendly to unions. The majority of the Center for Working Capital's Board of Directors are officers from the major unions in the US and inter-nationally. Since pension funds by law are required to invest in ways that are financially prudent, the ability to use these funds to promote organizing is limited. However, to the extent that high performance and worker-friendly policies are consistent with economic performance and unionization, these pension funds can be used to promote union programmes. As yet, active policies to promote unionization through the use of pension funds have been minor, but this is a potentially major source of union resurgence in the US, though pension laws may limit its application in the UK.

Overall, public policies need to be changed to increase the public policy costs of fighting unions in the US to at least the level in the UK, and they must include first contract arbitration for any type of resurgence in the US to be large. Public perception of unions as the major source for worker voice is essential before these policies are changed to include these provisions. Absent that transformation in public policy, and there is little chance that the union-focused policies that are being implemented by union leaders will be able to turnaround the decline in the US. In contrast, the combination of new union creativity toward organizing along with a more favourable public policy environment makes the chances of union revival more likely in the UK than the US. This is especially the case if the UK becomes more fully integrated into the EU with its focus on a social contract. These policies combined with a resurgent TUC could lead to a spurt in union density. If so, this would break the positive correlation of US and UK union density trends that has been the case throughout the post-World War II period.

Conclusions

This chapter has presented an overview of the comparative relationship of the changes in American and UK unionization. The focus has been on the relative costs and benefits of unionization for both workers and management. In the US, the wage differences of 20 to 25 per cent between union and non-union organizations in the private sector have encouraged management opposition to unionization and made it difficult for workers to organize new union members. In contrast, public policy penalties for violations of the law are small. In contrast, in the UK, union versus non-union wage differences in the private sector are small, and penalties for violations of the law are larger than in the US. Although the correlation between union densities in both countries is relatively high, when general trends are taken into account, there seems to be a weak but positive relationship between the US density and UK unionization rates. In spite of declining union density in the US, political contributions to political campaigns remain high, in part due to the importance of maintaining demand for public spending from which union members gain. The public sector remains a bright spot for unionization in both the US and UK. With large levels of political contributions by labour, the level of public sector unionization will likely remain steady.

Labour leaders in both nations have undertaken policies that may stop the decline in rates of unionization. Nevertheless, in the US, without a change in public policy that makes organizing easier, there is small likelihood that the decline in US unionzation will be stopped. Even with more favourable labour laws, structural economic changes still may dominate. Union policies like efforts to improve the productivity of union establishments, greater use of the Internet, union efforts at associate membership, and using pension programmes to gain more members are not likely to result in a spurt in members that is significant enough to quell the tide of declining density in the workforce. Although a union resurgence is unlikely, there are plausible circumstances that could lead to a turnaround like the one that occurred in the UK in the 1970s, even within the US.

Acknowledgements

The author would like to thank Maria Koumenta, Terry Risbey, and Yingying Wang for their excellent research assistance with this chapter.

Notes

1   Some organizing drives are occurring exclusively through the Internet. An example is an organizing effort by faculty at the University of Minnesota, Twin-Cities campus that took place solely through Internet signing of cards for an election. Although a huge majority of the faculty signed cards for the purpose of an election, the union barely lost the election for union representation 51 against 49 voting for the union. Under state law the union was not certified as the bargaining agent for the faculty and faded into perdition.

2   Although union membership has declined, per member expenditures have increased at an even faster rate. Consequently, the overall level of political expenditures has increased somewhat (Hirsch and Macpherson 2003; Dark 1996; US Census Bureau 1995, 1999, 2001).

3   In the US, more than 90 per cent of political contributions go to the Democratic Party, but several unions in the construction trades and the Teamsters are often supporters of the Republican Party.

Chapter 11

Trade unions in Germany

On the road to perdition?

Claus Schnabel

Key points

- Union membership in (West) Germany peaked in 1981 and has fallen since, as has union density. Currently less than one-quarter of employees in Germany are members of a trade union.
- The sustained decline in membership and density seems to have been the consequence of external factors (such as changes in the composition of the workforce) as well as internal factors (i.e. unions' own structures and policies).
- Several German unions merged, and the old system of industrial unionism was replaced by a small number of multi-sectoral unions.
- In the last 15 years, Germany has experienced a decentralization of collective bargaining and a substantial decline in bargaining coverage. Nevertheless still two out of three German employees work in an establishment that is covered either by multi-employer or single-employer bargaining.
- The German industrial relations system has not been able to transfer its institutions (such as multi-employer bargaining and co-determination) beyond manufacturing industries and the public sector into the growing sectors of private services and high technology.
- The fall in membership and bargaining coverage goes hand in hand with a decline in union bargaining power and with problems of political effectiveness.
- Union relations with the social-democratic party have soured in recent years after Chancellor Schröder pushed through reforms of the labour market and the welfare state against fierce opposition from the labour movement.
- Similarly to Britain, union perdition may be more likely than resurgence.

Structure of the labour movement in Germany

After World War II, the labour movement in Germany organized itself along different lines that all reflected a distinct break with the past. Socialist East Germany introduced the Confederation of Free German Trade Unions (*Freier Deutscher Gewerkschaftsbund*, or FDGB), which in effect was a state-controlled mass organization for labour engineered for putting planning decisions into practice that lacked most characteristics of free trade unions (such as bargaining autonomy, right to strike etc.). In the course of German unification, the FDGB and its individual member unions were disbanded during 1990. In capitalist West Germany, several trade unions and union peak organizations were set up that – in contrast to the union movement in the Weimar Republic – have stressed their ideological and political neutrality (see Keller 2004 for an overview). These so-called unitary trade unions included the member unions of the German Federation of Trade Unions (*Deutscher Gewerkschaftsbund*, DGB), the German Union of Salaried Employees (*Deutsche Angestellten-Gewerkschaft*, DAG) which became part of a merger with DGB unions and ceased to exist in 2001, and the German Civil Service Federation (*Deutscher Beamtenbund*, DBB) which organizes mainly, but not exclusively, civil servants. In addition to these unitary unions there exists a rather small Confederation of Christian Unions (*Christlicher Gewerkschaftsbund*, CGB), and there are a number of special organizations, for instance for executive staff, airline pilots, journalists and hospital doctors.

The DGB and its eight member unions form the most important labour organization in Germany, representing more than 80 per cent of union members. While the DGB is just a peak organization that is mainly responsible for political activities including lobbying, collective bargaining is conducted by its powerful member unions. These are organized centrally from the top down, with subdivisions at state, district and local levels. The DGB unions are organized on an industry basis, which means that they represent the interests not of particular occupations but of the employees working in a given industry or branch of activity. This implies that there should only be one union per establishment which all employees may join irrespective of their occupation or blue collar versus white collar status. This principle of industrial organization has not completely prevented inter-union rivalries and demarcation disputes, but it has helped to counteract overlap in the bargaining jurisdiction of different unions and managed to save transaction costs in collective bargaining.

While the organizational structure of the German union movement had been relatively stable for about four decades, starting in 1989 a number of mergers and takeovers have occurred in recent years (for a helpful graphical exposition see Waddington and Hoffmann 2000: 133 or Keller 2004: 218). In this process, the number of DGB affiliated unions was reduced from seventeen to eight, and the old system of industrial unionism was more and more replaced by a small number of multi-sectoral unions. These mergers and takeovers have been encouraged by changes in the employment structure, membership losses and decreasing financial resources of many unions. The biggest of these mergers, affecting five unions in both the public and the private service sector, resulted in the creation of the Unified Service Sector Union (*vereinte Dienstleistungsgewerkschaft*, or ver.di) in 2001 (see the case study). The number of unions can be expected to fall further since several unions seem to have problems surviving on their own.

Case study – mergers do not solve all union problems

Like in the UK, the German trade union movement has been characterized by a number of mergers and takeovers in recent years. In the biggest of these mergers five independent service-sector unions ceased to exist in March 2001: The Public Services, Transport and Traffic Union (ÖTV) with 1,480,000 members, the German Union of Salaried Employees (DAG) with 450,000 members, the German Postal Workers' Union (DPG) with 446,000 members, the Commerce, Banking and Insurance Union (HBV) with 441,000 members and the Media Union (IG Medien) with 175,000 members. They finally amalgamated in 2001 after a three-year process of legal procedures, internal conflicts and difficult negotiations, creating the Unified Service Sector Union (*vereinte Dienstleistungsgewerkschaft*, or ver.di). With almost 3 million members being employed in more than 1,000 professions ver.di was thought to be the largest union in the democratic world (for details see Keller 2001 and EIRO 2001).

This merger was not a marriage made in heaven but mainly a defensive reaction to increasing financial and organizational difficulties and new challenges. It was an ambitious project, not only because of the sheer number of unions and members involved. The membership of the new union is quite hetero-geneous, and ver.di encompasses a whole range of different trade union views and strategies ranging from 'social partnership' to 'countervailing power'. Ver.di is structured as a 'matrix' organization with a rather complex vertical structure (along geographical lines) and horizontal structure (with 13 sectoral areas). Within the trade union movement, the creation of ver.di brought together union activities in the public and private service sector and ended the previous situation of competition and demarcation disputes between individual service unions (but not disputes with other unions). One of the main aims of the merger was to achieve an integrated trade union policy for the entire service sector, including a common collective bargaining policy. Another aim was cost saving and achieving organizational synergy effects. Neither has manifested itself yet, and it remains to be seen whether ver.di will be more than the sum of its parts.

continued…

As organizing employees in the service sector has been a central problem for German unions, the creation of ver.di was also an attempt to become more attractive to potential members. However, as a multi-sectoral union ver.di appears not to be as close to its members as the five previous industrial unions were, and it has not been more successful in recruiting than its predecessors. On the contrary, ver.di membership has fallen from almost 3 million in 2000 to 2.6 million in 2003 – a 12 per cent reduction that was considerably higher than the average fall in membership for all German trade unions.

Membership problems

In the last decades trade unions in many countries have experienced severe membership losses and reductions in union density (see Ebbinghaus and Visser 2000; Visser 2003). Germany is no exception to this trend. Figure 11.1 shows that membership figures increased in the 1970s, reaching a peak in 1981. In this year 7.96 million people were organized in one of the member unions of the German Federation of Trade Unions (DGB), and total membership of all unions (i.e. including the members of the competing union federations DAG, DBB and CGB) was 9.56 million. In the 1980s, membership stagnated and union density, defined as the ratio of union members over employees, even fell in West Germany (see Müller-Jentsch and Ittermann 2000; Ebbinghaus and Visser 2000). For the unions, therefore, German unification in 1990 created a new and unexpected chance for organizational development.

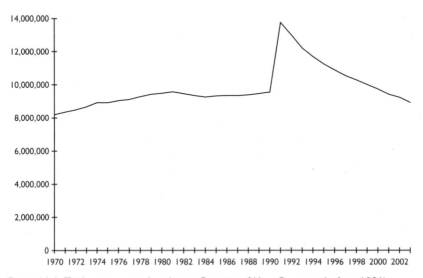

Figure 11.1 Trade union membership in Germany (West Germany before 1991)

In the course of the full-scale transfer of the West German institutional framework to the east, the DGB unions decided to expand to eastern Germany by applying a takeover model in which the East German state-controlled labour organization, the FDGB, was to voluntarily dissolve itself and recommend its members to transfer their enrolment to the appropriate branch union of the DGB. Following this strategy, the DGB unions managed to sign up more than 4.1 million members in eastern Germany in 1990 and 1991, which was almost one-half of all former FDGB members. However, due to the special modalities of membership recruitment, not all of the new members were highly motivated to join, and the membership boom directly after unification was a very special case which 'did not follow any "normal" patterns of union organizational development' (Fichter 1997: 87). Soon the trend reversed, with the DGB unions losing almost 800,000 members in 1992 and another 500,000 members in 1993, and membership in eastern Germany has continued to fall since. By the end of 1998, the last year for which disaggregate union statistics are available, the DGB unions had only 1.8 million members in eastern Germany, a loss of 56 per cent since 1991. Membership problems were aggravated by the fact that in the same period almost 1.2 million members turned their back on the DGB unions in western Germany (see Müller-Jentsch and Ittermann 2000). The only organization with growing membership in the 1990s was the German Civil Service Federation (DBB). Since 2001 total membership of all unions in united Germany is lower than it was in West Germany before unification. In 2003, total membership was just 8.92 million, and figures keep falling steadily.

The analysis of declining union membership and density is rendered difficult by the fact that only the DGB unions provided separate membership figures for eastern and western Germany, whereas the other unions have just presented figures for Germany as a whole. Moreover, official member statistics of all unions are inflated by a large (but not precisely known) number of retired members, preventing the calculation of meaningful union density figures. In order to circumvent these problems, representative survey data of employees in both parts of Germany taken from various waves of the ALLBUS, the German general social survey, can be used (see Schnabel and Wagner 2003, 2005). Table 11.1 presents – in intervals of four years – information on union density available from the ALLBUS since 1980. In contrast to usual calculations of density rates that rely on union figures and therefore include both active and retired members in the numerator (see e.g. Müller-Jentsch and Ittermann 2000), these data refer to employees only and enable us to calculate a more realistic net density rate defined as the percentage of union members among western and eastern German employees.

It is obvious from Table 11.1 that union density has fallen substantially in the last 20 years. Whereas in 1980 one in three West German employees was a union member, in 2000 this was only the case for one-quarter of western and less than one-fifth of eastern German employees. Shortly after unification,

Table 11.1 Union density: percentage of union members among German employees

Year	1980	1984	1988	1992		1996		2000	
	West	West	West	West	East	West	East	West	East
All	32.7	31.6	29.4	28.7	39.7	26.6	26.7	25.4	18.5
Male	39.6	38.7	37.5	36.0	35.8	33.8	28.8	31.0	20.8
Female	20.3	19.0	16.9	18.5	43.5	16.3	24.1	17.7	16.1
Blue collar	36.3	38.1	36.9	37.6	37.8	38.3	28.0	31.6	22.2
White collar	26.3	20.1	22.1	20.2	40.7	16.2	24.2	18.5	15.1
Civil servants	45.2	52.2	41.7	43.5	50.0	44.7	53.3	37.1	31.3

Source: Schnabel and Wagner (2003, 2005) based on ALLBUS data.

union density in eastern Germany reached almost 40 per cent in 1992, clearly above the western level of 28.7 per cent. By 2000, however, the picture was reversed: density in eastern Germany had fallen to 18.5 per cent, which is even lower than the western German density of 25.4 per cent. By and large, such a negative trend can be observed for men and women and for different groups of employees. In eastern and western Germany union density is lowest for white collar workers and highest for civil servants (*Beamte*). In 2000, density was also lower for women than for men in both parts of Germany whereas in 1992 this had not been the case in eastern Germany.

The determinants of union membership and its development over time have been analysed in a number of econometric studies (surveyed by Schnabel 2003). Aggregate time-series analyses in the business cycle tradition have shown that economic variables such as wage and price inflation, employment growth and unemployment influence union membership growth. In addition, the composition of the labour force plays a significant role, in particular in explaining long-run trends in unionization in West Germany (Carruth and Schnabel 1990).

Cross-sectional analyses at the level of individuals have identified a number of personal, occupational and firm characteristics as well as attitudinal and social variables that are associated with union membership. All studies find establishment size to be a significant determinant of unionization, but other significant covariates differ between studies depending on the data set and year analysed and on the econometric specification used. According to the most recent studies by Schnabel and Wagner (2003, 2005), in 2000 the probability of unionization was significantly higher for employees with left-wing views, for blue collar workers and for civil servants or public sector employees. With the exception of full time worker status, which is a significant determinant in western Germany only, the factors influencing individuals' probability of union membership seem to have converged over time between western and eastern Germany (see Schnabel and Wagner 2003). In addition,

Goerke and Pannenberg (2004) find that the individual willingness to join a union depends on industry-specific net union densities, a result which they interpret as reflecting social custom effects.

These results provide some (indirect) explanations for the decline in union density visible in Table 11.1. Since over the last 20 years the employment shares of full time workers, blue collar workers and civil servants have fallen considerably in Germany, the decline in aggregate union density is not surprising. While there still exist traditional union strongholds in public services and in manufacturing, union recruitment efforts have not been successful in the growing private service sector, among white collar workers, among young employees and among workers with atypical employment. 'German trade unions have remained strong in those areas where they have been traditionally strong, but are not gaining members in those areas where they have been traditionally weak' (Hassel 1999: 501). By and large, the present structure of union membership reflects the employment structure of the 1960s. German unions thus have not been able to adjust their membership composition to structural and occupational change.

In addition to structural effects, macroeconomic factors, the transition process in post-communist eastern Germany and union policies also play a role in the drastic fall in union membership and density since German unification (for detailed discussions see Fichter 1997 and Ebbinghaus 2003). The economic shock and the sudden exposure to world-market competition which unification meant for the hugely inefficient East German economy as well as unions' push for rapid wage convergence to western standards both resulted in substantial employment losses followed by union membership losses. While this is part of the story, the union density figures in Table 11.1 indicate that the unions also lost members among those who were employed.

Here again structural changes such as the widespread deindustrialization (in particular in eastern Germany) and the expansion of the service sector (in both parts) as well as the breaking up of the huge combines in eastern Germany, play a role. They have contributed to union membership problems since recruiting has proved more difficult in smaller workplaces and in a service-oriented economy. Recruiting new members is also hampered by organizational deficits, in particular by the fact that the unions have not been very successful in establishing effective workplace organization outside of large industrial plants (for a case study of union shop floor representation see Klikauer 2004). Moreover, in the course of the increasing individualization of society, traditional union slogans and collective policies are less and less able to attract core groups such as young and white collar employees. In eastern Germany many members left the unions in deep frustration because they had taken union demands for rapid wage convergence to be promises and because they did not feel well represented and integrated by the new unions from western Germany.

For some unions, in particular those that made large-scale investments in expanding to eastern Germany, membership losses have caused severe financial difficulties. In addition, an ever-increasing share of union members pay reduced fees since they are retired or unemployed. Natural consequences of declining revenues are staff reductions and organizational withdrawal from low membership areas. Less comprehensive organizational coverage, however, means that local union officials must attend to the needs of declining groups of members spread throughout ever larger areas, so that the remaining union members feel less integrated and cared for. The unions' dilemma is that saving costs by scaling down their regional and local presence and their services for members may result in a vicious circle of reduced benefits for members and falling membership.

These financial problems and the empirical evidence on membership described above paint a bleak picture for the future of the unions in Germany. Besides political attitudes (which might be difficult to influence by union actions) the most important determinants of union membership seem to be occupational characteristics and social norms. As the employment shares of blue collar workers, civil servants and full time workers have been falling constantly, union membership and density can be expected to decline further unless the unions manage to be more successful in recruiting growing groups of the labour force such as (part-time) female employees, white collar workers and employees in the private service sector. While union mergers helped to secure the financial resources of the labour movement, the resulting multi-sectoral unions are probably not very attractive for hitherto unorganized individuals with specific interests. Although following union pressure the rights of (independent, but union-dominated) works councils have been extended and their election has been made easier by the reform of the Works Constitution Act in 2001 (see Addison *et al.* 2004a), unions have not yet been able to profit from this political support meant to improve the chances for recruiting new members at the workplace.

Nobody knows whether there exists a minimum critical mass of membership or density below which union existence is not viable (as predicted in recent social custom models, see Schnabel 2003) and where this threshold lies. Nevertheless, with net union density approaching 20 per cent it is clearly high time for the unions to reverse the negative trend if they want to play further the important political and economic role which they still occupy in the German system of corporatism.

Changes in collective bargaining

Industrial relations in Germany are part of a system of corporatist group self-government which often delegates governance to certain organized groups and associations or to collective negotiations between them and which has resulted in 'joint governance of labour markets by employers associations and centralized industrial unions' (Streeck 1997: 243). Widespread organized cooperation between labour and capital ranges from employees' co-determination at the workplace and the company level over collective bargaining at the sectoral level to the tripartite governance of the Federal Labour Office by unions, employers associations and Federal Government. Structural conflicts between labour and capital are dealt with using a dual system of interest representation: while unions and employers associations are responsible for sectoral collective bargaining, works councils and management shape labour relations at company level. Although both groups of actors are formally independent, in reality they are mutually dependent, which used to result in a network of stable cooperation (see Jacobi *et al.* 1998; Hassel 1999; Müller-Jentsch and Weitbrecht 2003).

Within this system, special importance is given to rather centralized collective bargaining (see Schnabel 2000 and Keller 2004 for institutional details). In contrast to the UK, collective bargaining still predominantly takes place at the sectoral level, and here usually not at the federal but at the regional level, covering one federal state or a part of it. Multi-employer sectoral bargaining leads to binding collective agreements determining blue and white collar pay (usually annually) as well as job classifications, working time and working conditions (the latter elements over longer time periods). The regional negotiations within one sector are closely co-ordinated by the officials of the appropriate sectoral trade union and employers association, with 'pilot agreements' concluded in carefully selected bargaining districts being transferred to other districts of the same industry or sector. Even between sectors there is some co-ordination by unions and employers, which has led to an increasing uniformity of collective bargaining policy. Despite falling density at the aggregate level, unions' high density in strategic fields such as manufacturing (which traditionally is a wage leader in Germany) means that they are still in a position to negotiate pace-setting collective agreements.

The most important topics for negotiations in the last 25 years have been wage increases, employment security, and the reduction or more flexible design of working time. As is typically the case in wage negotiations, the strongest trade union in terms of membership, the Metalworkers' Union (*IG Metall*, IGM), took the lead in pushing for working time reduction. Its campaign peaked in 1984 with the biggest industrial dispute in post-war history. This six-week strike and subsequent collective bargaining rounds led to the step-by-step reduction of the average weekly working time set in collective bargaining from 40.0 hours in 1984 to 37.4 hours in 2003 in western Germany and to 39.1 hours in eastern Germany. While weekly working time in western German metalworking is even lower at just 35 hours, the IGM in 2003 had to call off a four-week strike in the eastern German metalworking industry after failing to push through a 35-hour working week (down from the current 38 hours) there, too. This defeat is widely seen as a heavy blow to IGM and the entire German trade union movement. More and more employers demand to return to a 40-hour working week, and in 2004 quite a few firms (most notably Siemens) managed to push through such a lengthening of weekly working time with no extra pay for the workers involved by threatening to move production units and jobs abroad.

Concerning wage determination, nominal contract wages in West Germany in the past usually increased in line with productivity and consumer prices, with unemployment exerting just a minor dampening effect on wage rises (for an empirical analysis see Carruth and Schnabel 1993). By ignoring the interests of unemployed 'outsiders' and redistributing productivity increases resulting from lay-offs, the trade unions (who mainly represent the employed 'insiders') pushed through excessive wage increases which resulted in temporary employment losses becoming permanent. The problem of high wage increases was exacerbated by reductions in working time and by growing non-wage labour cost arising from the German transfer system. In the light of these problems and of growing unemployment and a corresponding reduction in their bargaining power, the trade unions have adopted a more moderate, employment-oriented wage policy in the years since 1996, which has helped to improve the international competitiveness of German companies and to secure jobs.

The fact that collectively negotiated wages in Germany, which are relatively generous by international comparison, serve as quasi-minimum wages for each industry and apply to companies in very different situations has increasingly turned into a problem. In order not to endanger the solidarity of their members, trade unions and employers associations are often not very interested in differentiated wage increases. This has led to a 'one-size-fits-all mentality', which does not allow for differentiated negotiations according to sectors and regions, despite formally independent sectoral trade unions and collective bargaining areas. Furthermore, since collective contract wages have increased so much, the scope for differentiation via wage drift (i.e. plants paying premiums over and above the contract wage) has narrowed considerably. Even if there are different wage agreements in different industries, there is still the problem within each industry that sectoral collective agreements can hardly take into account the particular situation of individual companies. In addition, there is criticism that collective agreements have tried to regulate too many details and have limited the flexibility of the plants.

Therefore more and more employers have complained about the current system of wage determination and are reluctant to bind themselves to a collective agreement. In most sectors there has been an increasing but not officially quantified tendency to resign from employers' associations. Also, more and more companies hesitate to join an employers' association if this implies that they become subject to a collective agreement. As a consequence, in many branches new employers' associations have been founded which will neither conclude, nor be bound by, branch-level collective agreements.

Even firms that still believe in the virtues of collective bargaining often have changed course in that they now prefer single-employer to multi-employer bargaining. The number of firms concluding their own firm-level agreements has almost tripled since 1990. The problem for the unions is that both developments increase the costs of negotiating collective agreements that cover a large share of employees.

A special case in point is eastern Germany where trade unions have been driving hard for wage convergence to western standards – with detrimental consequences for employment. Although effective hourly wages are still below those in western Germany, labour productivity is even lower, so that average unit labour costs in eastern Germany are higher than in western Germany, and many firms have problems in paying the collectively agreed minimum wages. Therefore, many small and medium sized companies do not belong to an employers' association and they pay lower wages, mostly through informal agreement with their workforce. The latter also happens in companies which are bound by collective agreements (where it is a violation of the law), but the collective bargaining parties tacitly put up with it.

While the extent of such illegal deviations from industry-wide collective agreements is not known, there is some information on the erosion of collective bargaining coverage over time (see Kohaut and Schnabel 2003; Ellguth and Kohaut 2004). Representative data from the IAB Establishment Panel show that between 1995 and 2003 the coverage rate of sectoral multi-employer bargaining fell from 53 to 43 per cent of all western German establishments with one or more employees. In eastern Germany this coverage rate dropped from 28 per cent of establishments in 1996 to 21 per cent in 2003. In 2003, about 3 per cent of western German and 5 per cent of eastern German establishments made use of single-employer bargaining. The rest, that is the majority of western German and almost three-quarters of eastern German establishments, were not bound anymore by collective agreements. About 43 per cent of these establishments, however, used sectoral agreements as a point of reference for determining pay and working conditions (see Table 11.2).

Since coverage rates are positively associated with establishment size, the picture becomes brighter when calculating the coverage rate of employees. Table 11.2 makes clear that almost 70 per cent of western German employees work in an establishment that is covered either by multi-employer or single-employer bargaining. In eastern Germany, this coverage rate of employees is 54 per cent. In both parts of Germany bargaining coverage rates are highest in the public sector, in the mining and energy sector as well as in banking and insurance whereas they are quite low in business-related services and in agriculture. Econometric analyses find that the probability of multi-employer collective bargaining rises with the size of an establishment, depends on the composition of its workforce and is significantly lower for young establishments, which is consistent with the observed fall in coverage rates over time (see Kohaut and Schnabel 2003).

Table 11.2 Collective bargaining coverage in western and eastern Germany (percentage of establishments and employees covered in 2003)

Establishment size interval (number of employees)	Multi-employer sectoral collective agreement		Single-employer collective agreement		No collective agreement(share of firms using sectoral agreement as a point of reference in parentheses)	
	West	East	West	East	West	East
1 to 9	37.4	16.9	2.1	3.9	60.5 (39.7)	79.1 (41.3)
10 to 49	55.1	31.2	3.2	6.9	41.7 (56.2)	61.9 (51.8)
50 to 199	62.4	47.3	8.4	14.5	29.2 (60.1)	38.2 (59.0)
200 to 499	70.8	57.2	10.5	19.9	28.7 (55.6)	22.9 (57.2)
500 and above	80.0	70.8	11.3	19.8	8.7 (53.6)	9.4 (66.8)
All establishments	42.6	20.9	2.7	5.0	54.7 (42.9)	74.1 (43.3)
All employees	62.1	42.6	7.6	11.4	30.3 (52.9)	46.0 (52.0)

Source: IAB Establishment Panel, own calculations.

The mounting criticism regarding the current system of wage determination, the erosion of bargaining coverage, and the rise of illegal wild-cat agreements have prompted the social partners in most branches to gradually modernize the collective bargaining system in order to bring companies back into the legal framework of sectoral agreements. While both trade unions and employers' associations have an obvious interest in retaining the rather centralized, corporatist collective bargaining system, they have slowly come to accept that they must give firms more freedom and flexibility to regulate working conditions at company level. Over recent years they have introduced certain elements of flexibility and decentralization into sectoral collective agreements, which shift bargaining competence to the company level. According to the German Works Constitution Act the social partners at plant level (i.e. the management and the works council) are usually not allowed to conclude works agreements on collective bargaining issues because these are to be dealt with by trade unions and employers. The only exception is when the relevant trade union and employers' association delegate issues to the plant level by stating this explicitly in their sectoral collective agreement through the introduction of 'opening clauses' which define the scope and limits of plant-level regulations (for details, see Hassel 1999 and Schnabel 2000).

Since the mid-1980s, a growing tendency towards the use of opening clauses has been observed in the field of working time. In exchange for the step-by-step reduction of weekly working hours trade unions had to accept the introduction of opening clauses in most of the branch-level collective agreements. These allowed for plant-level negotiations between management and works council on the distribution of working time in order to increase productivity by detaching individual working time from the operating hours of the establishment. Over the years, this has resulted in an increasingly flexible use of working time at the plant level. For instance, regular working hours can differ for different groups of employees, individual working time can vary in a certain corridor without overtime bonuses etc. being paid, or 'working time accounts' allow companies to deviate temporarily from the agreed average weekly working time by compensating the worker with free time within a specified period.

A new stage in this development towards modernization and decentralization of collective bargaining has been reached by agreements in several industries which for the first time agreed opening clauses relating to the core of wages and salaries. These opening clauses enable the social partners at plant level to conclude works agreements which deviate from the branch-level collective agreement within limits stated therein, but in most cases the collective bargaining parties (i.e. trade union and employers' association) retain the right to veto such a works agreement. In 1997, for instance, after threats of several companies to leave the employers' association, the social partners in the chemical and rubber industry in western Germany introduced such an opening clause with veto rights in the national pay framework agreement. The opening clause allows companies to reduce the collectively agreed wage by up to 10 per cent for a limited period of time in order to save jobs and/or improve competitiveness. It should be noted, however, that opening clauses may only be used jointly by company management and works council, and that neither party is allowed to use strikes or lock-outs when negotiating a works agreement.

Over the last few years, different sorts of opening clauses concerning wages have been introduced in many branches in western and eastern Germany. Either by means of such opening clauses or – where they do not exist – by wild-cat agreements with company management, employees often have tried to secure their jobs and to prevent shifting employment abroad by making certain concessions which lower production costs. Most big companies signed so-called 'employment pacts' or 'alliances for jobs' with their workforce which typically contain a package of measures aimed at boosting competitiveness and securing jobs such as increased working time flexibility and limitations on pay increases in exchange for employment guarantees (see Rehder 2003).

In the face of globalization and mounting international competition more and more companies are looking for ways to opt out of the German collective bargaining system if they are not offered legal options for adjusting pay and working conditions to firm-specific needs, for example via opening clauses. Therefore, in December 2003, the mediation committee of the two chambers of the German parliament adopted a joint declaration which asks the trade unions and employers' associations to agree to more opening clauses within sectoral collective agreements. The leading opposition political parties have even presented draft bills aimed at changing bargaining law in order to give firms more freedom to depart from collectively agreed standards. If they want to prevent government intervention and stabilize high coverage rates (on which their political influence is partly based), trade unions and employers' associations have no alternative but to further modernize and decentralize the German system of collective bargaining.

The decentralization of the German system of industrial relations

The rising number of firms opting out of employers' associations and multi-employer bargaining, their growing tendency to conclude company agreements with trade unions or (often illegally) with their workforce, and the introduction of opening clauses in collective agreements all illustrate that the German system of industrial relations is in a process of decentralization. The introduction of opening clauses means a substantial shift of regulative competence from the sectoral to the plant level. By adjusting general, sectoral collective agreements to the specific situation in the plants, the plant-level parties and their relationship gain in importance whereas the collective bargaining parties – the employers' associations and trade unions – lose some of their former power. In particular the trade unions have hesitated to decentralize industrial relations because they fear a loss of influence in favour of the formally independent company works councils (Schnabel 2000; Keller 2004).

According to the German Works Constitution Act, works councils may be set up in all establishments with at least five permanent employees following a petition by a small group of workers or by a trade union represented in the establishment. Although in practice just one in six establishments do have a works council, larger plants are much more likely to have elected one, so that more than 50 per cent of employees work in establishments with works councils (see Addison *et al.* 2004a). Works councillors are elected in a secret ballot for a four-year term of office, and they represent the entire workforce of an establishment, not only union members. Works councils are formally independent of the unions, but since about three out of five works councillors are union members, ties between both institutions are close, and works councils can be regarded as 'pillars of union security' (Müller-Jentsch 1995: 61).

The law provides the works council with far-reaching rights of information and consultation (on issues such as manpower planning, changes in work processes, the working environment, job content, etc.), and even with an explicit set of co-determination rights on social and personnel matters. Examples of those areas in which the works council has joint decision-making authority with management are the commencement and termination of working hours, principles of remuneration, pay arrangements including the fixing of job and bonus rates, the regulation of overtime and reduced working time, holiday arrangements, health and safety measures, and hiring and firing decisions. Works councils are excluded, however, from reaching agreement with the employer on wages and working conditions that are settled or normally settled by collective agreements between unions and employers' associations at sectoral level, unless the latter explicitly authorize works agreements of this type via an opening clause. The law also does not give works councils the right to strike and asks them to work together with the employer 'in a spirit of mutual trust ... for the good of the employees and of the establishment' (for details see Müller-Jentsch 1995; Addison *et al.* 2004a).

Due to the shift of competences from sectoral bargaining to the company level and other factors favouring decentralization, works councils can now be regarded as 'the pivotal institution of the German industrial relations system, their position *vis-à-vis* the union having been continually strengthened' (Müller-Jentsch 1995: 55). Although works councils can restrict management authority, delay decision-making and reduce company profits (see Addison *et al.* 2004b for a survey of their economic effects), employers have increasingly accepted works councils and their functions in the last 25 years. While works councils are mainly made up of union members they often behave in a much more pragmatic and flexible way than the more political and ideological trade unions. In general, works councils support management policies for modernization and rationalization of production if the establishment's economic position will benefit and if dismissals can be avoided. Managers therefore quite frequently take advantage of the works councils' authority over the workforce by asking them to share responsibility not only for awkward personnel matters but also for certain strategic decisions (Jacobi *et al.* 1998). Mainly due to the challenges of globalization and technical change, this sort of cooperation at plant level has gained in importance, with works councillors often co-managing the restructuring of plants and processes. In recent years, this cooperation has even included the unavoidable downsizing of many firms.

In addition to the developments in working time and pay determination sketched above, since the mid-1980s several managerial measures have also led to a decentralization of industrial relations and to greater importance being attached to the plant level. These measures, such as the introduction of new technologies and organizational settings, were due to worldwide technological and structural changes as well as increased international competition. As in several other countries, new forms of employee involvement such as quality circles and teamwork have been introduced as part of a human resource management policy by many German firms, and new actors such as work-groups and production teams have gained in importance, but they have not made traditional structures obsolete yet (see Jacobi *et al.* 1998).

A more serious problem for trade unions is that like bargaining coverage, works councils coverage seems to decline over time, not least because the industrial relations system has not been able to transfer its institutions beyond manufacturing industries into the growing sectors of private services and high technology. Today fewer than 10 per cent of German establishments are covered by both a binding collective agreement and a works council (Ellguth and Kohaut 2004). In the past, works councils were able to feed trade unions with new members and to supervise the implementation of sectoral agreements, whereas trade unions assisted works councils in their local bargaining function. These mutually supportive functions are difficult to maintain in a climate of decentralization pressures and institutional erosion. The decreasing coverage of works councils in the private sector undermines the traditional recruitment mechanisms of German trade unions, which may result in further reductions of union density and (finally) of bargaining coverage. In light of these institutional developments, which were aggravated by German unification, many observers express 'serious doubts about the future of a successful model of co-operative modernization' (Hassel 1999: 483).

Current problems and new challenges – Germany following the UK?

Trade unions in Germany have more facets and face more external and internal problems than could be discussed here (for extended reviews see the volumes by Schroeder and Weßels 2003 and by Müller-Jentsch and Weitbrecht 2003). Some of the main developments sketched above may sound familiar to observers of unionism in Britain while others differ substantially from the British experience (which is not surprising given the different institutional settings). Taking the reverse perspective, German industrial relation experts and trade unionists sometimes ask whether their system is going the British way, perhaps with a delay of 10 to 20 years. While the lack of truly comparative research precludes any definite answers, it may be worthwhile to have a look at some of the major tendencies and try to assess the extent of similarities between the two countries.

Probably the most serious problem of German and British unions is their crumbling membership. In (West) Germany, union membership figures peaked in 1981 and have fallen since, as has union density. In the UK, the fall in membership started two years earlier but has come to a halt in 1998 (Kelly, this volume). Calculations by Metcalf (this volume) suggest that long run union density will be around 20 per cent in Britain – a level almost reached in Germany today! In both countries the sustained decline in membership and density seems to have been the consequence of external factors (such as changes in the composition of the workforce) as well as internal factors (i.e. unions' own structures and policies). The resulting financial problems have not made union revitalization easier (see also Willman, this volume). Union mergers have been one consequence, but it is an open question whether a smaller number of larger unions are really better suited for the modern world (see also Gospel, this volume). Like in the UK and the US (Freeman, this volume), unions in Germany have made innovative use of modern information and communication technologies to deliver union services and conduct campaigns. It must be doubted, however, whether this is sufficient to compensate for the loss of face-to-face contacts and for organizational withdrawal from low membership areas. Although everybody agrees that recruiting new members is of paramount importance for union survival, neither in Britain nor in Germany have trade unions (and external advisors) been able to identify promising and successful strategies for convincing increasingly heterogeneous groups of employees to join the unions.

Both countries also have experienced a decentralization of collective bargaining and a substantial decline in bargaining coverage in the last decades, with Britain taking the lead. At first sight decentralization trends at industry level, say in the metalworking industry, are stunningly comparable, although they are separated by 15 to 20 years. A closer look shows that in the UK bargaining coverage is generally lower and single-employer bargaining is relatively more important (Zagelmeyer 2004; Gospel, this volume). In contrast, multi-employer collective bargaining still dominates in Germany, even though there has been a substantial shift of bargaining competences to the plant level in sectoral agreements, and more and more firms leave this regime and switch to single-employer bargaining. As with membership, unions in both countries seem to have had problems in organizing new establishments (see e.g. Machin 2000 for UK evidence) which implies that bargaining coverage can be expected to decline further, in particular in the private sector.

Despite these similarities, the gradual erosion of the German system of multi-employer bargaining should not be misinterpreted as a convergence to the British system. While Britain has a tradition of voluntarism and non-legalism, Germany still enjoys a solid legal framework for collective bargaining including legislative support for multi-employer bargaining. For German unions it will be crucial to keep (or gain) control of increasing workplace bargaining, which in turn will depend on the delicate relationship between the unions and the institutionally independent works councils – an institutional setting that is quite different from Britain and that may lead to substantially different results in the long run.

In Germany, as in the UK, the fall in membership and bargaining coverage goes hand in hand with a decline in bargaining power (which of course is also the result of other factors such as globalization) and with problems of legitimacy and political effectiveness. Unions have not been very successful in opposing calls for higher flexibility (demanded by employers) and deregulation (initiated not only by conservative but also by social-democratic governments). The result has been increasing decentralization, although the corporatist German path – gradual reforms within the system via opening clauses, political round tables etc. – may be categorized as 'organized' in contrast to the 'disorganized' decentralization experienced in many other countries (see also Keller 2004).

Interestingly, the standing of the unions seems not to have benefited as much as expected from the fact that in the last years Britain has had a Labour government and Germany has had a social-democratic Chancellor. To be sure, like in the UK (Kelly, this volume), the German government coalition of the social-democratic and the green party passed several laws and regulations that were demanded and influenced by the unions, such as the reform of the Works Constitution Act. Union relations with the government and the social-democratic party have soured, however, since March 2003 when Chancellor Schröder outlined to parliament his reform programme for reinvigorating the stagnating German economy, known as 'Agenda 2010'. This included reforms of the labour market and the welfare state (such as changes in job protection law and in unemployment insurance and social assistance benefits) that were demanded by many economists and were also supported by the employers. Although the trade unions rebuked Mr Schröder for his 'socially unbalanced' reforms and although they tried to organize mass demonstrations against the Agenda 2010, they (and the union-dominated left wing of the social-democratic party) have not been able to stop the reforms. The insight of Kelly (this volume) that unions 'have not yet demonstrated a degree of political effectiveness sufficient to overcome their limited bargaining effectiveness' also applies to Germany.

In the political arena as well as in the fields of collective bargaining and industrial relations the German unions face difficult decisions, in particular whether to behave more pragmatically and try to influence reforms or to strictly oppose them for ideological reasons. Behind the mask of a unified labour movement in Germany there is a whole range of different union views and strategies. These range from 'social partnership' (strongly supported and successfully implemented by the chemical and energy union IGBCE) to 'countervailing power' against employers and government alike (as proposed by the two biggest unions IGM and ver.di). It is high time for the unions to discuss and define what they stand for in the twenty-first century and to find convincing strategies for reversing the various economic and political trends working against them. Like in Britain, perdition may be more likely than resurgence (Metcalf, this volume). However, although the German unions sometimes look like dinosaurs, it may be a bit premature to relegate them to a museum of extinct species.

Appendix

Trade union numbers, membership and density

Andy Charlwood and David Metcalf

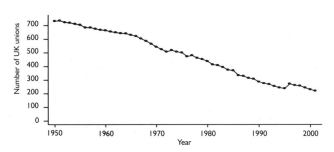

Figure A.1 Number of trade unions, 1950–2001 (Source: Table A.1, column 1)

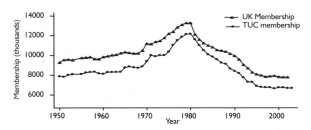

Figure A.2 Membership of trade unions headquartered in the UK and membership of TUC afflliated trade unions, 1950–2002 (Source: Table A.1, columns 2 and 8)

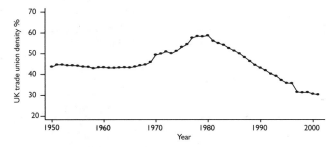

Figure A.3 UK trade union density, 1950–2003 (Source: Table A.1, column 4)

Table A.1 The number of trade unions in trade union membership and membership density in the UK, 1950–2003

	1	2	3	4	5	6	7	8	9	10	11	12	13
	Number of trade unions headquartered in the UK (Certification Officers)	Membership of trade unions headquartered in the UK (thousands) (Certification Officers)	Employees in employment in the UK[1] (thousands)	UK trade union density[2] %	Membership of trade unions in GB (thousands) (Certification Officers)	Employees in employment in GB (thousands)	GB trade union density[3] %	Membership of TUC unions (thousands)	GB trade union density (BSAS)[4] %	UK trade union density (LFS)[5] %	GB trade union density (LFS)[6] %	GB trade union density (WERS)[7] %	GB trade union density (GHS)[8] %
1950	732	9,288	21,054	44.1	9,009	20,591	43.8	7,883					
1951	735	9,535	21,171	45.0	9,249	20,682	44.7	7,828					
1952	723	9,588	21,266	45.1	9,300	20,826	44.7	8,020					
1953	720	9,527	21,347	44.6	9,241	20,786	44.5	8,089					
1954	711	9,566	21,347	44.6	9,241	20,786	44.5	8,094					
1955	704	9,741	21,911	44.5	9,449	21,399	44.2	8,107					
1956	685	9,778	22,179	44.1	9,485	21,652	43.8	8,264					
1957	685	9,829	22,333	44.0	9,534	21,797	43.7	8,305					
1958	675	9,639	22,288	43.2	9,350	21,767	43.0	8,337					
1959	668	9,623	22,006	43.7	9,334	20,983	44.5	8,176					
1960	664	9,835	22,489	43.7	9,540	21,450	44.5	8,128					
1961	655	9,916	22,825	43.4	9,619	21,789	44.1	8,299					
1962	649	10,014	23,024	43.5	9,714	22,006	44.1	8,313					
1963	643	10,067	23,060	43.7	9,765	22,060	44.3	8,315					
1964	641	10,218	23,356	43.7	9,911	22,362	44.3	8,326					
1965	630	10,325	23,621	43.7	10,015	22,619	44.3	8,771					
1966	622	10,254	23,253	44.1	9,946	22,787	43.7	8,868					
1967	604	10,188	22,808	44.7	9,882	22,347	44.2	8,787					
1968	586	10,200	22,650	45.0	9,894	22,186	44.6	8,726					
1969	565	10,479	22,619	46.3	10,165	22,148	45.9	8,876					
1970	543	11,187	22,624	49.5	10,851	21,993	49.3	9,402					
1971	525	11,135	22,122	50.3	10,800	21,648	49.9	10,002					
1972	507	11,359	22,121	51.4	11,018	21,650	50.9	9,895					

1	2	3	4	5	6	7	8	9	10	11	12	13	14
1973	519	11,456	22,664	50.6	11,112	22,182	50.1	10,001					
1974	507	11,764	22,789	51.6	11,411	22,297	51.2	10,002					
1975	501	12,193	22,556	54.1	11,827	22,213	53.2	10,364					50
1976	473	12,386	22,577	54.9	12,014	22,048	54.5	11,036					
1977	481	12,846	22,631	56.8	12,460	22,126	56.3	11,516					
1978	462	13,112	22,762	57.6	12,719	22,246	57.2	11,865					
1979	453	13,289	23,145	57.4	12,890	22,611	57.0	12,128					
1980	438	13,289	22,965	57.9	12,890	22,432	57.5	12,173				65	
1981	414	12,106	21,870	55.4	11,743	21,362	55.0	11,601					
1982	408	11,593	21,395	54.2	11,245	20,896	53.8	11,006					
1983	394	11,236	21,054	53.4	10,899	20,557	53.0	10,510					
1984	375	10,994	21,229	51.8	10,664	20,731	51.4	10,082	49			58	
1985	370	10,821	21,414	50.5	10,496	20,909	50.2	9,855	47				
1986	335	10,539	21,379	49.3	10,223	20,874	49.0	9,586	47				
1987	330	10,475	21,586	48.5	10,160	21,071	48.2	9,243	46				
1988	315	10,376	22,266	46.6	10,065	21,736	46.3	9,127	46				
1989	309	10,158	22,656	44.8	9,853	22,133	44.6	8,652	–	39.0		47	
1990	287	9,947	22,887	43.5	9,649	22,370	43.1	8,405	44	38.1			
1991	275	9,585	22,682	42.3	9,298	21,707	42.8	8,193	40	37.5			
1992	268	9,048	22,335	40.5	8,777	21,359	41.1	7,763	43	35.8			
1993	254	8,700	22,006	39.5	8,439	21,039	40.1	7,303	–	35.1			
1994	243	8,278	22,084	37.5	8,030	21,103	38.1	7,298	40	33.6			
1995	238	8,089	22,414	36.1	7,846	21,410	36.7	6,895	–	32.1	32.3		
1996	271	7,982	23,598	33.8	7,743	21,765	35.6	6,790	36	31.2	31.5		
1997	261	7,841	24,195	32.4	7,606	22,205	34.3	6,757	36	30.2	30.4	36	
1998	257	7,894	24,722	31.9	7,657	24,108	31.8	6,756	34	29.6	29.9		
1999	243	7,940	25,042	31.7	7,702	24,416	31.5	6,639	33	29.5	29.6		
2000	230	7,823	25,337	30.9	7,588	24,946	30.4	6,750	32	29.4	29.5		
2001	220	7,796	25,496	30.6	7,762	25,254	29.9	6,746	33	28.8	29.1		
2002	197	7,797	25,975	30.0	7,736	25,312	29.9	6,685	31	29.0	29.0		
2003	–	–	–	–	–	–	–	6,691	32	29.0	29.1		

Notes to Table A.1

1 Since 1997, The Annual Abstract has described 'employees in employment' as 'employee jobs'. This reflects the fact that some employees may have more than one job.

2 The numerator is the number of members of UK headquartered unions deflated by 0.9915 to take account of members in the Republic of Ireland and overseas. For further information see the explanatory notes. The denominator is employees in employment.

3 The numerator is the number of members of UK unions deflated by 0.9705 to account for members in Northern Ireland, the Republic of Ireland and Overseas. The denominator is employees in employment.

4 British Social Attitudes Survey: GB employees who work more than ten hours a week only.

5 Labour Force Survey UK employees.

6 Labour Force Survey GB employees.

7 Workplace Employment Relations Survey (previously known as the Workplace Industrial Relations Survey): employees in GB workplaces with 25 or more employees.

8 General Household Survey.

Sources for Table A.1

Number of trade unions headquartered in the UK; membership of trade unions headquartered in the UK; and employees in employment (UK and GB): all from the Office for National Statistics (ONS) *Annual Abstract of Statistics*, published annually by HM Stationery Office, London and available online at www.nationalstatistics.gov.uk since 2002. Note that since 1997, the heading 'employees in employment' has been re-labelled 'employee jobs'.

TUC Membership: TUC General Council Report 2002, supplemented by information supplied by the TUC Information Service.

Labour Force Survey: Brook (2002: 344), Hicks (2000: 332) and Hicks and Palmer (2004: 100). The sample is drawn from all adults resident in the UK. Employees are asked whether or not they are members of a trade union or staff association.

General Household Survey: authors' own calculations. The sample is drawn from all adults resident in Great Britain. Employees were asked whether or not they were members of a trade union or staff association.

British Social Attitudes Survey: calculated by Alex Bryson at the authors' request. The sample is drawn from all adults resident in Great Britain. Employees who work ten or more hours a week are asked whether or not they are members of a trade union or staff association.

Workplace Employment Relations Survey: Millward *et al.* (2000: 87). The sample is British workplaces with more than 25 employees. Managers were asked to provide information on the number of employees at their workplace and the number of union members at their workplace.

Explanatory notes

The number of trade unions

Between 1950 and 1975, records of the number of trade unions headquartered in the UK were collated by civil servants at the Department of Employment and published annually in the *Department of Employment Gazette* and the *Annual Abstract of Statistics*. These records were collated in co-operation with the Registrar General for Friendly Societies, who had a statutory role in regulating trade union activities and who maintained a list of trade unions that had chosen to register with him. Not all trade unions chose to register. Department for Employment records covered both registered and unregistered unions.

As a result of the 1974 Trades Union and Labour Relations Act, statutory responsibility for maintaining records of trade unions and trade union membership passed to the Certification Officers (COs) of Great Britain and Northern Ireland. This Act also changed the statutory definition of a trade union. From 1975 onwards, only organizations that appeared to satisfy the new statutory definition of a trade union under section 28 of the Act were included in the figures collected by the CO and subsequently published in the *Gazette* and *Annual Abstract*. This had the effect of excluding 31 organizations which had previously been included in the published totals. Therefore, the figures for years before 1975 are not precisely comparable with the figures from 1975 onwards.

We were unable to establish precisely which organizations were excluded from the published totals as a result of this change. Without this information we were unable to attempt the task of making the figures consistent by adding the excluded organizations to the post-1975 figures or removing the excluded organizations from the pre-1975 figures. It is possible that the information that will allow this task to be performed will become available once the civil service records for 1975 and 1976 are released to the public.

After 1988 the COs started to collect information on organizations that appeared to fulfil the statutory definition of a trade union, but which chose not to register. These 'unlisted' trade unions are not directly comparable with the organizations that were excluded from the *Gazette/Annual Abstract* figures as a result of the 1974 Act. They were not included in the figures published in *Gazette/Labour Market Trends* and the *Annual Abstract* until 1999, although they can be found in the COs' reports from 1988 onwards.

To maintain consistency with the 1975–87 period, we exclude them from the figures reported here.

Until 1996, the compilers of the official trade union statistics were careful to avoid 'double counting' of unions. Double counting can occur if an autonomous branch of a trade union registers in addition to the parent union. From 1996 onwards, the compilers of the statistics have not avoided double counting. Since the change has been made, the only example of 'double counting' on the lists is the National Union of Mineworkers (NUM). This change has had the effect of increasing the number of trade unions by 17 and means that the pre-1996 figures are not consistent with the figures from 1996 onwards.

Note also that in 1996, the reporting of the official trade union statistics changed. In the *Labour Market Trends* (formerly *Gazette*) article on trade unions, figures now refer to the number of trade unions headquartered in Great Britain only. Figures reported in the UK Annual Abstract of Statistics continued to refer to unions headquartered in the United Kingdom. This change does not affect the figures reported here.

Trade union membership

The changes to the methods for collecting and recording information about trade unions outlined above also mean that trade union membership figures from the certification officer are not consistent over time. Specifically:

- The change in the statutory definition of a trade union in 1974 had the effect of reducing total trade union membership by 167,000 so figures before 1975 are not consistent with the post-1975 figures.
- Because 'double counting' is not taken into account after 1995, the figures for 1996 onwards are not consistent with the pre-1996 figures because the membership of the National Union of Mineworkers will be counted twice, once in the returns submitted by the NUM and again in the returns submitted by the regional branches. However, the effect of this change is minimal because between 1996 and 2001, the membership of the NUM fluctuated between 13,000 and 22,000, at most just 0.3 per cent of total union membership.

Note also the change in the reporting of the COs' membership figures after 1995. COs' figures reported in *Labour Market Trends* from 1996 onwards refer to membership of unions headquartered in Great Britain, including members in Northern Ireland and overseas, but not members of unions head-quartered in Northern Ireland. Again, this does not change the figures reported here.

The published figures for membership (and the number of trade unions) were often subject to revision because some trade unions failed to observe the year-end deadline for completing their annual returns to the Certification Officers. Consequently we observe some variation in both the number of unions and the number of union members reported for the same year in different editions of the *Gazette* and *Annual Abstract*. Figures reported here are from the most recent *Gazette* or *Annual Abstract*. For example, the figures for 1950 come from the 1960 *Annual Abstract* rather than the 1951 *Gazette* because the figures published in 1951 were subject to revision.

GB union membership

The raw UK membership figures reported in column two include members in branches overseas and in the Republic of Ireland. Until 1978, the annual *Gazette* article provided information on the number of members in branches in Northern Ireland, the Irish Republic and overseas. The mean proportion of UK membership in Northern Ireland, the Republic of Ireland and overseas for the period 1950–78 was 0.0295. There was little variation in this figure over time. Therefore, the figures for GB membership in column five are the UK figures deflated by 0.9705.

Trade union density

Producing a time-series of UK union density

Before calculating the proportion of employees in union membership for the UK, it is first necessary to remove members in the Republic of Ireland and overseas from the raw COs' figures. As the mean proportion of members of UK unions in branches in the Irish Republic or overseas was 0.0085 during the period 1950–78, the UK figures were deflated by 0.9915 before union density was calculated.

Other issues

Total union membership from the Certification Officers includes retired members, unemployed members, self-employed members and members serving in HM Armed Forces. The latter number may have been significant during the 1950s and early 1960s when apprentices undertaking National Service were likely to have been maintained on their union's books. National Service ended in 1961, so the number of union members in HM Armed Forces after that date is likely to be trivial.

The number of retired, unemployed and self-employed members is more difficult to ascertain. The inclusion of these members in the calculation of union density biases density upwards. However, we lack the data to establish the proportion of retirees, unemployed and self-employed in union membership over time. Bailey and Kelly (1990) attempted to adjust for these factors by deflating the number of union members by 0.923. The problem with Bailey and Kelly's approach is that it assumes that the proportion of union members who are retired, unemployed and self-employed does not vary over time.

Estimates of union density may also be biased upwards if unions systematically over-report the number of members that they have. Systematic misreporting of membership may occur as a result of administrative shortcomings on the part of the union, or perhaps as a result of a political decision taken by the union leadership to enhance the political standing of the trade union within the forums of the TUC and Labour Party (if the union is affiliated to these bodies). Political factions within unions may also misrepresent membership figures for their own purposes. One of us was a union branch secretary in the mid-1990s so has some anecdotal experience of the factors which lead to membership misreporting.

The branch in question was a white-collar branch of a general union. The branch's membership had been dominated by a few large defence-related factories which closed in the early 1990s. When the defence factories had been open, the membership of the branch had been around 1,500. Most of these members had paid through check-off (where the employer deducts union subscriptions direct from wages and pays them to the union). When the factories closed and the members were made redundant, very few formally resigned from the union, but very few made arrangements to continue paying their subscriptions. As a result, by 1996 the branch had a notional membership of 1,100 members, but a paying membership (including retired members) of just 450. Attempts to 'clean up' the branch membership register met a number of obstacles. First, the membership department at the union's head office simply did not have the systems in place to respond to requests from the branch to remove members. Second, there was evidence that the senior leadership of the union were happy to allow this state of affairs to continue, because if they acknowledged the scale of membership loss across the union they would see a significant loss of prestige and influence within the TUC and Labour Party (where votes are determined by the number of members affiliated). Third, the branch had a history of supporting one of the two political factions which operated in the union. If membership of the branch remained at more than 600, the branch enjoyed enhanced representation rights at the union's annual conference and regional council. Consequently there was some pressure from members and from within the political faction to keep membership above 600. As a result, it was over four years before the branch membership was adjusted downwards to its true level following the factory closures.

We can get some sense of the scale of this type of problem by observing what happened when two unions, MSF and the AEEU, merged to form AMICUS. At the time of the merger, MSF claimed a membership of 332,000 and AEEU claimed membership of 730,000 – which would have resulted in a joint membership of around one million. Yet immediately after the merger just 693,000 ballot papers were distributed to members in elections for the new union's executive committee. It was also notable that after the 1984 law was introduced – requiring unions to ballot for industrial action and in the election of union General Secretaries – the number of ballot papers distributed was often noticeably smaller than the membership previously claimed.

Finally, it is also important to note that estimates of density may be biased downwards because employees who hold more than one job will be counted as employees more than once. There have also been a number of changes to the methodology for estimating the number of employee jobs over the years, so the time-series of employees in employment is not internally consistent.

Bibliography

Ackers, P., Marchington, M., Wilkinson, A. and Goodman, J. (1992) 'The use of cycles? Explaining employee involvement in the 1990s', *Industrial Relations Journal*, 23(4): 268–83.

Addison, J.T. and Belfield, C. (2000) 'The impact of financial participation and employee involvement on financial performance: an estimation using the 1998 WERS', *Scottish Journal of Political Economy*, 47(5): 571–83.

—— (2001) 'Updating the determinants of firm performance: estimation using the 1998 WERS', *British Journal of Industrial Relations*, 39(4): 341–66.

Addison, J.T. and Hirsch, B. (1997) 'The economic effects of employment regulation: what are the limits?', in B. Kaufman *Government Regulation of the Employment Relationship*, Madison, WI: Industrial Relations Research Association.

Addison, J.T., Bellmann, L., Schnabel, C. and Wagner, J. (2004a) 'The reform of the German Works Constitution Act', *Industrial Relations*, 43(2): 392–420.

Addison, J.T., Schnabel, C. and Wagner, J. (2004b) 'The course of research into the economic consequences of German works councils', *British Journal of Industrial Relations*, 42(2): 255–81.

Ashenfelter, O. and Johnson, G. (1969) 'Bargaining theory, trade unions and industrial strike activity', *American Economic Review*, 59: 35–49.

ATL (2000) *Performance Management and You: Advice and Information for Members*, London: Association of Teachers and Lecturers.

—— (2001) *Setting Objectives: Advice and Information for Members*, London: Association of Teachers and Lecturers.

ATL, NASUWT, NUT, PAT and UCAC (2001) 'Joint submission to STRB, September 2001'.

Bach, S. (1990) 'Competitive tendering and contracting out: prospects for the future', in H. Cook (ed.) *The NHS/Private Health Sector Interface*, Harlow: Longman.

—— (1998) 'NHS pay determination and work re-organisation', *Employee Relations*, 20(6): 565–76.

—— (2002) 'Public-sector employment relations reform under Labour: muddling through on modernization?', *British Journal of Industrial Relations*, 40(2): 319–39.

Bach, S. and R.K. Givan (2004) 'Public service unionism in a restructured public sector: challenges and prospects?', in J. Kelly and P. Willman (eds) *Union Organization and Activity*, London: Routledge.

Bailey, R. and Kelly, J. (1990) 'An index measure of British trade union density', *British Journal of Industrial Relations*, 28(2): 267–70.

Bain, G.S. (1970) *The Growth of White Collar Unionism*, Oxford: Oxford University Press.

Bain, G.S. and Clegg, H.A. (1974) 'A strategy for industrial relations research in Britain', *British Journal of Industrial Relations*, 12(1): 91–113.

Bain, G.S. and Elsheikh, F. (1976) *Union Growth and the Business Cycle*, Oxford: Blackwell.

Bain, G.S. and Price, R. (1980) *Profiles of Union Growth*, Oxford: Blackwell.

BBC News Online (2004) 'Unions hail two-tier worker deal', 20 July.

Behrens, M., Hamann, K. and Hurd, R. (2004) 'Conceptualizing labour union revitalization', in C.M. Frege and J. Kelly (eds) *Varieties of Unionism: Strategies for Union Revitalization in a Globalizing Economy*, Oxford: Oxford University Press.

Bender, K. and Sloane, P. (1998) 'Job satisfaction, trade unions and exit-voice revisited', *Industrial and Labor Relations Review*, 51(2): 222–40.

Bennett, J.T. and Kaufman, B.E. (2001) 'The future of private sector unionism in the US', *Journal of Labor Research*, 22(2): 227–8.

Benson, J. and Gospel, H. (2004) 'The emergent enterprise union? A conceptual and comparative analysis', King's College London, Mimeo.

Bernstein, A. (2004) 'Can this man save labor?', *Business Week*, 3899: 13 September.

Bewley, H. and Fernie, S. (2003) 'What do unions do for women?', in H. Gospel and S. Wood (eds) *Representing Workers: Trade Union Recognition and Membership in Britain*, London: Routledge.

Bibby, A. (2004) 'Building up an international trade union community in the net', available online at www.andrewbibby.com.

Blanchard, O. (2001) 'Final remarks', in T. Boeri, A. Brugiavini and L. Calmfors (eds) *The Role of Unions in the Twenty-first Century*, Oxford: Oxford University Press.

Blanchflower, D. and Bryson, A. (2003) 'Changes over time in union relative wage effects in the UK and the USA revisited', in J.T. Addison and C. Schnabel (eds) *International Handbook of Trade Unions*, Cheltenham: Edward Elgar.

Blanchflower, D. and Freeman, R. (1992) 'Unionism in the United States and other advanced OECD countries', in M.F. Bognanno and M.M. Kleiner (eds) *Labor Market Institutions and the Future Role of Unions*, Cambridge, MA: Blackwell.

Blanchflower, D.G., Millward, N. and Oswald, A.J. (1991) 'Unionism and employment behaviour', *The Economic Journal*, 101: 815–34.

Blau, F. and Kahn, L. (2000) 'Gender differences in pay', *Journal of Economic Perspectives*, 14(4): 75–99.

Blau, P.M. and Scott, W.R. (1963) *Formal Organization*, London: Routledge.

Boyer, G. (1988) 'What did unions do in nineteenth century Britain?', *Journal of Economic History*, 48(2): 319–32.

Brewer, M., Goodman, A., Myck, M., Shaw, J. and Shephard, A. (2004) *Poverty and Inequality in Britain: 2004*, London: The Institute for Fiscal Studies.

Brook, K. (2002) 'Trade union membership: an analysis of data from the autumn 2001 LFS', *Labour Market Trends*, July: 343–54.

Brown, W. (2003) 'Industrial relations and the economy 1939–1999', in R. Floud and P. Johnson (eds) *The Economic History of Britain*, 3rd edn, Cambridge: Cambridge University Press.

Brown, W., Deakin, S., Hudson, M., Pratten, C. and Ryan, P. (1998) *The Individualisation of Employment Contracts in Britain*, Department of Trade and Industry Employment Relations Research Series 4, London: HMSO.

Brown Johnson, N. and Jarley, N. (2004) 'Justice and union participation: an extension and test of mobilization theory', *British Journal of Industrial Relations*, 42(3): 543–62.

Bryson, A. (1999) 'Are unions good for industrial relations?', in R. Jowell, J. Curtice, A. Park and K. Thomson (eds), *British Social Attitudes: The 16th Report*, Aldershot: Ashgate.

—— (2001a) *Union Effects on Workplace Governance 1983–1998*, Policy Studies Institute Discussion Paper No. 8.

—— (2001b) *Have British Workers Lost their Voice, or Have they Gained a New One?*, Policy Studies Institute Research Discussion Paper 2.

—— (2001c) *Employee Voice, Workplace Closure and Employment Growth: A Panel Analysis*, Policy Studies Institute Discussion Paper No.6.

Bryson, A. and Gomez, R. (2005) 'Why have workers stopped joining unions? Accounting for the rise in never-membership in Britain', *British Journal of Industrial Relations*, forthcoming.

Bryson, A. and McKay, S. (1997) 'What about the workers?', in R. Jowell, J. Curtice, A. Park, L. Brook, K. Thomson and C. Bryson (eds) *British Social Attitudes: The 14th Report*, Aldershot: Ashgate.

Bryson, A., Cappellari, L. and Lucifora, C. (2003) 'Does union membership really reduce job dissatisfaction?', Catholic University of Milan, Discussion Paper 34, April.

Bryson, A., Gomez, R. and Willman, P. (2004) 'The end of the affair? The decline in employers' propensity to unionize', in J. Kelly and P. Willman (eds) *Union Organization and Activity*, Routledge: London.

Buchanan, R. (1981) 'Union concentration and the largest unions', *British Journal of Industrial Relations*, 19(2): 232–7.

Budd, J. and McCall, B. (2004) 'Unions and unemployment insurance benefit receipts: evidence from the current population survey', *Industrial Relations*, 43(2): 339.

Burchell, B. (2002) 'The prevalence and redistribution of job insecurity and work intensification', in B. Burchell, D. Ladipo and F. Wilkinson (eds) *Job Insecurity and Work Intensification*, London: Routledge.

Cairnes, J. (1874) *Some Leading Principles of Political Economy Newly Expounded*, London: Macmillan.

Card, D. and Freeman, R. (2004) 'What have two decades of British economic reform delivered?', in R. Blundell, D. Card and R. Freeman (eds) *Seeking a Premier League Economy*, Chicago, IL: University of Chicago Press for NBER.

Carrol, G. and Hannan, M. (2000) *Organisations in Industry*, Oxford: Oxford University Press.

Carroll, L. (1872) *Through the Looking Glass, and What Alice Found There*, London: Macmillan.

Carroll, M.R. (1923) 'Recent tendencies in the American labor movement', in R.F. Hoxie (ed.) *Trade Unionism in the United States*, New York: Appleton.

Carruth, A. and Disney, R. (1988) 'Where have two million trade union members gone?', *Economica*, 55: 1–19.

Carruth, A. and Schnabel, C. (1990) 'Empirical modelling of trade union growth in Germany, 1956–1986: Traditional versus cointegration and error correction methods', *Weltwirtschaftliches Archiv*, 126: 326–46.

—— (1993) 'The determination of contract wages in West Germany', *Scandinavian Journal of Economics*, 95: 297–310.

Carvel, J. (2003) 'Inspectors slam PFI hospital in report', *The Guardian (UK)*, Manchester and London.

CBI (2004) *Competition: A Catalyst for Change in the Prison Service*, London: CBI, available online at www.cbi.org.uk.

Centre for Economic Performance Panel Survey of Performance Management for Teachers in England and Wales.

Center for Working Capital (2004), available online at www.centerforworkingcapital.org/who/.

Certification Office, *Annual Reports*, various years.

Chandler, A.D. (1962) *Strategy and Structure*, Cambridge, MA: MIT Press.

—— (1977) *The Visible Hand*, Cambridge, MA: Harvard University Press.

—— (1990) *Scale and Scope: The Dynamics of Industrial Capitalism*, Cambridge, MA: Harvard University Press.

Charlwood, A. (2002) 'Why do non-union employees want to unionise?', *British Journal of Industrial Relations*, 40(3): 463–91.

—— (2004a) 'Influences on trade union organising effectiveness in Britain', *British Journal of Industrial Relations*, 42(1): 69–95.

—— (2004b) 'The new generation of trade union leaders and prospects for union revitalization', *British Journal of Industrial Relations*, 42(2): 379–97.

Child, J., Loveridge, R. and Warner, M. (1973) 'Towards an organisational study of trade unions', *Sociology*, 71(1): 71–91.

Clark, A. (1996) 'Job satisfaction in Britain', *British Journal of Industrial Relations*, 34(2): 189–217.

Clark, P.F. (2001) *Building More Effective Unions*, Ithaca, NY: ILR Press.

Clegg, H.A. (1960) *A New Approach to Industrial Democracy*, Oxford: Blackwell.

—— (1976) *Trade Unionism under Collective Bargaining: A Theory Based on Comparisons of Six Countries*, Oxford: Blackwell.

—— (1979) *The System of Industrial Relations in Great Britain*, Oxford: Blackwell.

—— (1985) *A History of British Trade Unions since 1889: Volume 2, 1910–1933*, Oxford: Clarendon Press.

—— (1994) *A History of British Trade Unions since 1889: Volume 3, 1934–1951*, Oxford: Clarendon Press.

Clegg, H. and Flanders, A. (1954) *The System of Industrial Relations in Great Britain: Its History, Law, and Institutions*, Oxford: Blackwell.

Clegg, H., Fox, A. and Thompson, P. (1964) *A History of British Trade Unions since 1889: Volume 1, 1889–1910*, Oxford: Clarendon Press.

Colling, T. (1999) 'Tendering and outsourcing: working in the contract state', in S. Corby and G. White (eds) *Employee Relations in the Public Services*, London: Routledge.

—— (2000) 'Personnel management in the extended organization', in S. Bach and K. Sisson (eds) *Personnel Management: A Comprehensive Guide to Theory and Practice*, Oxford: Blackwell.

Commons, J.R. (1909) 'American shoemakers 1648–1895: a sketch of industrial evolution', *Quarterly Journal of Economics*, 24: 39–84.

—— (1918) *History of Labor in the United States*, Vols 1–2, New York: Macmillan.

—— (1919) *Industrial Goodwill*, New York: Macmillan.

—— (1924) *Legal Foundations of Capitalism*, New York: Macmillan.

—— (1934) *Institutional Economics*, Madison, WI: University of Wisconsin Press.

Commons Select Committee on Health (2002) *The Role of the Private Sector in the NHS*, London: United Kingdom Parliament.

Conant, J.L. (1993) 'The role of managerial discretion in union mergers', *Journal of Economic Behaviour and Organisation*, 30: 49–62.

Cowley, P. and Stuart, M. (2003) 'When sheep bark: the Parliamentary Labour Party, 2001–2003', Paper to the PSA Election Conference, Cardiff, September.

Cronin, J.E. (2004) *New Labour's Pasts: The Labour Party and its Discontents*, London: Pearson Longman.

Cropanzano, R. and Ambrose, M.L. (2001) 'Procedural and distributive justice are more similar than you think: a monistic perspective and a research agenda', in J. Greenberg and R. Cropanzano (eds) *Advances in Organizational Justice*, Stanford, CA: Stanford University Press.

Cropanzano, R. and Greenberg, J. (1997) 'Progress in organizational justice: tunnelling through the maze', in C.L. Cooper and I.T. Robertson (eds) *International Review of Industrial and Organizational Psychology*, Chichester: John Wiley.

Crouch, C. (1979) *The Politics of Industrial Relations*, Glasgow: Fontana.

Croucher, R. (1982) *Engineers at War*, London: Merlin.

Cully, M., Woodland, S., O'Reilly A. and Dix, G. (1999) *Britain at Work: As Depicted by the 1998 Workplace Employee Relations Survey*, London: Routledge.

Dark, T.E. (1996) 'Organized labor and the Congressional Democrats: reconsidering the 1980s', *Political Science Quarterly*, 111(1): 83–104.

Darlington, R. (2000) 'The creation of the e-union: the use of ICT by British unions', paper given at Internet Economy Conference, Centre for Economic Performance, London School of Economics, 7 November, available online at http://members.tripod.co.uk/rogerdarlington/E-union.html.

Davies, R. (2004) 'Contracting out and the retention of employment model in the National Health Service', *Industrial Law Journal*, 33(2): 95–120.

Denny, K. and Nickell, S. (1991) 'Unions and investment in British manufacturing industry', *British Journal of Industrial Relations*, 29(1): 113–21.

DfEE (1998) *Teachers Meeting the Challenge of Change*, London: Department for Education and Employment.

—— (1999) *Teachers: Meeting the Challenge of Change: A Technical Consultation Document on Pay and Performance Management*, London: Department for Education and Employment.

—— (2000) *The Education (School Teachers' Pay and Conditions) (No.4) Order 2000*, London: HMSO.

DfES (2001) Written evidence from the Department for Education and Skills, *Evidence from the Department for Education and Skills to the School Teachers' Review Body on the Pay and Conditions of Employment of School Teachers – 2001/2002*, London: Department for Education and Skills.

—— (2002) 'Performance pay points', Letter from Secretary of State, Estelle Morris to Head teachers in England, 5 March.

—— (2004) Written evidence from the Department for Education and Skills: additional issues, *Evidence from the Department for Education and Skills to the School*

Teachers' Review Body on the Pay and Conditions of Employment of School Teachers – February 2004, London: Department for Education and Skills.

Department of Employment (1971) *British Labour Statistics*, London: HMSO.

Department of Health (2003) *Private Finance and Investment*, London: Department of Health.

Department of Trade and Industry (2003) *Review of the Employment Relations Act (1999)*, London: Department of Trade and Industry.

Diamond, W. and Freeman, R. (2001) 'British workplace representation and participation survey', London: London School of Economics, Centre for Economic Performance.

—— (2002) 'Will unionism prosper in cyberspace? The promise of the Internet for employee organization', *British Journal of Industrial Relations*, 40(3): 569–96.

Dickens, L. and Hall, M. (2003) 'Labour law and industrial relations: a new settlement?', in P. Edwards (ed.) *Industrial Relations: Theory and Practice 2e*, Oxford: Blackwell.

Donaldson, L. (1995) *American Anti-Management Theories of Organization; A Critique of Paradigm Proliferation*, Cambridge: Cambridge University Press.

—— (1999) *Performance Driven Organisational Change*, Thousand Oaks, CA: Sage.

Donovan Commission (1968) *Report of the Royal Commission on Trade Unions and Employers' Associations 1965–1968* (Chairman: Lord Donovan). Cmnd 3623, London: HMSO.

Dunlop Commission on the Future of Worker–Management Relations (1994) *Fact-finding Report*, Washington, DC: US Department of Labor and Department of Commerce.

Dunnigan, M.G. and Pollock, A.M. (2003) 'Downsizing of acute inpatient beds associated with private finance initiative: Scotland's case study', *British Medical Journal*, 326 (26 April 2003): 905.

Durcan, J.W., McCarthy, W.E.J. and Redman, G.P. (1983) *Strikes in Post-war Britain*, London: Allen & Unwin.

Ebbinghaus, B. (2003) 'Die Mitgliederentwicklung deutscher Gewerkschaften im historischen und internationalen Vergleich', in W. Schroeder and B. Weßels (eds) *Die Gewerkschaften in Politik und Gesellschaft der Bundesrepublik Deutschland*, Wiesbaden: Westdeutscher Verlag.

Ebbinghaus, B. and Visser, J. (2000) *Trade Unions in Western Europe since 1945*, Basingstoke: Macmillan.

Edwards, P.K. (1988) 'Patterns of conflict and accommodation', in D. Gallie (ed.) *Employment in Britain*, Oxford: Blackwell.

—— (2000) 'Discipline: towards trust and self-discipline', in S. Bach and K. Sisson (eds) *Personnel Management*, Oxford: Blackwell.

—— (ed.) (2003) *Industrial Relations; Theory and Practice*, Oxford: Blackwell.

Edwards, P.K. and Bain, G.S. (1988) 'Why are unions becoming more popular? Trade unions and public opinion in Britain', *British Journal of Industrial Relations*, 26(3): 311–26.

Ellguth, P. and Kohaut, S. (2004) 'Tarifbindung und betriebliche Interessenvertretung: Ergebnisse des IAB-Betriebspanels 2003', *WSI Mitteilungen*, 57: 450–4.

Employment Tribunals Service (2003) available online at www.employmenttribunals. gov.uk/default.asp.

Engels, F. (1892) 'The condition of the working class in England in 1844', English edition pamphlet.

European Commission (2003) *Employment in Europe 2003*, Luxembourg: Office for Official Publications of the European Communities.

European Industrial Relations Observatory (EIRO) (2001) 'Unified service sector union (ver.di) created', available online at www.eiro.eurofound.ie/print/2001/04/feature/de0104220f.html (accessed 4 August 2004).

Ewing, K.D. (1987) *The Funding of Political Parties in Britain*, New York: Cambridge University Press.

Fairbrother, P. (2002) 'Unions in Britain', in P. Fairbrother and G. Griffin (eds) *Changing Prospects for Trade Unions*, London: Continuum.

Farber, H. and Western, B. (2001) 'Accounting for the decline of unions in the private sector, 1973–1998', *Journal of Labor Research*, 22(2): 459–86.

—— (2002) 'Ronald Reagan and the politics of declining union organization', *British Journal of Industrial Relations*, 40(3): 385–402.

Fichter, M. (1997) 'Trade Union Members: A vanishing species in post-unification Germany', *German Studies Review*, 20: 83–104.

Fiorito, J., Jarley, P. and Delaney, J.T. (1993) 'National union effectiveness', *Research in the Sociology of Organisations*, 12: 117–37.

—— (2001) 'National unions as organizations', *Research in Personnel and Human Resource Management*, 20: 231–68.

Fischbacher, M. and Beaumont, P. (2003) 'PFI, public–private partnerships and the neglected importance of process: stakeholders and the employment dimension', *Public Money and Management*, 23(3): 171–6.

Flanders, A. (1974) 'The tradition of voluntarism', *British Journal of Industrial Relations*, 12(3): 352–70.

Folger, R. and Cropanzano, R. (1998) *Organizational Justice and Human Resource Management*, Thousand Oaks, CA: Sage.

Forth, J. and Millward, N. (2000) 'The determinants of pay levels and fringe benefit provision in Britain', London, National Institute for Economic and Social Research, Discussion Paper 171.

—— (2002) *The Growth of Direct Communication*, London: Chartered Institute of Personnel and Development.

Foster, P. and Scott, D. (1998) 'Conceptualising union responses to contracting out municipal services, 1979–97', *Industrial Relations Journal*, 29(2): 137–50.

Fox, A. (1985) *History and Heritage*, London: Allen & Unwin.

Fox, R., email message, 12 July 2004.

Franks, J., Mayer, C. and Rossi, S. (2004) 'Spending less time with the family: the decline of family ownership in the UK', European Corporate Governance Institute Working Paper, London, 1–35.

Freeman, R. (1985) 'Why are unions faring poorly in NLRB representation elections?', in T.A. Kochan (ed.) *Challenges and Choices Facing American Labor*, Cambridge, MA: MIT Press.

—— (1988) 'Contraction and expansion: the divergence of private sector and public sector unionism in the US', *Journal of Economic Perspectives*, 2(2): 63–88.

—— (1996) 'Spurts in union growth: defining moments and social processes', in M. Bordo, C. Goldin and E. White (eds) *The Defining Moment: The Great Depression and the American Economy in the Twentieth Century*, Chicago, IL: University of Chicago Press.

—— (2004) 'Wage indicator web surveys: how to overcome statistical problems and maximize their scientific value', PowerPoint presentation at Amsterdam Institute of Advanced Labor Studies, European Launch Woliweb, 8 July.

Freeman, R. and Diamond, W. (2003) 'Young workers and trade unions', in H. Gospel and S. Wood (eds) *Representing Workers: Union Recognition and Membership in Britain*, London: Routledge.

Freeman, R. and Ichniowski, C. (1988) *When Public Sector Workers Unionize*, Chicago, IL: University of Chicago Press.

Freeman, R. and Medoff, J. (1984) *What Do Unions Do?*, New York: Basic Books.

Freeman, R. and Pelletier, J. (1990) 'The impact of industrial relations legislation on British union density', *British Journal of Industrial Relations*, 28(2): 141–64.

Freeman, R. and Rehavi, M. (2004) 'Future unionism today: how union reps use the web', mimeo, London School of Economics.

Freeman, R. and Rogers, J. (1993) 'Who speaks for us? Employee representation in a non-union labor market', in B.E. Kaufman and M.M. Kleiner (eds) *Employee Representation: Alternatives and Future Directions*, Madison, WI: Industrial Relations Research Association.

—— (1999) *What Workers Want*, Ithaca, NY: ILR Press.

—— (2002a) 'Open source unionism: beyond exclusive collective bargaining', *WorkingUSA: The Journal of Labor and Society*, 7(2) (Spring): 3–4. Available online at http://www.workingusa.org/2002sp/fulltext/osunionsim.htm.

—— (2002b) 'A proposal to American labor', *The Nation*, 274 (24 June): 18–24.

Frege, C.M., Heery, E. and Turner, L. (2004) 'Comparative coalition building and the revitalization of the labour movement', in C.M. Frege and J. Kelly (eds) *Varieties of Unionism: Strategies for Union Revitalization in a Globalizing Economy*, Oxford: Oxford University Press.

Friedman, M. (1951) 'Some comments on the significance of labor unions for economic policy', in D. McCard Wright (ed.) *The Impact of the Union*, New York: Harcourt and Bruce.

Friedman, R.A. and Podolny, J. (1992) 'Differentiation of boundary-spanning roles; labor negotiations and implications for role conflict', *Administrative Science Quarterly*, 37: 28–47.

Furnham, A. (1997) *The Psychology of Behaviour at Work: The Individual in the Organization*, Hove: Psychology Press.

Gall, G. (2004) 'Trade union recognition in Britain, 1995–2002: turning a corner?', *Industrial Relations Journal*, 35(3): 249–70.

Gall, G. and McKay, S. (1999) 'Developments in union recognition and derecognition in Britain, 1994–1998', *British Journal of Industrial Relations*, 37(4): 601–14.

Geroski, P. (2001) 'Exploring the niche overlaps between organisational ecology and industrial economics', *Industrial and Corporate Change*, 10(2): 507–40.

Glover, J. (2002) 'Explained: Labour Party funding', *The Guardian*, 22 July.

GMB (2002a) *Who are the Real Wreckers?*, London: GMB.

—— (2002b) 'PFI: the "retention of employment" policy for PFI in NHS', Briefing Note for GMB by Public Service Insight.

Goerke, L. and Pannenberg, M. (2004) 'Norm-based trade union membership: evidence for Germany', *German Economic Review*, 5: 481–504.

Goldstein, J. (1952) *The Government of British Trade Unions*, London: Allen & Unwin.

Gosling, T. (2003) *Openness Survey Paper*, available online at http://www.ippr.org.

Gospel, H. (1992) *Markets, Firms, and the Management of Labor in Modern Britain*. Cambridge: Cambridge University Press.

Gospel, H. and Fiedler, A. (2004) Database of top 100 firms by employment, 1906, 1935, 1955, 1972, 1992/5/8, mimeo, Centre for Economic Performance, London School of Economics.

Gospel, H. and Pendleton, A. (2003) 'Financial markets, corporate governance, and the management of labour', *British Journal of Industrial Relations*, 41(3): 557–82.

Gospel, H. and Willman, P. (2003) 'Dilemmas in worker representation – information, consultation, and negotiation', in H. Gospel and S. Wood (eds) *Representing Workers: Trade Union Recognition and Membership in Britain*, London: Routledge.

Grassman, S. (1980) 'Long-term trends in openness of national economies', *Oxford Economic Papers*, 23(1): 123–33.

Gray, H. (2001) 'It pays to be family friendly', *CentrePiece*, 8(3): 2–7.

Green, F., Machin, S. and Wilkinson, D. (1999), 'Trade unions and training practices in British workplaces', *Industrial and Labor Relations Review*, 52(2): 179–95.

Green, F. and Tsitsianis, N. (2004) 'Can the changing nature of jobs account for national trends in job satisfaction?', UKC Discussion Papers in Economics, 04/06.

Greenberg, J. (1990) 'Organizational justice: yesterday, today and tomorrow', *Journal of Management*, 16(2): 399–433.

Grow, D. (2004) 'Steelworkers trying to resuscitate unions', Minneapolis, MN: Star Tribune.

Guardian, The (2003) 'Government strikes deal to end "two-tier" pay', Manchester and London.

Hall, B. (2004) 'Blair woos unions with deals on workers' rights', *The Financial Times*, 25 July.

Hamann, K. and Kelly, J. (2003) 'The domestic sources of differences in labour market policies', *British Journal of Industrial Relations*, 41(4): 639–63.

—— (2004) 'Political action as a recipe for union revitalization', in C.M. Frege and J. Kelly (eds) *Varieties of Unionism: Strategies for Union Revitalization in a Globalizing Economy*, Oxford: Oxford University Press.

Hammer, T.H. (2000) 'Non-union representational forms: an organizational behavior perspective', in B. Kaufman and D. Taras (eds) *Non-Union Employee Representation; History, Contemporary Practice and Policy*, New York: M.E. Sharpe.

Hannah, L. (1983) *The Rise of the Corporate Economy*, London: Methuen.

Hannan, M.T. and Carrol, G. (1992) *Dynamics of Organisational Populations*, Oxford: Oxford University Press.

—— (2000) *The Demography of Corporation and Industries*, Princeton, NJ: Princeton University Press.

Hannan, M.T. and Freeman, J. (1987) 'The ecology of organizational founding; American labor unions, 1836–1985', *American Journal of Sociology*, 92: 910–43.

—— (1988) 'The ecology of organizational mortality; American labor unions, 1836–1985', *American Journal of Sociology*, 94: 25–52.

Hassel, A. (1999) 'The erosion of the German system of industrial relations', *British Journal of Industrial Relations*, 37(3): 483–505.

Hay, C. (1999) *The Political Economy of New Labour: Labouring Under False Pretences?*, Manchester: Manchester University Press.

Hayek, F. (1980) *1980s Unemployment and the Unions*, Hobart Paper 87, Institute of Economic Affairs.

Hebson, G., Grimshaw, D. and Marchington, M. (2003) 'PPPs and the changing public sector ethos', *Work, Employment and Society*, 17(3): 481–501.

Heery, E. (1997a) 'Performance-related pay and trade union de-recognition', *Employee Relations*, 19(3): 208–21.

—— (1997b) 'Performance-related pay and trade union membership', *Employee Relations*, 19(5): 430–42.

Heery, E. and Salmon, J. (2000) 'The insecurity thesis', in E. Heery and J. Salmon (eds) *The Insecure Workforce*, London: Routledge.

Heery, E., Conley, H., Delbridge, R., Simms, M. and Stewart, P. (2004) 'Trade union responses to non-standard work', in G. Healy, E. Heery, P. Taylor and W. Brown (eds) *The Future of Worker Representation*, Basingstoke: Palgrave.

Heery, E., Simms, M., Delbridge, R., Salmon, J. and Simpson, D. (2000) 'The TUC's organising academy: an assessment', *Industrial Relations Journal*, 31(5): 400–15.

Heery, E., Simms, M., Simpson, D., Delbridge, R. and Salmon, J. (2003) 'Trade union recruitment policy in Britain: form and effects', in G. Gall (ed.) *Union Organizing: Campaigning for Trade Union Recognition*, London: Routledge.

Hersch, J. (1991) 'Equal employment opportunity law and firm profitability', *Journal of Human Resources*, 26(1): 139–53.

Hicks, J. (1931) *The Theory of Wages*, New York: Macmillan.

Hicks, S. (2000) 'Trade union membership 1998–99: an analysis of data from the Certification Officer and the Labour Force Survey', *Labour Market Trends*, July: 329–40.

Hicks, S. and Palmer, T. (2004) 'Trade union membership: estimates from the autumn 2003 Labour Force Survey', *Labour Market Trends*, March: 99–101

Hirsch, B. and Macpherson, D.A. (2003) 'Union membership and coverage database from the current population survey', *Industrial and Labor Relations Review*, 56(2): 349–54.

Hirsch, B. and Schumacher, E. (2001) 'Private sector union density and the wage premium: past, present and future', *Journal of Labor Research*, 22(3): 487–518.

Hoxie, R.F. (1923) *Trade Unionism in the United States*, New York: Appleton.

Hyman, R. (1971) *Marxism and the Sociology of Trade Unionsm*, London: Pluto Press.

—— (2001) 'The methods of international trade unionism', in B. de Wilde (ed.) *The Past and Future of International Unionism*, Gent: AMSAB.

Institute of Economic Affairs (1984) *From Taff Vale to Tebbit* (by Charles Hadson), London: Institute of Economic Affairs.

IPPR (2001) *Building Better Partnerships: The Final Report of the Commission on Public Private Partnerships*, London: IPPR.

IRS (2003) 'End of the road for the two-tier workforce?', *IRS Employment Review* 771 (17 March): 14–16.

Jacobi, O., Keller, B. and Müller-Jentsch, W. (1998) 'Germany: facing new challenges', in A. Ferner and R. Hyman (eds) *Changing Industrial Relations in Europe*, Oxford: Blackwell.

Jarley, P., Fiorito, J. and Delaney, J.T. (1997) 'A structural contingency approach to bureaucracy and democracy in US National Unions', *Academy of Management Journal*, 40: 831–61.

Javeline, D. (2003) 'The role of blame in collective action: evidence from Russia', *American Political Science Review*, 97(1): 107–21.

Jensen, M.C. and Meckling, W.H. (1976) 'Theory of the firm: managerial behavior, agency costs, and ownership structure', *Journal of Financial Economics*, 3: 305–60.

Jowell, R. *et al.*, *British Social Attitudes*, various co-authors, various years.

Kahn-Freund, O. (1972) *Labour and the Law*, London: Stevens.

—— (1977) *Labour Relations: Heritage and Adjustment*, Oxford: Oxford University Press.

Kaufman, B. (2004a) *Theoretical Perspectives on Work and the Employment Relationship*, Champaign, IL: IRRA.

—— (2004b) 'What do unions do? Insights from theory', in J. Bennett and B. Kaufman (eds) *What Do Unions Do? The Evidence Twenty Years Later* (*Journal of Labor Research*, 25(3): 351–82).

—— (2004c) 'Historical insights: the early institutionalists on trade unionism', in J. Bennett and B. Kaufman (eds) *What Do Unions Do?: The Evidence Twenty Years Later* (*Journal of Labor Research*, 25(4): 501–20).

Kaufman, B. and Levine, D.I. (2000) 'An Economic analysis of employee representation', in B. Kaufman, and D. Taras (eds), *Non-Union Employee Representation; History, Contemporary Practice and Policy*, New York: M.E. Sharpe.

Kay, J. (2003) 'The embedded market', in A. Giddens (ed.) *The Progressive Manifesto*, Cambridge: Polity.

Keller, B. (2001) 'The biggest trade union in the world', *Mitbestimmung: international edition 2001*, available online at www.boeckler.de/cps/rde/xchg/SID-3D0AB75D-BCA8E22D/hbs/hs.xsl/index.html (accessed 6 August 2004).

—— (2004) 'Employment relations in Germany', in G.J. Bamber, R.D. Lansbury and N. Wailes (eds) *International and Comparative Employment Relations*, 4th edn, London: Allen & Unwin.

Kelly, J. (1998) *Rethinking Industrial Relations: Mobilization, Collectivism and Long Waves*, London: Routledge.

Kelly, J. and Badigannavar, V. (2004) 'Union organizing' in J. Kelly and P. Willman (eds) *Union Organization and Activity*, London: Routledge.

Kelly, J. and Hamann, K. (2005) 'Social pacts and the puzzle of trade union strength in Europe', Paper to the IRRA Conference, Philadelphia, January 2005.

Kelly, J. and Willman, P. (2004) 'Introduction', in J. Kelly and P. Willman (eds) *Union Organization and Activity*, London: Routledge.

Klandermans, B. (1997) *The Social Psychology of Protest*, Oxford: Blackwell.

Kleiner, M.M. (2001) 'Intensity of management resistance: understanding the decline of unionisation in the private sector', *Journal of Labor Research*, 22(3): 519–40.

Kleiner, M.M. and Ham, H. (2002) 'Do industrial relations institutions impact economic outcomes? International and US state-level evidence', NBER Working Paper 8729.

Klikauer, T. (2004) 'Trade union shopfloor representation in Germany', *Industrial Relations Journal*, 35(1): 2–18.

Knoke, D. (1990) *Organizing for Collective Action: The Political Economics of Associations*, New York: Aldine de Gruyter.

Knowles, K.G.J.C. (1952) *Strikes*, Oxford: Blackwell.

Kohaut, S. and Schnabel, C. (2003) 'Zur Erosion des Flächentarifvertrags: Ausmaß, Einflussfaktoren und Gegenmaßnahmen', *Industrielle Beziehungen*, 10: 193–219.

Labour Market Trends, July 2002.

Labour Party (2001) *Ambitions for Britain: Labour's Manifesto 2001*, London: The Labour Party.

Labour Research Department (2003) 'Unions welcome two-tier workforce code', *Labour Research*, 92(3): 5.

Lawler, E.E. III (1971) *Pay and Organizational Effectiveness*, New York: McGraw-Hill.

Lee, D. and Wolpin, K. (2004) 'Intersectoral labor mobility and the growth of the service sector', University of Pennsylvania Working Paper 04–036.

Lee, E. (1996) *The Labour Movement and the Internet: The New Internationalism*, London: Pluto Press.

—— (1999) 'From Internet to "international": the role of the global computer communications network in the revival of working class internationalism', Paper presented to the 'Marxism on the Eve of the Twenty-first Century' conference, 18–21 March, Elgersburg, Germany.

—— (2004) 'The Labour website of the year: a brief history', 11 January, available online at www.ericlee.me.uk/archive/000068.html.

Litwin, A. (2000) 'Trade unions and industrial injury in Great Britain', Centre for Economic Performance Discussion Paper 468, London School of Economics.

Locke, E.A. and Latham, G.P. (2002) 'Building a practically useful theory of goal setting and task motivation: a 35-year odyssey', *American Psychologist*, 57(9): 705–17.

Lott, J.R. and Roberts, R.D. (1995) 'The expected penalty for committing a crime: an analysis of minimum wage violations', *Journal of Human Resources*, 30(2): 397–408.

Ludlam, S. and Taylor, A. (2003) 'The political representation of the labour interest in Britain', *British Journal of Industrial Relations*, 41(4): 727–49.

Machin, S. (2000) 'Union decline in Britain', *British Journal of Industrial Relations*, 38(4): 631–45.

—— (2001) 'Does it still pay to be in or to join a union?', mimeo, London: LSE, Centre for Economic Performance.

—— (2004) 'Trade union decline, new workplaces and new workers', in H. Gospel and S. Wood (eds) *Representing Workers: Union Recognition and Membership in Britain*, London: Routledge.

Makinson, J. (2000) *Incentives for Change: Rewarding Performance in National Government Networks*, London: Public Services Productivity Panel, HM Treasury.

Maltby, P. and Gosling, T. (2003) *Ending the 'Two-tier' Workforce*, London: Institute for Public Policy Research.

Marsden, D. (2000) 'Teachers before the threshold', Discussion Paper No. 454, London: LSE, Centre for Economic Performance.

—— (2001) 'The rate for the job', *CentrePiece*, 6: 28–32.

—— (2003) 'Renegotiating performance: the role of performance pay in renegotiating the effort bargain', Discussion Paper No. 578, London: LSE, Centre for Economic Performance.

—— (2004) 'The role of performance-related pay in renegotiating the 'effort bargain': the case of the British public service', *Industrial and Labor Relations Review*, 57(3): 350–70.

Marsden, D. and French, S. (1998) 'What a performance: performance-related pay in the public services', Special Report, London: LSE, Centre for Economic Performance.

Marsden, D. and Richardson, R. (1994) 'Performing for pay? The effects of 'merit pay' on motivation in a public service', *British Journal of Industrial Relations*, 32(2): 243–62.

Marsden, D., French, S. and Kubo, K. (2001) 'Does performance pay de-motivate, and does it matter?', Discussion Paper No. 503, London: LSE, Centre for Economic Performance.

Marsh, H. (2002) 'Changing pressure-group politics: the case of the TUC 1994–2000', *Politics*, 22(3): 143–51.

Marshall, A. (1890) *Principles of Economics*, 1st edn, London: Macmillan.

—— (1892) *Elements of Economics of Industry*, London: Macmillan.

Martin, D.L. (1980) *An Ownership Theory of the Trade Union*, Berkeley, CA: University of California Press.

Marx, K. (1867) *Das Kapital*, Vol. 1, Hamburg: Otto Meissner.

Masters, M.F. and Jones, R. (1999) 'The hard and soft sides of union political money', *Journal of Labor Research*, 20(3): 297–327.

McCarthy, W. (1967) *The Role of Shop Stewards in Industrial Relations*, Research Paper Number 1, Donovan Royal Commission.

McCarthy, Lord (1999) *Fairness at Work and Trade Union Recognition: Past Comparisons and Future Problems*, London: Institute of Employment Rights.

McCulloch, J. (1823) 'Wages', *Encyclopedia Britannica*, 4th edn.

McIlroy, J. (1998) 'The enduring alliance? Trade unions and the making of New Labour, 1994–1997', *British Journal of Industrial Relations*, 36(4): 537–64.

Menzes-Filho, N. and Van Reenen, J. (2003) 'Unions and innovation: a survey of the theory and empirical evidence', in J. Addison and C. Schnabel (eds) *International Handbook of Trade Unions*, Cheltenham: Edward Elgar.

Metcalf, D. (1990a) 'Industrial relations and the "productivity miracle" in British manufacturing industry in the 1980s', *Australian Bulletin of Labour*, 16(2): 65–76.

—— (1990b) 'Union presence and labour productivity in British manufacturing industry', *British Journal of Industrial Relations*, 28(2): 249–66.

—— (1993) 'Industrial relations and economic performance', *British Journal of Industrial Relations*, 31(2): 255–83.

—— (1999) 'The British national minimum wage', *British Journal of Industrial Relations*, 37(2): 171–201.

—— (2003) 'Unions and productivity, financial performance and investment: international evidence', in J. Addison and C. Schnabel (eds) *International Handbook of Trade Unions*, Cheltenham: Edward Elgar.

—— (2004) 'British unions: resurgence or perdition?', Discussion Paper, Centre for Economic Performance, London School of Economics.

Metcalf, D., Hansen, K. and Charlwood, A. (2001) 'Unions and the sword of justice: unions and pay systems, pay inequality, pay discrimination and low pay', *National Institute of Economic Review*, 176: 61–75.

Michels, R. (1915, reprinted 1962) *Political Parties: A Sociological Study of the Oligarchic Tendencies of Modern Democracy*, New York: Dover.

Middlemas, K. (1980) *Politics in Industrial Society*, London: Deutsch.

Milkovich, G.T. and Wigdor, A.K. (eds) (1991) *Pay for Performance: Evaluating Performance Appraisal and Merit Pay*, Washington, DC: National Academy Press.

Mill, J.S. (1848) *Principles of Political Economy*, 1st edn, London: Longmans, Green and Co.

Millward, N., Bryson, A. and Forth, J. (2000) *All Change at Work*, London: Routledge.

Millward, N., Forth, J. and Bryson, A. (2001) *Who Calls the Tune at Work?*, Joseph Rowntree Foundation, Work and Opportunity Series, No. 25.

Milner, S. (1995) 'The coverage of collective pay-setting institutions: 1895–1990', *British Journal of Industrial Relations*, 33(1): 69–91.

Minkin, L. (1991) *The Contentious Alliance: Trade Unions and the Labour Party*, Edinburgh: Edinburgh University Press.

Moore, S. (2004) 'Union mobilization and counter-mobilization in the statutory recognition process', in J. Kelly and P. Willman (eds) *Union Organization and Activity*, London: Routledge.

Morris, T.J., Storey, J., Wilkinson, A. and Cressey, P. (2001) 'Industry change and union mergers in British retail finance', *British Journal of Industrial Relations*, 39(2): 237–56.

Müller-Jentsch, W. (1995) 'Germany: from collective voice to co-management', in J. Rogers and W. Streeck (eds) *Works Councils – Consultation, Representation, and Cooperation in Industrial Relations*, Chicago, IL: University of Chicago Press.

Müller-Jentsch, W. and Ittermann, P. (2000) *Industrielle Beziehungen: Daten, Zeitreihen, Trends 1950–1999*, Frankfurt am Main: Campus.

Müller-Jentsch, W. and Weitbrecht, H. (eds) (2003) *The Changing Contours of German Industrial Relations*, Munich: Rainer Hampp Verlag.

Murray, L. (1980) 'Trade unions and the state', Granada Lecture.

National Association of Citizens Advice Bureaux *Annual Reports, Various Years*, London: NACAB.

National Association of Schoolmasters Union of Women Teachers (NASUWT) (1999) *Appraisal is a Fresh Start*, Birmingham: National Association of Schoolmasters Union of Women Teachers.

National Association of Schoolmasters Union of Women Teachers (NASUWT) and Secondary Heads Association (SHA) (2000) *NASUWT Performance Management: Teachers, Team Leaders: A Practical Guide*, National Association of Schoolmasters Union of Women Teachers and Secondary Heads Association.

National Union of Teachers (NUT) (1999) *Teaching at the Threshold. The NUT Response to the Government's Green Papers: Meeting the Challenge of Change – England; and The Best for Teaching and Learning – Wales*, London: National Union of Teachers.

—— (2000) *NUT Launches Threshold Watch as Confusion and Inconsistency Hit Government Scheme*, Media Centre: National Union of Teachers.

New York Herald (1891) Samuel Gompers Library and Archives, Volume 3, 11 January.

Nickell, S., Jones, P. and Quintini, G. (2002) 'A picture of job insecurity facing British men', *The Economic Journal*, 112: 1–27.

OECD (2004a) *Employment Outlook 2004*, Paris: Organisation for Economic Cooperation and Development.

—— (2004b) *Performance-related Pay Policies for Government Employees: Main Trends in OECD Member Countries*, Paris: HRM Working Party Meeting 7–8 October, Organisation for Economic Cooperation and Development.

Office of the Deputy Prime Minister (2003) *Circular: Best Value Performance Improvement*, London: ODPM.

Office of Government Commerce (2003) *Signed Deals List as of the 4th April 2003*, London: Office of Government Commerce.

Office of National Statistics, *Labour Market Trends*, Stationery Office (monthly publication).

O'Grady, F. and Nowak, P. (2004) 'Beyond the new unionism', in J. Kelly and P. Willman (eds) *Union Organization and Activity*, London: Routledge.

Oxenbridge, S. and Brown, W. (2002) 'The two faces of partnership? An assessment of partnership and cooperative employers/trade union relations', *Employee Relations*, 24(3): 262–76.

Pass, K. (2004) Interview with Nick McCarthy, London, April.

Pattie, C. (2004) 'Re-electing New Labour', in S. Ludlam and M.J. Smith (eds) *Governing as New Labour: Policy and Politics Under Blair*, London: Palgrave.

Pelling, H. (1968) *The History of British Trade Unionism*, London: Macmillan.

Pencavel, J. (1991) *Labor Markets Under Trade Unionism*, Oxford: Basil Blackwell.

—— (2004) 'The surprising retreat of union Britain', in R. Blundell, D. Card and R. Freeman (eds) *Seeking a Premier League Economy*, Chicago, IL: University of Chicago Press for NBER.

Perlman, S. (1949) *A Theory of the Labour Movement*, New York: August M. Kelly.

Pfeffer, J. (1997) *New Directions for Organization Theory; Problems and Prospects*, New York: Oxford University Press.

Phelps-Brown, H. (1965) *The Growth of British Industrial Relations*, London: Macmillan.

—— (1986) *The Origins of Trade Union Power*, Oxford: Oxford University Press.

—— (1990) 'The counter-revolution of our times', *Industrial Relations*, 29(1): 1–14.

Professional Association of Teachers (1999) *Official Response to the Green Paper*, Derby: Professional Association of Teachers.

Ramsay, H. (1977) 'Cycles of control: worker participation in sociological and historical perspective', *Sociology*, 11(3): 481–506.

Rehder, B. (2003) *Betriebliche Bündnisse für Arbeit in Deutschland*, Frankfurt am Main: Campus.

Reid, A. (2004) *United We Stand*, London: Allan Lane.

Rewards and Incentives Group (2004) 'Performance pay progression', Rewards and Incentives Group.

Ricardo, D. (1817) *On the Principles of Political Economy and Taxation*, London: John Murray.

Richards, D. and Smith, M.J. (2004) 'The "hybrid state": Labour's response to the challenge of governance', in S. Ludlam and M.J. Smith (eds) *Governing as New Labour: Policy and Politics Under Blair*, London: Palgrave.

Ross, A. (1948) *Trade Union Wage Policy*, Berkeley, CA: University of California Press.

Royal College of Nursing (2000) *An RCN Guide to the Private Finance Initiative*. London: Royal College of Nursing.

—— (2003a) *Report of 2002 Congress and Report of Council*, London: Royal College of Nursing.

—— (2003b) *Programme and Key Information*, London: Royal College of Nursing.

Ruane, S. (2000) 'Acquiescence and opposition: the private finance initiative in the National Health Service', *Policy and Politics*, 28(3): 411–24.

Sandy, R. and Elliott, R. (1996) 'Unions and risk: their impact on the level of compensation for fatal risk', *Economica*, 63: 291–309.

Schnabel, C. (2000) 'The German system of collective bargaining under stress: reforming or abolishing the Flächentarifvertrag?', in S.J. Silvia (ed.) *Unemployment Ebbs in Germany: Explanations and Expectations*, Washington, DC: American Institute for Contemporary German Studies.

—— (2003) 'Determinants of trade union membership', in J.T. Addison and C. Schnabel (eds) *International Handbook of Trade Unions*, Cheltenham: Edward Elgar.

Schnabel, C. and Wagner, J. (2003) 'Trade union membership in eastern and western Germany: convergence or divergence?', *Applied Economics Quarterly*, 49: 213–232.

—— (2005) 'Determinants of trade union membership in West Germany: evidence from micro data, 1980–2000', *Socio-Economic Review* 3: 1–24.

School Teachers' Review Body (2000a) *Ninth Report*, London: School Teachers' Review Body.

—— (2000b) *Special Review of the Threshold Standards for Classroom Teachers and Related Matters*, London: School Teachers' Review Body.

—— (2001) *Tenth Report*, London: School Teachers' Review Body.

—— (2003) *Thirteenth Report*, London: School Teachers' Review Body.

—— (2004) *Thirteenth Report – Part 2: 2004*, London: School Teachers' Review Body.

Schroeder, W. and Weßels, B. (eds) (2003) *Die Gewerkschaften in Politik und Gesellschaft der Bundesrepublik Deutschland*, Wiesbaden: Westdeutscher Verlag.

Senior, N. (1841) *Commission for Inquiring into the Condition of the Unemployed Hand-Loom Weavers in the United Kingdom*, Parliamentary Papers, X.

Shaw, E. (2004) 'The control freaks? New Labour and the party', in S. Ludlam and M.J. Smith (eds) *Governing as New Labour: Policy and Politics Under Blair*, London: Palgrave.

Shostak, A. (1999) *Empowering Labor Through Computer Technology*, Armonk, NY: M.E. Sharpe.

Smith, P. and Morton, G. (2001) 'New Labour's reform of Britain's employment law: the devil is not only in the detail but in the values and policy too', *British Journal of Industrial Relations*, 39(1): 119–38.

Streeck, W. (1997) 'German capitalism: does it exist? Can it survive?', *New Political Economy*, 2: 237–56.

Studenmund, P. (2002) *Econometrics: A Practical Guide*, Reading, MA: Addison-Wesley.

Supiot, A. (1999) *Transformation of Labour and Future Labour Law in Europe*, Brussels: European Commission.

Surowiecki, J. (2004) *The Wisdom of Crowds*, New York: Doubleday.

Tarrow, S. (1994) *Power in Movement: Social Movements, Collective Action and Politics*, New York: Cambridge University Press.

Terry, M. (2003) 'Partnership and the future of trade unions in the UK', *Economic and Industrial Democracy*, 24(4): 485–507.

Tijdens, K., van Klaveren, M. and Wetzels, C. (2004) 'Research on the wage indicator survey data', PowerPoint presentation at Amsterdam Institute of Advanced Labor Studies, European Launch Woliweb, 8 July.

Tilly, C. (1978) *From Mobilization to Revolution*, New York: McGraw Hill.

Timmins, N. (2004) 'Union claims success on two-tier workforces', *Financial Times*, 21 July.

Timmins, N. and Turner, D. (2003) 'New clinics' reliance on NHS staff under fire', *Financial Times*, 11 September.

Trades Union Congress (TUC), 'Workers of the world-wide-web, unite!', available online at www.tuc.org.uk/organisation/tuc-6803.f0.cfm.

—— *General Council Reports*, various years, London: Trades Union Congress.

—— *TUC Directory*, various years, London: Trades Union Congress.

—— (1999) *British Trade Unionism: the Millenial Challenge*, Consultative Document, May.

—— (2003) *Things Have Got Better – Labour Market Performance 1992–2002*, London: Trades Union Congress.

—— (2004) 'Low ebb union/government relations must be replaced by shared vision for the workplace', London: Trades Union Congress, Press Release, 6 March.

Turner, H.A. (1962) *Trade Union Growth, Structure, and Policy*, London: Allen & Unwin.

Ulman, L. (1955) *The Rise of the National Trade Union*, Cambridge, MA: Harvard University Press.

Undy, R., Ellis, V., McCarthy, W. and Halmos, A. (1981) *Change in Trade Unions*, London: Hutchinson.

Undy, R., Fosh, P., Morris, H. Smith, P. and Martin, R. (1996) *Managing the Unions*, Oxford: Clarendon Press.

Undy, R. and Martin, R. (1984) *Ballots and Trade Union Democracy*, Oxford: Blackwell.

Unions21 (2004) *What Next for the Unions?*, London: Unions21.

UNISON (2002a) *PFI: Failing Our Future*, London: UNISON.

—— (2002b) *UNISON Political Fund Review*, London: UNISON.

—— (2003a) *UNISON Annual Report 2002/03*, London: UNISON.

—— (2003b) *Unison Conference backs Carillion Strikers*, London: UNISON.

—— (2004) *Put an End to the Two Tier Workforce Warns UNISON*, Press Release, 26 April, London: UNISON.

US Census Bureau (1995) *Statistical Abstract of the United States: 1995*.

—— (1999) *Statistical Abstract of the United States: 1999*.

—— (2001) *Statistical Abstract of the United States: 2001*.

Vaarlem, A., Nuttall, D. and Walker, A. (1992) 'What makes teachers tick? A study of teacher morale and motivation', Clare Market Papers 4, London: LSE, Centre for Educational Research.

Verma, A. and Kochan, T. (2004) *Unions in the 21st Century*, Basingstoke: Palgrave.

Visser, J. (2003) 'Unions and unionism around the world', in J.T. Addison and C. Schnabel (eds) *International Handbook of Trade Unions*, Cheltenham: Edward Elgar.

Waddington, J. (1995) *The Politics of Bargaining: The Merger Process and British Trade Union Structural Development*, London: Mansell.

Waddington, J. and Hoffmann, R. (2000) 'The German union movement in structural transition: defensive adjustment or setting a new agenda?', in R. Hoffmann, O. Jacobi, B. Keller and M. Weiss (eds) *Transnational Industrial Relations in Europe*, Düsseldorf: Hans Böckler Stiftung.

Ward, S.J. and Lusoli, W. (2003) 'Dinosaurs in cyberspace? British trade unions and the Internet', *European Journal of Communication*, 18(2): 147–79.

Waterman, P. and Wills, J. (2001) *Place, Space and the New Internationalism*, Oxford: Blackwell.

Webb, S. and Webb, B. (1894, 1920) *History of Trade Unionism*, London: Chiswick Press.

—— (1897, 1920) *Industrial Democracy*, London: Longman.

Wedderburn, K.W. (1972) 'Labour law and labour relations in Britain', *British Journal of Industrial Relations*, 10(2): 270–90.

Weekes, B., Mellish, M., Dickens, L. and Lloyd, J. (1975) *Industrial Relations and the Limits of Law*, Oxford: Blackwell.

Weil, D. (1997) 'Implementing employment regulation: insights on the determinants of the regulatory performance', in B. Kaufman (ed.) *Government Regulation of the Employment Relationship*, Madison, WI: Industrial Relations Research Association.

Whittington, R. and Mayer, M. (2000) *The European Corporation: Strategy, Structure, and Social Science*, Oxford: Oxford University Press.

Wilkinson, D. (2000) 'Collective bargaining and workplace financial performance in Britain', mimeo, Policy Studies Institute.

Williamson, O.E. (1975) *Markets and Hierarchies*, New York: Free Press.

Willman, P. (1996) 'Merger propensity and merger outcomes among UK unions, 1986–1995', *Industrial Relations Journal*, 27(4): 331–9.

—— (2001) 'The viability of trade union organisation: a bargaining unit analysis', *British Journal of Industrial Relations*, 39(1): 97–117.

—— (2004) 'Structuring unions; the administrative rationality of collective action', in J. Kelly and P. Willman (eds) *Union Organization and Activity*, London: Routledge.

Willman, P. and Morris, T.J. (1995) 'Financial management and financial performance in British trade unions', *British Journal of Industrial Relations* 33(2): 289–95.

Willman, P., Morris, T.J. and Aston, B. (1993) *Union Business; Trade Union Organisation and Financial Reform in the Thatcher Years*, Cambridge: Cambridge University Press.

Wills, J. (2004) 'Organising the low paid: east London's living wage campaign as a vehicle for change', in G. Healy, E. Heery, P. Taylor and W. Brown (eds) *The Future of Worker Representation*, Basingstoke: Palgrave.

Winchester, D. (1983) 'Industrial relations research in Britain', *British Journal of Industrial Relations*, 21(1): 100–14.

Wing, M. (2003) *Ending the Two-tier Workforce: A Comprehensive Solution?*, London: IPPR.

Wintour, P. (2004) 'Unions bury hatchet with Labour', *The Guardian*, 26 July.

Wood, S. and Godard, J. (1999) 'The statutory union recognition procedure in the Employment Relations Bill: a comparative analysis', *British Journal of Industrial Relations*, 37(2): 203–45.

Woodcock, G. (1968) 'Trade unions and government', Lecture, Leicester University.

Zagelmeyer, S. (2004) *Governance Structures and the Employment Relationship: Determinants of Employer Demand for Collective Bargaining in Britain*, Oxford: Peter Lang.

Index